بسم الله الرحمن الرحيم

سنة الأشاعرة

شهادة علماء الأمة وأدلتهم

AHL AL-SUNNA: THE ASHʿARĪS

The Testimony and Proofs of the Scholars

Shaykh Ḥamad al-Sinān
Shaykh Fawzī al-ʿAnjarī

Forewords by
Shaykh Wahba al-Zuḥaylī
Shaykh Muḥammad Saʿīd Ramaḍān al-Būṭī

Translated by
Abdul Aziz Suraqah

SUNNI PUBLICATIONS

First Edition, January 2016
First Print, January 2016

ISBN 978-90-79294-22-0

Ahl al-Sunna: The Ashʿaris
The Testimony and Proofs of the Scholars

Shaykh Hamad al-Sinan
Shaykh Fawzi al-ʿAnjari

Forewords by:
Shaykh Wahba al-Zuhayli
Shaykh Muhammad Saʿid Ramadan al-Buti

Translated by:
Abdul Aziz Suraqah

Cover Design by:
Amina Hiba

Printed by:
Ten Brink
Meppel, the Netherlands

Published by:
Sunni Publications
Rotterdam, the Netherlands
www.sunnipubs.com
info@sunnipubs.com

Transliteration Table

ا/آ/ى	ā	ظ	ẓ
ب	b	ع	ʿ
ت	t	غ	gh
ث	th	ف	f
ج	j	ق	q
ح	ḥ	ك	k
خ	kh	ل	l
د	d	م	m
ذ	dh	ن	n
ر	r	ه	h
ز	z	و	w/ū
س	s	ي	y/ī
ش	sh	ة	a
ص	ṣ	ء	ʾ
ض	ḍ	أ	a/u
ط	ṭ	إ	i

List of Symbols

عَزَّ وَجَلَّ	Mighty and Majestic is He
سُبْحَانَهُ وَتَعَالَى	Exalted and Sublime is He
صَلَّى ٱللَّٰهُ عَلَيْهِ وَسَلَّمَ	Allah's prayers and salutations be upon him
عَلَيْهِ ٱلسَّلَامُ	Peace be upon him
رَضِيَ ٱللَّٰهُ عَنْهُ	May Allah be pleased with him
رَضِيَ ٱللَّٰهُ عَنْهَا	May Allah be pleased with her
رَضِيَ ٱللَّٰهُ عَنْهُمَا	May Allah be pleased with them both
رَضِيَ ٱللَّٰهُ عَنْهُمْ	May Allah be pleased with them

أهل السنة الأشاعرة

شهادة علماء الأمة وأدلتهم

AHL AL-SUNNA: THE ASHʿARĪS

The Testimony and Proofs of the Scholars

Shaykh Ḥamad al-Sinān
Shaykh Fawzī al-ʿAnjarī

Forewords by
Shaykh Wahba al-Zuḥaylī
Shaykh Muḥammad Saʿīd Ramaḍān al-Būṭī

Translated by
Abdul Aziz Suraqah

SUNNI PUBLICATIONS

Table of Contents

بسم الله الرحمن الرحيم

FOREWORD BY SHAYKH WAHBA AL-ZUḤAYLĪ

ALL PRAISE IS DUE TO ALLAH, the Lord of the Worlds; the good end is for the godfearing; and there is no punishment except against the transgressors. May prayers and salutations be upon our master Muḥammad, the Seal of the Prophets and Emissaries, and upon his Family and Companions entirely.

To my two noble brothers, Ustādh Ḥamad al-Sinān and Ustādh Fawzī al-ʿAnjarī, may Allah aid them: I thank you both for your noble letter and extend my deep appreciation for this beautiful effort you have put forth to gather the statements of the scholars and reliable Imāms concerning the Ashʿarīs and the two Imāms, Abū al-Ḥasan al-Ashʿarī and Abū Manṣūr al-Māturīdī.

You have presented a fair and balanced view and clarified the truth and made clear the correct path, detailing the history of the development of these two schools which are nearly identical and without any substantial differences between them. These two Imāms have been followed by Muslims the world over, as the Qurʾān carries many angles of interpretation, and the revealed texts have many possible understandings, and it is impossible for the people of knowledge to deny the presence of figurative language in the Qurʾān and the Prophetic Sunna.

Examples of figurative language include the ambiguous revealed texts, whose wording is upheld and whose meaning is entrusted to Allah ﷻ. So there should be no extreme denial [*taʿṭīl*] like that of the Jahmiyya, nor should there be an affirmation of resemblance [*tashbīh*] as is done by the Mujassima (anthropomorphists). The essence of what it means to believe in the Exalted Entity [Allah] and His beautiful names and lofty attributes is encapsulated in the noble verse: ﴾*There is nothing like unto Him, and He is All-Hearing, All-Seeing.*﴿

That said, the Islamic nation has been tested by a faction that hastily accuses others of error and rushes to utter pronouncements that others are misguided—all without due process and deliberation—even though the entire body of Sunnis entrust to Allah the unequivocal meaning and intent [of His words]. We are with the majority of the *Salaf* in taking the position of non-specific interpretation [*tafwīḍ*] and entrusting the meanings to Allah. By the same token, specific figurative interpretation [*ta'wīl*] is a matter of scholarly judgement and our basis for it is found among certain Companions—with the knowledge that had it been an obvious error or danger to the faith, the noble Companions would have criticized those who engaged in it, albeit without altering or leaving the general meanings indicated in those text.

As such, it behoves us to advise the faction bent on accusing other Muslims of disbelief and misguidance to contemplate carefully and deliberate on these matters so they do not fall into disbelief themselves. May Allah guide us and them to the straight path.

بسم الله الرحمن الرحيم

FOREWORD BY SHAYKH MUḤAMMAD SAʿĪD RAMAḌĀN AL-BŪṬĪ

ALL PRAISE IS DUE TO ALLAH, He in Whose hand is the dominion and is All-Powerful over everything. May prayers and salutations be upon our master Muḥammad who was sent as a mercy to the worlds, and upon his Family and Companions entirely. To proceed:

Indeed, Imām Abū al-Ḥasan ʿAlī b. Ismāʿīl al-Ashʿarī (260–330 AH) was one of the notable figures from the early community [*Salaf*] and one of the most prominent of them in knowledge and uprightness upon the methodology of the Book of Allah and the Sunna of His Messenger ﷺ. Anyone who feigns ignorance of this reality is simply disputing the historical record and pretending to be blind to what is obvious to all who can see.

Imām al-Ashʿarī did not innovate a novel belief or found a new school of thought; rather, he codified the way of the *Salaf* and defended the truth upon which the Messenger of Allah ﷺ left his Companions. This has been acknowledged by virtually all of the leading scholars of Qurʾānic exegesis [*tafsīr*], Ḥadīth, and jurisprudence [*fiqh*] in his time.

Anyone who attempts to deny this reality that was acknowledged by the Imāms of the *Salaf* is a slanderer against the *Salaf*—a liar in his claim of emulating their way and loving them. Imām al-Ashʿarī's followers who came after him were just like his direct followers in his time, so whoever belittles them or detracts from their status, or accuses them of reprehensible innovation, then he has essentially accused all of the Imāms who were the cream of the *Salaf* and the best of them in their age—who were the thronging majority and the trustworthy carriers of the Book of Allah and Sunna of His Messenger ﷺ.

I once asked one of those who declare the followers of Imām al-Ashʿarī to be blameworthy innovators and belittle them and speak without restraint regarding them: What problem exactly do you find with them, and what innovation have they brought that gives you reason to deem them corrupt? He answered me: "They negate the Qurʾān with their innovated figurative interpretation!" I said to him: There is not a single word for which they have given a figurative interpretation except that it was first interpreted as such by one of the Imāms of the *Salaf*; for the path to understanding the meaning of the word is subject to qualified independent judgment and the word can encompass more than one understanding. Don't you know that there were some among the *Salaf* who gave a figurative interpretation to the act *istawā*ʾ mentioned in Allah's words: ❴*Then He rose* [*istawā*ʾ] *to the heaven and it was smoke.*❵ Don't you know that there were some from the *Salaf* who gave a figurative interpretation to the word "face" in the words of the Most Exalted: ❴*And the face of Your Lord remains, the Possessor of Majesty and Grandeur.*❵ Don't you know that there were some from the *Salaf* who gave a figurative interpretation to the word "laughter" in the statement of the Messenger of Allah ﷺ: "Your Lord laughed at what you two did tonight." Don't you know that there were some from the *Salaf* who gave a figurative interpretation to the word "attend" in the statement of the Most Exalted: ❴*We shall attend to you, O mankind and jinn.*❵[1]

Do any of those take pride in ascribing themselves to the *Salaf* fail to give a figurative interpretation to the phrase "He loves them" found in the statement of the Most Exalted: ❴*Allah will soon bring a people whom He loves and who love him.*❵ And do any among them fail to give a figurative interpretation to the "withness" mentioned in the statement of the Most Exalted: ❴*And He is with you wherever you may be*❵ and a figurative interpretation of the word "closer" in the statement of the Most Exalted: ❴*And We are closer to him than his jugular vein.*❵

Why, then, do you allow for yourselves what you do not allow for those are not lesser than you in knowledge? Nay, you know very well that they are the righteous examples for this Umma. Why is the figurative interpretation of the Ashʿarīs—which was deduced and deemed sound from clear proof borne of

---

[1] See al-Bayhaqī's *Al-Asmā*ʾ *wal-Ṣifāt* as well as al-Khaṭṭābī's commentary on Abū Dāwūd [*Maʿālim al-Sunan Sharḥ Abī Dāwūd*] where he discusses the Ḥadīth "Your Lord laughed at what you two did tonight."

independent scholarly effort—considered a cancelling [of Allah's attributes] and a blameworthy innovation, while your figurative interpretation—which we might not support ourselves—is sourced to the *Salaf* and deemed pure and upright and not considered a cancelling [of Allah's attributes] or even a figurative interpretation?

In the past we used to say: "May Allah kill ignorance, for how often does it veil the intellect from the truth"—but today we say may Allah kill blind bigotry, for how often does it veil one's eyes from seeing the resplendence of the sun on the horizon!

As such, I thank these two brothers for their efforts in making available and known the basics of belief and their supporting proofs—which is difficult and no small task, and thus deserving of thanks and astonishment, for in the past it was said "The hardest thing to do is simplify the simple." The two authors have successfully managed to achieve just that here and add clarity to the truth and further simplify it to hearts and minds.

I am certain that ignorance cannot resist and overcome the lucidity found in this work; however, with regards to blind bigotry, I am certain that it is prepared to sweep away this world and the Next so that nothing remains before it save spectres of illusion that it can utilize and defend.

Inasmuch as I thank these two brothers and pray to Allah for them, I also pray for those who are stuck in the prison of bigotry, and I ask that Allah honour them with a safe and swift release before it is too late and before they are engulfed in darkness and the shadows of their prison are mixed with the shadows of punishment in the Hereafter against which nothing will avail them.

أهل السنة الأشاعرة

شهادة علماء الأمة وأدلتهم

AHL AL-SUNNA: THE ASHʿARĪS

The Testimony and Proofs of the Scholars

Shaykh Ḥamad al-Sinān
Shaykh Fawzī al-ʿAnjarī

بسم الله الرحمن الرحيم

INTRODUCTION

ALL ABUNDANT AND GREAT PRAISE IS DUE TO ALLAH, as it attains His good pleasure. May prayers and salutations be upon the choicest and most elect of His creation, and upon his progeny, Companions, and allies.

The basis of this research came in the form of small writings we compiled in response to questions given to us by some university students regarding the Ashʿarīs, asking if they are from Ahl al-Sunna wal-Jamāʿa. We thought that those writings would quench the thirst and prove sufficient, but we were proven wrong after receiving many follow-up questions on the topic. This all comes at a time in which both common and educated people have heard different things, and the issue has reached a critical mass. It has reached the point where a Muslim will abandon his fellow Muslim and refuse to greet him or pray behind him, all because the latter is an Ashʿarī! There is no might or power except by Allah, the Most High and Exalted! The Ashʿarī school of Ahl al-Sunna has become an insult and accusation that one seeks to exonerate himself from if ascribed to him!

This school has always carried the banner of Ahl al-Sunna wal-Jamāʿa; it has always defended the constants of this Umma and its doctrine; and it has always confronted the floods of blameworthy innovation and deviance and their adherents. In reality, this school is merely an extension of the way of the Companions and followers and those after them among Ahl al-Sunna. This school is followed by over ninety percent of the Islamic Umma: its great bulk, its scholars, and its common folk.

One of the reasons why we felt it a duty to write this research was to play a role in removing the coverings of ignorance that have enveloped the minds of the Muslims regarding matters of extreme importance. In the past, these issues were well known to all; however, in our times hardly anyone knows them! Moreover, a certain group has taken part in this ignorance and oppression against the school. They are a folk who desired goodness but they did wrong. They failed to understand the reality of the Ashʿarī doctrine regarding specific figurative interpretation [*taʾwīl*] and non-specific interpretation [*tafwīḍ*], so as a result they levelled charges of misguidance against it, even though it does not call for such browbeating and accusations.

The issue of figurative interpretation and non-specific interpretation has never represented a danger or existential threat to this Umma. It was never seen as something so problematic by the scholars of the Muslims that it called for indictments and name-calling. Both figurative interpretation and non-specific interpretation have been reported from the pious predecessors and neither resulted in accusations of misguidance or blameworthy innovation. That being the case, why do we make them a cause for accusations? Why do we make them an obstacle for the unity of Ahl al-Sunna wal-Jamāʿa during a time in which we are in dire need of unity?

In the past, we used to avoid discussions on this topic for fear of introducing the common folk to issues they didn't need—especially the issue of Allah's attributes and the ambiguous texts that the pious predecessors forbade others from delving into and ordered the people to pass on by referring them to clear-cut verses and texts. On the other hand, when certain people delved into this subject matter and described Allah, the Exalted, with things that are inappropriate and impossible for Him, and on top of that, got the common folk involved and accused the notables of this religion and the scholars of this Umma with misguidance, it was inevitable that we enter through this door and clarify the truth and defend the scholars of the Umma, even if we detest getting involved in this.

As an Umma, we possess many means for unity, agreement, and harmony that other nations do not possess. For us to neglect those means and causes for unity and to feign ignorance about them is one of the greatest of wrongs. For us to focus on side-issues in jurisprudence and doctrine and turn them into fundamentals upon which the religion is based is one of the most severe of injustices.

Today we are in dire need of unity and harmony in order to rescue our Umma from the darkness in which it wallows. We are unable to achieve unity with the methodology of reckless and wrongful accusations of innovation against the notables of our history and the pillars of our heritage and civilization. Moreover, we are unable to achieve unity by spreading divisions and classifying the Muslims into "misguided," "innovators," "heretics," "grave worshippers" and so on.

The Umma will not achieve its liberation unless it returns to the well-spring and refers back to its roots and origin. It must develop a generation of Muslims who know their religion and the real worth of their scholars. There must be a generation that understands the value of constructive dialogue in pursuit of the truth, and it must be open to differences of opinion that are a part of human nature. We have always attempted to emphasize these points in all of our researches—including this one. In this research, we have avoided the ad hominem attacks of others, and we firmly believe that calm dialogue with proof and evidence is the shortest path to reality.

In this research, we have gathered the statements of the notable Imāms and fully referenced every quote back to its source in order to stick to a sound methodology. In most cases, our efforts were only in arranging and organizing the material—with the occasional comment here and there. Everything else besides our comments are texts and statements from the scholars directed to the reader and his or her intellect. Having said that, this topic is too detailed to be encompassed in a limited number of pages; however, due to its sensitivity and seriousness, this is all that space has allowed.

In conclusion, this is only a small effort. Perhaps Allah, the Exalted, will bless it and benefit those who read it, just as He blessed the essays and researches that preceded it. We ask Allah, the Exalted, to grant us success in authoring more researches that will help shed light on the path to Allah, the Exalted, and play a role in building a solid Islamic consciousness.

All might and strength is by Allah. To Him is the refuge in achieving every desire. We rely upon Him and take Him as our support. He is sufficient for us and He is the best disposer of affairs.

Ahl al-Sunna: The Ashʿarīs

The Testimony and Proofs of the Scholars

Chapter One

The Meaning of the Term *Ashʿarī*

The term Ashʿarī is used for one who follows the way of Imām Abū al-Ḥasan al-Ashʿarī in doctrine out of guided conviction and not servile conformism [*taqlīd*]. Imām Abū al-Ḥasan—may Allah have mercy upon him—is like others who firmly held the banner of the way of the early generations, in order for those who see them to be guided. Ascription to him [in the matters of doctrine] is similar to ascription to Imām Abū Ḥanīfa, Mālik, Shāfiʿī, and Aḥmad—may Allah be pleased with all of them—in the branches of jurisprudence. So even though they disagreed about the methods of deriving and extracting legal rulings, they were in agreement regarding the sources from which they took and the springs from which they drew.

In the fundamentals of the religion, Imām Abū al-Ḥasan al-Ashʿarī was similar to them in that he took only from the Holy Qurʾān and noble Sunna and treaded the path of the *Salaf* and ascribed himself to it. He is who he is only because he shed light on the path and was taken as its spokesman and made it well known to the Umma after people of blameworthy innovations and desires sought to extinguish it.

Imām Tāj al-Dīn al-Subkī—may Allah have mercy upon him—said:

> You should know that Abū al-Ḥasan did not innovate a novel opinion or develop a new doctrine. He only confirmed the doctrine of the *Salaf* and defended the way of the noble Companions of Allah's Messenger ﷺ. Ascription to him is only due to the fact that he was considered a spokesman for the way of the *Salaf* and had held firmly to it and established proofs and evidence for it. The one who follows him in that and treads his path in proofs is called an Ashʿarī...
>
> Shaykh al-Islam, ʿIzz al-Dīn b. ʿAbd al-Salām, mentioned that his [al-Ashʿarī's] doctrine was unanimously agreed upon by the Shāfiʿīs, Mālikīs, Ḥanafīs, and the virtuous Ḥanbalīs. [He mentioned] that his contemporaries who

> agreed with him included the Shaykh of the Mālikīs in his time, Abu ʿAmr b. al-Ḥājib, and the Shaykh of the Ḥanafīs, Jamāl al-Dīn al- Ḥaṣīrī.[2]

Al-Ḥāfiẓ Abū Bakr al-Bayhaqī—may Allah have mercy upon him—who was from the third rank of those who followed Imām al-Ashʿarī,[3] said:

> Until the time came for our Shaykh, Abū al-Ḥasan al-Ashʿarī—may Allah have mercy upon him. He did not invent anything in the religion of Allah or bring a blameworthy innovation. Rather, he took the statements of the Companions, the followers, and those after them among the Imāms, regarding the fundamentals of the religion and aided them with additional commentary and clarification and demonstrated that their beliefs and what the Sacred Law brought in matters of creed are rationally sound—contrary to the claims of the people of vain desires who said that some of it does not withstand rational scrutiny.
>
> His elucidations strengthened what was not [previously expounded upon] from Ahl al-Sunna wal-Jamāʿa and aided the beliefs of the past Imāms, such as Abū Ḥanīfa and Sufyān al-Thawrī from the people of Kufa, al-Awzāʿī and others from the people of the Levant, Mālik and al-Shāfiʿī from the people of the two Sacred Sanctuaries [Mecca and Medina], as well as those who traversed their way in the Ḥijāz and other lands, such as Aḥmad b. Ḥanbal and others from the people of Ḥadīth, Layth b. Saʿd and others, and Abū ʿAbdullāh Muḥammad b. Ismāʿīl al-Bukhārī and Abū al-Ḥusayn Muslim b. al-Ḥajjāj al-Naysabūrī—the two Imāms of the people of Prophetic reports, as well as the authors of the *Sunan* collections around which the Sacred Law revolves—may Allah be pleased with all of them.

Al-Ḥāfiẓ Ibn ʿAsākir—may Allah have mercy upon him—said:

---

[2] *Al-Ṭabaqāt*: 3:365.

[3] See: *Tabyīn Kadhib al-Muftarī*: p. 103, and *Al-Ṭabaqāt al-Kubrā*: 3:397.

> We do not concede that Abū al-Ḥasan invented a fifth school. He only established the doctrines of Ahl al-Sunna that were made obscure by the innovators. He explained the doctrines of the four [Imāms] who went before him —and others—that were vague, and he renewed the signposts of the Sacred Law that were obliterated by the rejection of the transgressors. Our ascription to him in matters pertaining to Divine Oneness does not mean that we blindly follow him and rely solely upon him in those matters; Rather, we agree with him in his method regarding Divine Oneness because of the soundness of its proofs—not out of servile conformism. Those among us who ascribe themselves to him only do so in order to be distinguished from the innovators who do not hold [his] beliefs, such as the various groups of the Muʿtazila, Jahmiyya, Karrāmiyya, anthropomorphists, Sālimiyya, and other groups of innovators and corrupt doctrines.
>
> Al-Ashʿarī was tasked with refuting them and he was able to subdue them and expose their innovations to those who did not know. We do not see the four Imāms differing in the fundamentals of the religion. On the contrary, we see that they were in agreement regarding their belief in the Oneness and transcendence of Allah, and they were united in their negation of resemblance [*tashbīh*] from the Pre-eternal ﷻ. Al-Ashʿarī—may Allah have mercy upon him—was upon their methodology. There is no blame on one who ascribes himself to him in this manner. No success is hoped for one who repudiates his [al-Ashʿarī's] correct doctrine. If believing in Divine transcendence and shunning resemblance [between Allah and His creation] is considered Ashʿarism, then all of the believers in Divine Oneness are Ashʿarīs! False accusations against a faction that ascribes itself to a believer in Divine Oneness will not harm in the least.[4]

See how he declared that ascription to Imām al-Ashʿarī is in contradistinction to the people of blameworthy innovations and desires, and that he and those who ascribe themselves to him are upon the way of the *Salaf* and the four Imāms. He also said:

---

[4] *Tabyīn Kadhib al-Muftarī*, p. 359.

> And they [the Ash'arīs] are strict in their adherence to the Book and the Sunna; they shun the causes that lead to dissension; they are patient in their religion during times of affliction and trial; and they are victorious over their enemy without taking revenge or feuding. They do not abandon the Qur'ān and the Prophetic proofs and they do not follow the way of the Mu'aṭṭila (deniers) and Qadariyya in the rational sciences. Rather, in matter of doctrine, they gather between revelatory evidence and rational proofs. They avoid the extremism of the Mu'tazila, eschew the ways of the deniers, and they repudiate the negligence of the anthropomorphists and corporealists. With proofs, they expose the doctrines of the false sects. They reject the ways of the Jahmiyya; they disdain the Karrāmiyya and the Sālimiyya; they invalidate the beliefs of the Qadariyya; and they reject the doubts of the Jabriyya... Their doctrine is the most moderate of doctrines; their drinking-source contains the sweetest drink; their positions are the noblest of positions; and their ranks are the greatest of ranks. The insult of a detractor has no effect upon them, and the injury of an injurious person leaves no mark upon them.[5]

Imām al-Murtaḍā al-Zabīdī—may Allah have mercy upon him—said:

> It should be known that neither Imām Abū al-Ḥasan nor Abū al-Manṣūr—may Allah be pleased with them and reward them with good on behalf of Islam—innovated an opinion from their own selves or derived a [distinct] doctrine; they only confirmed the doctrines of the *Salaf* and defended the way of the Companions of Allah's Messenger ﷺ... Both of them debated with the people of blameworthy innovation and misguidance until the innovators were cut down and fled in defeat.[6]

These are the Ash'arīs: the followers of Imām Abū al-Ḥasan al-Ash'arī. So who, then, was this illustrious Imām?

---

[5] Ibid., p. 397.
[6] *Itḥāf al-Sāda al-Muttaqīn*: 2:7.

CHAPTER TWO

THE BIOGRAPHY OF IMĀM ABŪ AL-ḤASAN AL-ASHʿARĪ

HE IS THE SCHOLARLY IMĀM; the pious and righteous; the helper of the Sunna, religious knowledge, and the distinguishing marks of the Muslims—ʿAlī the son of Ismāʿīl, the son of Abī Bishr Isḥāq, the son of Sālim, the son of Ismāʿīl, the son of ʿAbdullāh, the son of Mūsā, the son of Bilāl, the son of Abī Burda, who was the son of the Companion of Allah's Messenger ﷺ Abū Mūsā ʿAbdullāh b. Qays al-Ashʿarī ؓ.

He was the Shaykh of the way of Ahl al-Sunna wal-Jamāʿa and the Imām of the theologians. He was born in the year 260 AH. He initially followed the Muʿtazilī school of al-Jubbāʾī and remained upon that doctrine for approximately forty years. He became an expert in the doctrine of the Muʿtazila and became one of their leaders and a sword against their opponents.

When Allah willed to give victory to His religion and aid the Sunna of His Prophet ﷺ, He made al-Ashʿarī realize the falsehood of the Muʿtazila school. He would start to have doubts about some of the doctrinal beliefs of the Muʿtazila, and when he would ask his teachers about those matters he would not find suitable answers.

After Allah, the Exalted, showed him the truth, he went out to the congregational Mosque, ascended the pulpit, and loudly proclaimed: "O people! Whoever knows me, knows me. Whoever does not know me, I shall tell him who I am. I am so-and-so, the son of so-and-so. I used to believe in the createdness of the Qurʾān, that Allah will not be seen by the ocular vision in the Hereafter, and that the servants create their own actions. Here and now I repent from the doctrine of the Muʿtazila and I will strive to refute them and lay bare their weaknesses.

"O people! I was only away from you for this period of time because I was investigating. All evidence became equal in my eyes and nothing seemed preponderant over anything else. I sought guidance from Allah, the Exalted, and He guided me to the doctrine that I have placed in these books of mine. I have cast aside everything I used to believe just as I cast aside this garment of mine."

It is mentioned that he then took his outer garment and threw it, and gave people some of the books he authored on the doctrine of the people of truth and the path of the community of jurists and Ḥadīth scholars.

The scholars mention that before Abū al-Ḥasan al-Ashʿarī, the people of blameworthy innovation would raise their heads in pride, but after he gained ascendency over them, he humiliated them.

Many notable Imāms took from him—may Allah have mercy upon him—such as: Imām Abū al-Ḥasan al-Bāhilī al-Baṣrī, Imām Abū ʿAbdullāh b. Mujāhid al-Baṣrī, Imām Abū Muḥammad al-Ṭabarī—better known as al-ʿIrāqī—Imām Abū Bakr al-Qaffāl al-Shāshī, and Imām Abū Sahl al-Ṣuʿlūkī al-Naysabūrī—may Allah have mercy upon all of them.

Many notable Imāms took from his companions, such as: the Imām, Qāḍī Abū Bakr al-Bāqillānī, Imām Abū al-Ṭayyib b. Abī Sahl al-Ṣuʿlūkī, Imām Abū ʿAlī al-Daqqāq, Imām al-Ḥākim al-Naysabūrī, Imām Abū Bakr b. Fūrak, the Ḥadīth master Abū Nuʿaym al-Aṣfahānī, and others whose good mention has adorned the pulpits and whose lives have given fragrance to the books—may Allah have mercy upon all of them. They left behind students who were the notables of the world and the stars of guidance.

The people of the Sunna followed the footsteps of the *Salaf* ﷺ and raised the banner of the Sunna by aiding al-Ashʿarī's school all over the world, and it has reached everywhere by the day and the night. He left behind many written works. It is said that he authored over two-hundred works.[7]

Imām Abū al-Ḥasan al-Ashʿarī—may Allah have mercy upon him—died in the year 324 AH. The people of the Sunna wept at his passing and grieved over losing him, whereas the people of blameworthy innovation felt respite and comfort. May Allah be pleased with him.[8]

---

[7] See: *Al-Ṭabaqāt al-Shāfiʿiyya*, 3:360.

[8] This biography is summarized from *Tabyīn Kadhib al-Muftarī*, *Ṭabaqāt al-Shāfiʿiyya*, and *Miftāḥ al-Saʿāda*.

Chapter Three

Did al-Ashʿarī Die upon a Different Doctrine?

Some people believe that Imām Abū al-Ḥasan al-Ashʿarī—may Allah have mercy upon him—went through three stages in his life:

One: the period in which he was a Muʿtazilī, which lasted for about forty years.

Two: the period in which he followed ʿAbdullāh b. Saʿīd b. Kullāb.

Three: the period in which he returned to the doctrine of the *Salaf* and Ahl al-Sunna.

Those who believe this claim deduce from it that the Ashʿarīs followed Imām al-Ashʿarī in his second stage in which he followed ʿAbdullāh b. Saʿīd b. Kullāb. According to them, ʿAbdullāh b. Saʿīd b. Kullāb was not a Sunni, and the Ashʿarīs are really following him and not Imām al-Ashʿarī, because in his third stage, Imām al-Ashʿarī actually retracted from his belief in the doctrine of ʿAbdullāh b. Saʿīd b. Kullāb and wrote his book *Al-Ibāna* and other books based upon the doctrine of the *Salaf*.

This is the gist of their claim. Before we respond to it and demonstrate its scientific and historical inaccuracy, we would first like to examine the underlying premises it holds. This claim contains three premises:

- Imām al-Ashʿarī went through three stages in his life: following the doctrine of the Muʿtazila, following the doctrine of Ibn Kullāb, and returning to the methodology of Ahl al-Sunna wal-Jamāʿa.

- ʿAbdullāh b. Saʿīd b. Kullāb was not upon the methodology of Ahl al-Sunna wal-Jamāʿa.

- The book *Al-Ibāna* represents the third stage of Imām al-Ashʿarī's life, signalling his return to the way of the pious predecessors.[9]

REFUTING THE FIRST PREMISE

Imām Abū al-Ḥasan al-Ashʿarī—may Allah have mercy upon him—is one of the signposts of the Muslims. Much attention is given to him and his words. He was not an obscure personality or someone whose condition was unknown to the people; especially considering the seriousness of the issue we are discussing. If this claim was true, and al-Ashʿarī did in fact go through three stages in his life, then it must have been mentioned by the historians and it would have undoubtedly spread as far and wide as his reported retraction from the doctrine of the Muʿtazila. There is not a single biographer who mentioned his life except that he also mentioned al-Ashʿarī's ascension upon the pulpit and his public repudiation of the Muʿtazila doctrine. Have any of the historians mentioned anything about al-Ashʿarī's alleged retraction from ʿAbdullāh b. Saʿīd b. Kullāb's methodology?

When reviewing the books of history we find no indication of this whatsoever. Quite the contrary, we find that all of the historians were unanimous in reporting that, when Imām Abū al-Ḥasan left the Muʿtazila and their doctrine, he embraced the methodology of the pious predecessors and wrote books according to their way, such as his *Al-Ibāna* and other works written in defence of the doctrine of the people of truth.

Imām Abū Bakr b. Fūrak—may Allah have mercy upon him—said: "Shaykh Abū al-Ḥasan ʿAlī b. Ismāʿīl al-Ashʿarī ﵀ went from following the doctrine of the Muʿtazila to aiding the doctrine of Ahl al-Sunna wal-Jamāʿa with rational proofs, and he wrote books on that."[10]

---

[9] We mention this for argument's sake. The investigative scholars and researchers posit that the book *Al-Lumaʿ* was written by al-Ashʿarī after *Al-Ibāna*. Please refer to the introduction to *Al-Lumaʿ* by Ustādh Ḥamūda Ghurāba, the comments of al-Kawtharī in his edition of *Al-Sayf al-Ṣaqīl* (p. 123), his comments in *Tabyīn Kadhib al-Muftarī* (p. 392), and the introduction to *Al-Ibāna* written by Shaykh Fawqiyya Ḥusayn (pp. 79–80).

[10] *Tabyīn Kadhib al-Muftarī*, p. 127.

Ibn Khallikān said: "He was the master of the fundamentals, the one who aided the doctrine of the Sunna... Abū al-Ḥasan was first a Muʿtazilī, and then on a Friday, in the congregational Mosque, he repented from his belief in divine justice[11] and the createdness of the Qurʾān."[12]

Imām al-Dhahabī said: "It has reached us that Abū al-Ḥasan repented and ascended the pulpit of Basra and said: 'I used to believe in the createdness of the Qurʾān, ...now I repent and I shall refute the Muʿtazila.'"[13]

Ibn Khaldūn—may Allah have mercy upon him—said in his *Muqaddima*:[14] "Until Shaykh Abū al-Ḥasan al-Ashʿarī appeared and debated some of their Shaykhs on the issue of best interests [*al-ṣalāḥ wal-aṣlaḥ*][15] and rejected their path. He held the views of ʿAbdullāh b. Saʿīd b. Kullāb, Abū al-ʿAbbās al-Qalānisī, and al-Ḥārith al-Muḥāsibī among the followers of the *Salaf* and the path of the Sunna."

So we see here that after he repented from the doctrine of the Muʿtazila, Abū al-Ḥasan al-Ashʿarī held the views of ʿAbdullāh b. Saʿīd b. Kullāb, al-Qalānisī, and al-Muḥāsibī; and all of them were upon the path of the *Salaf* and the Sunna. This is found in all of the books of history that mentioned Imām Abū al-Ḥasan's biography: *Tārīkh Baghdād* of Khaṭīb al-Baghdādī, *Ṭabaqāt al-Shāfiʿiyya* of al-Subkī, *Shadharāt al-Dhahab* of Ibn ʿImād, *Al-Kāmil* of Ibn Athīr, *Tabyīn Kadhib al-Muftarī* of Ibn ʿAsākir, *Tartīb al-Madārik* of Qāḍī ʿIyāḍ, *Ṭabaqāt al-Shāfiʿiyya* of Ibn Qāḍī Shuhba, *Ṭabaqāt al-Shāfiʿiyya* of al-Isnawī, *Al-Dībāj* of Ibn Farhūn and *Mirʾāt al-Jinān* of al-Yāfiʿī, and others. All of them were unanimous that Imām Abū al-Ḥasan was upon the way of the *Salaf* and the Sunna after he repented from the doctrine of the Muʿtazila.

---

[11] Divine justice [*ʿadl*] here refers to the belief of the Muʿtazila that Allah is obliged to do what is "just"—to bestow His mercy and punishment according to a prior and intrinsic deservedness of beings. According to Sunni doctrine, this contradicts Allah's power and makes Him subordinate to something else. [t]

[12] *Wafiyāt al-Aʿyān*, 3:284.

[13] *Siyar ʿAlām al-Nubalāʾ*, 15:89.

[14] *Muqaddima*, p. 853.

[15] That is, the belief of the Muʿtazila who stated that it is necessary for Allah to observe benefit and what is in the best interest of creation. [t]

In addition to this, if this alleged retraction of Imām Abū al-Ḥasan was true, the first people to know about it and transmit it would have been his companions and students. His students, companions, and followers knew best about him. Certainly they were the closest to him and the most acquainted with his states, beliefs and opinions, especially in such an important issue as this in which people would be motivated to report it, and especially coming from a major Imām like Imām Abū al-Ḥasan. When reviewing the statements of his companions and the companions of his companions, we do not find any indication that would prove this alleged retraction. On the contrary, we find that they were all in agreement that after Imām Abū al-Ḥasan forsook the doctrine of the Muʿtazila he followed the way of the *Salaf*, like al-Muḥāsibī, Ibn Kullāb, al-Qalānisī, al-Karābisī, and others.

Take, as an example, the works of the one who gave aid to the Ashʿarī school, Qāḍī Abū Bakr al-Bāqillānī—may Allah have mercy upon him—like *Al-Inṣāf* and *Al-Tamhīd* and others, and take the works of Ibn Fūrak, Abū Bakr al-Qaffāl al-Shāshī, Abū Isḥāq al-Shīrāzī, Abū Bakr al-Bayhaqī, and others among his companions and the companions of his companions and their students. There is no mention or indication in any of these works of this alleged retraction.

Is it even conceivable that Imām Abū al-Ḥasan—a pivotal figure of great importance—could have retracted his doctrine and abandoned it without the retraction being mentioned by any of his companions or students? Can you in any way believe that he secretly retracted from his beliefs even though he had publically abandoned the Muʿtazila doctrine, on the pulpit of the Muʿtazila, and announced it to all?

Of course not. This claim is false. The truth of the matter is that Imām Abū al-Ḥasan only went through two stages in his life: the stage of following the doctrine of the Muʿtazila, and the stage of retracting and following the way of the *Salaf*. No one who claims otherwise has a shred of evidence or even a semblance of proof.

Those who make this claim rely upon the Imām's style of writing found in *Al-Ibāna* and other essays. In those works, Imām Abū al-Ḥasan followed the way of non-specific interpretation [*tafwīḍ*], which was the way of the majority of the *Salaf*.

When they read Imām Abū al-Ḥasan's works expressing non-specific interpretation, they deduced that he opposed the view of Ibn Kullāb whom they claimed was not upon the way of the *Salaf*.

Is there anything in *Al-Ibāna*—which was written according to the way of the *Salaf* and is one of the last, if not *the* last, of his books—that contradicts the way of 'Abdullāh b. Sa'īd b. Kullāb? Or to word it differently: was 'Abdullāh b. Sa'īd b. Kullāb on a path that opposed the path of the *Salaf* as it was expressed in Imām Abū al-Ḥasan's *Al-Ibāna*? This inevitably leads us to the second premise.

Refuting the Second Premise

First of all, we concede that after he abandoned the doctrine of the Mu'tazila, Imām Abū al-Ḥasan followed the way of 'Abdullāh b. Sa'īd al-Kullāb. We agree with the claimants in this part of the premise. However, they differ with us regarding Ibn Kullāb's way. We believe that his path and the path of the *Salaf* was one in reality, because Ibn Kullāb was among the Imāms of Ahl al-Sunna wal-Jamā'a and he followed the path of the pious predecessors.

Al-Tāj al-Subkī said:

> In any case, Ibn Kullāb is from Ahl al-Sunna... I saw that Imām Ḍiyā' al-Dīn al-Khaṭīb, the father of Imām Fakhr al-Dīn al-Rāzī, mentioned 'Abdullāh b. Sa'īd b. Kullāb at the end of his book *Ghāya al-Marām fī 'Ilm al-Kalām*. He wrote: "Among the Sunni theologians during the reign of al-Ma'mūn was 'Abdullāh b. Sa'īd al-Tamīmī, who demolished the Mu'tazila in the gathering of al-Ma'mūn and exposed them with his rhetorical skills."

Al-Ḥāfiẓ Ibn 'Asākir—may Allah have mercy upon him—said:

> I read from a letter from the handwriting of the Ḥadīth scholar of Egypt, 'Alī b. Baqā' al-Warrāq that was written by the Mālikī jurist, Abū Muḥammad 'Abdullāh b. Abī Zayd al-Qayrawānī who was the leading scholar of Mālik's school in the Maghreb during his time. He wrote it to 'Alī b. Aḥmad b. Ismā'īl al-Baghdādī al-Mu'tazilī as a response to a letter written by the latter to the Mālikīs of Qayrawān in which he offered them advice that would convert them

> to the Mu'tazila doctrine. [Within the letter—produced in full by Ibn 'Asākir—it reads:]... "And you attributed him to innovation then you did not mention a statement from him that can be identified as an innovation or be used to call him an innovator. We know of no one who has accused Ibn Kullāb of innovation. What has reached us is that he closely follows the Sunna and takes it upon himself to refute the Jahmiyya and other innovators..."[16]

This is a powerful testimony from Imām Ibn Abī Zayd—may Allah have mercy upon him—regarding Ibn Kullāb and his close adherence to the Sunna and refutations against the innovators and that he knew of no one who accused him of innovation.

[Shaykh Muḥammad Zāhid] Al-Kawtharī commented on this [in his edition of *Tabyīn Kadhib al-Muftarī*]: "He was the Imām of the Sunni theologians during the time of Aḥmad and he used to keep the company of al-Ḥārith b. Asad. Some people who are weak in theology attack him..."

Al-Kawtharī then proceeded to examine the issues that caused some to attack him and he explained how those issues are not distant from the Sacred Law and the intellect.

Ibn Qāḍī Shuhba said: "He was one of the major theologians and he was from Ahl al-Sunna. His path and the path of al-Ḥārith al-Muḥāsibī were followed by Abū al-Ḥasan al-Ash'arī."[17]

Jamāl al-Dīn al-Isnawī said: "He was one of the major theologians and he was from Ahl al-Sunna... Al-'Abādī mentioned him in the rank of Abū Bakr al-Ṣayrafī and said: 'He is one of our companions among the theologians.'"[18]

Imām al-Dhahabī said: "The man is the closest of the theologians to the Sunna; nay, he is among their debaters."[19]

Shaykh Shu'ayb al-Arna'ūṭ commented on this [in his edition of al-Dhahabī's *Siyar*]: "He was the Imām of Ahl al-Sunna and its reference in his time. Imām al-Ḥaramayn [al-Juwaynī] described him in *Al-Irshād*, saying: 'He is from our companions.'"

---

[16] *Tabyīn Kadhib al-Muftarī*, p. 405.
[17] *Ṭabaqāt al-Shāfi'iyya*, 1:78.
[18] *Ṭabaqāt al-Shāfi'iyya* of *al-Isnawī*: 2:178.
[19] *Siyar 'Alām al-Nubalā'*, 11:175.

We have already mentioned the statement of Ibn Khaldūn: "He held the views of ʿAbdullāh b. Saʿīd b. Kullāb, Abū al-ʿAbbās al-Qalānisī and al-Ḥārith al-Muḥāsibī among the followers of the *Salaf* and the path of the Sunna." Here, he described him as a follower of the *Salaf*, and that Imām al-Ashʿarī held his views, and the views of al-Qalānisī and al-Muḥāsibī: all followers of the *Salaf* and upon the way of the Sunna.

ʿAllāma Kamāl al-Dīn al-Bayāḍī—may Allah have mercy upon him—said:

> That is because al-Māturīdī detailed the doctrine of the Imām [Abū Ḥanīfa] and his Sunni companions who appeared before al-Ashʿarī. There has never been an era bereft of those who aid and manifest the religion. He [al-Ashʿarī] was also preceded in that [aiding the doctrine of Ahl al-Sunna] by Imām Abū Muḥammad ʿAbdullāh b. Saʿīd al-Qaṭṭān.[20]

In other words, Imām Ibn Kullāb preceded Imām Abū al-Ḥasan in aiding the religion and manifesting the Sunna.

Al-Ḥāfiẓ Ibn Ḥajar said in his biography of Ibn Kullāb, after mentioning the statement of Ibn al-Nadīm [who was a Muʿtazilī]: "He was from the *Ḥashawī* riff-raff": "What he means is that [a *Ḥashawī* is] whoever is upon the way of the *Salaf* by abandoning figurative interpretation of the verses and Ḥadīth reports about the Divine attributes; they are also called the people of non-specific interpretation [*mufawwiḍa*]."[21]

Imām al-Shahrastānī said:

> Until the time of ʿAbdullāh b. Saʿīd al-Kullābī [*sic*], Abū al-ʿAbbās al-Qalānisī, al-Ḥārith b. Asad al-Muḥāsibī. They were from the generality of the *Salaf*; however, they engaged in speculative theology and aided the doctrines of the *Salaf* with theological proofs and rational evidence. Some of them wrote books and some of them taught. Then there was the debate that took place between Abū al-Ḥasan al-Ashʿarī and his teacher regarding the issue

[20] *Ishārāt al-Marām min ʿIbārāt al-Imām*, p. 23.
[21] *Lisān al-Mīzān*, 3:291.

> of best interest [*al-ṣalāḥ wal-aṣlaḥ*]. They debated and al-Ash'arī then switched camps and assisted their [the Sunni] doctrine with theological methods and it became a school of Ahl al-Sunna and the term *Ash'ariyya* replaced the term *Ṣifātiyya.*[22]

We will go further and say that not only was Imām al-Ash'arī upon the methodology of Ibn Kullāb, but it was also the same doctrine of the major Imāms like Imām al-Bukhārī—may Allah have mercy upon him. Al-Ḥāfiẓ Ibn Ḥajar—may Allah have mercy upon him—said:

> In all that al-Bukhārī cited concerning the explanation of rare words, he quoted from the people of that science, such as Abū 'Ubayda, al-Naḍir b. Shumayl, al-Farrā', and others. As for the matters of jurisprudence, most of it is taken from al-Shāfi'ī, Abū 'Ubayd, and their likes. As for the matters of theology [*masā'il kalāmiyya*], most of it is taken from al-Karābisī, Ibn Kullāb, and their likes.

All of these citations clearly show that Imām 'Abdullāh b. Sa'īd b. Kullāb was upon the way of the *Salaf* and the Sunna.

WHAT WERE THE ACCUSATIONS AGAINST IBN KULLĀB?

If the Imāms clarified this matter, then why was 'Abdullāh b. Sa'īd b. Kullāb accused of opposing the way of the *Salaf*? Ibn 'Abd al-Barr explained a bit about this in his biographical notice for al-Karābisī. He said:

> There was a strong friendship between him [al-Karābisī] and Aḥmad b. Ḥanbal, but when the former opposed the latter regarding the Qur'ān, their friendship turned into enmity. Both of them would speak ill about the other. This is because Aḥmad used to say: "Whoever says that the Qur'ān is created is a Jahmī; whoever says that the Qur'ān is the speech of Allah but does not say that it is uncreated or created is *wāqifī* (hesitant); and whoever says: 'My pronunciation of the Qur'ān is created' is an innovator."

---

[22] *Al-Milal wal-Niḥal*, p. 81.

> Now, al-Karābisī, ʿAbdullāh b. Kullāb, Abū Thawr, Dāwūd b. ʿAlī and their rank used to say that the Qur'ān spoken by Allah is an attribute among His attributes and cannot be created; the recitation of the reader and his speaking with the Qur'ān is his own acquisition and action; that is created and is a *ḥikāya* (narration) of Allah's speech...
>
> The Ḥanbalī companions of Aḥmad b. Ḥanbal had forsaken al-Karābisī, declared him an innovator, and spoke ill about both him and all who spoke with his belief in that matter.

This is the reason why ʿAbdullāh b. Kullāb was rebuked and why some said he was not upon the way of the Sunna and the *Salaf*. This matter becomes even clearer if we understand that these Imāms engaged in speculative theology in order to refute the opponents and expose their deviancy. Now, Aḥmad used to hate the way of speculative theology as a method for clarifying the truth, and he used to prefer stopping at where the *Salaf* stopped. This is undoubtedly the truth as long as there is no pressing need for speculative theology.

Al-Tāj al-Subkī—may Allah have mercy upon him—said: "We say as Aḥmad used to say: the correct view is that there should be no engaging in speculative theology as long as there is no pressing need for it."[23]

No matter what the case may be, the view for which ʿAbdullāh b. Kullāb was declared and innovator does not entail the description of blameworthy innovation or being against the way of the *Salaf*, especially if we consider that this doctrine on the pronunciation of the Qur'ān was held by many illustrious Imāms from the Umma of Islam, such as those mentioned by Ibn ʿAbd al-Barr.

Others who held this belief include Imām al-Bukhārī, Imām Muslim, al-Ḥārith al-Muḥāsibī, Muḥammad b. Naṣr al-Marwazī, and others. The problems that occurred between al-Bukhārī and his Shaykh al-Dhuhalī were only because of this issue. Imām al-Bukhārī wrote a book on this topic called *Khalq Afʿāl al-ʿIbād* in order to support his viewpoint and refute his opponents.

---

[23] *Al-Ṭabaqāt al-Kubrā*, 2:119.

Al-Tāj al-Subkī—may Allah have mercy upon him—said: "The truth regarding the issue of pronunciation is with him [al-Bukhārī]; no one of intellect among creation doubts that his pronunciation is from his contingent actions that are created by Allah, the Exalted. The only reason Imām Aḥmad ﷺ rebuked it was because of its repugnant expression."[24] As for Imām Muslim, he used to openly declare his belief in the issue of pronunciation and did he not conceal it.[25]

Al-Ḥāfiẓ Ibn Kathīr—may Allah have mercy upon him—said in his biographical entry for al-Karābisī:

> Aḥmad b. Ḥanbal used to speak negatively about him because of the issue of pronunciation, and he [al-Karābisī] used to speak negatively about Aḥmad as well, and for that reason the people abstained from taking from him [al-Karābisī]. I say: What I have seen from him is that he said: "The speech of Allah is uncreated from every angle, except that my pronunciation of the Qur'ān is created. Whoever does not believe that one's pronunciation of the Qur'ān is created is a disbeliever." This is also relayed from al-Bukhārī and Dāwūd b. ʿAlī al-Ẓāhirī. Imām Aḥmad used to shut this door in order to close the discussion regarding the createdness of the Qur'ān.[26]

Another Imām who believed that the pronunciation of the Qur'ān is created was Imām Muḥammad b. Jarīr al-Ṭabarī—may Allah have mercy upon him. This is one of the issues for which he was rebuked by some of the bigoted Ḥanbalīs.

Al-Ḥāfiẓ Ibn Kathīr said:

> Some turmoil took place between al-Ṭabarī and the Ḥanbalīs—I believe it was because of the issue of pronunciation—and he was accused of Shiʿism. They requested that a debate take place between him and them, so Ibn Jarīr came for the debate but no one among them showed up.

---

[24] Ibid., 2:13.

[25] See: *Siyar ʿAlām al-Nubalā'*, 12:453, 12:572.

[26] *Ṭabaqāt al-Fuqahā' al-Shāfiʿīn*, 1:133.

> The Ḥanbalīs exaggerated about this issue and became very bigoted regarding it. They maintained that the belief in pronunciation led to the belief in the createdness of the Qurʾān. The matter is not as they claimed; and indeed, the truth cannot be safeguarded by falsehood, and Allah knows best.[27]

Yes. The Qurʾān is the uncreated speech of Allah and an attribute from the attributes of His Exalted Essence; however, this truth cannot be safeguarded by the falsehood of denying the contingency and creation of what subsists within a created being and rebuking those who speak of it.

The truth in this matter is with al-Karābisī, Ibn Kullāb, al-Bukhārī, Abū Thawr, Dāwūd, al-Muḥāsibī, al-Ṭabarī, and others upon their path. As For Imām Aḥmad b. Ḥanbal ﵀—and by extension, those who believe as he did—his words are interpreted as closing the door of this discussion so as to prevent the belief in pronunciation from leading to belief in the createdness of the Qurʾān itself.

Imām al-Dhahabī said: "There is no doubt that what al-Karābisī innovated and explained in the question of the pronunciation and that it is created is the truth, but Imām Aḥmad refused it in order that it not lead to a belief in the createdness of the Qurʾān, so in this sense, he shut the door."[28]

He also said: "He [al-Karābisī] used to say that the speech of Allah is uncreated and that the pronunciation of the Qurʾān is created. If by that he meant the utterance [*tallafuẓ*], then that is fine, for our actions are created. On the other hand, if he meant that the uttered content [*al-malfūẓ*] is created, then this is what Aḥmad and the *Salaf* censured and considered Jahmism."[29]

Undoubtedly, the first view was the belief of al-Karābisī, Ibn Kullāb, al-Bukhārī, Muslim, Abū Thawr, Dāwūd, and those who shared with them in this belief. In general, this issue is not so serious as to warrant charges of innovation.

---

[27] *Al-Bidāya wal-Nihāya*, 11:145, *Al-Kāmil*, 7:8, *Al-Siyar*, 14:272, and *Al-Wāfī fī al-Wafiyāt*: 2:284.

[28] *Siyar ʿAlām al-Nubalāʾ*, 12:82.

[29] *Mīzān al-ʿItidāl*, 1:544.

Al-Ḥāfiẓ Abū Bakr al-Aʿyīn said: "The Shaykhs of Khorasan are three: Qutayba, ʿAlī b. Ḥajar, and Muḥammad b. Mihrān al-Rāzī, and its men are four: ʿAbdullāh b. ʿAbd al-Raḥmān al-Samarqandī, Muḥammad b. Ismāʿīl al-Bukhārī before there appeared from him what appeared..." Imām al-Dhahabī commented on this statement:

> That which appeared from Muḥammad [al-Bukhārī] is a minor issue that was differed over between the Imāms regarding the belief in the createdness of the Qur'ān and it is called "the question regarding the actions of the readers." The majority of the Imāms and the *Salaf* and latter generations were of the view that the Qur'ān is the revealed and uncreated speech of Allah—and this is what we take as our religion with Allah.

Imām Aḥmad's abandonment of these Imāms does not necessitate that they were opposed to the way of the *Salaf*, especially considering that the truth in this issue was on their side, as Imām al-Dhahabī explained. Al-Dhahabī also said:

> This Imām [Aḥmad] did not believe in delving into these matters for fear of it leading to the belief in the createdness of the Qur'ān. He believed that abstaining from this is more fitting: we believe in Allah, the Exalted, His Angels, His Books, His Messengers, His decree, the Resurrection, and the appearance before Allah on the Day of Recompense. If these lines were explained with all their detail and evidence they would come in five volumes. Nay, that is found and explained by those who pursue it. The Qur'ān contains a healing and a mercy for the believers. It is known that the utterance is from the acquisition of the reader and is not the uttered content; the reading is other than the content; and the recitation and its goodness and melody is other than recited content. The voice of the reader is from his own acquisition for he performs the act of pronunciation and brings out the voice, the movement, and the utterance, and he articulates the words from his created vocals; he did not originate the words of the Qur'ān or its arrangement, composition, or meanings...

He then narrated a report from al-Ḥākim with his chain up to Fawrān, the companion of Aḥmad: "Al-Athram and Abū 'Abdullāh al-Mu'īṭī asked me to request some personal time with Abū 'Abdullāh [Aḥmad] so I could ask him about our companions who differentiate between the pronunciation and what is relayed [*maḥkī*]. I asked him about this and he replied: 'The Qur'ān is uncreated, however it is dealt with in statement and action. As for our actions, they are created.' I further asked him: 'Does their belief in the pronunciation include them within the fold of the Jahmiyya?' He replied: 'No, the Jahmiyya are those who say that the Qur'ān is created.'"

In *Al-Asmā' wal-Ṣifāt*, Imām al-Bayhaqī reported from 'Abdullāh b. Aḥmad b. Ḥanbal who said: "I heard my father say: 'Whoever says that my pronunciation of the Qur'ān is created—intending thereby the Qur'ān—is a disbeliever.'" Al-Bayhaqī commented:

> I say: This restriction that his son 'Abdullāh memorised from him "...intending thereby the Qur'ān..." went unnoticed by those who reported an opposite view from him regarding pronunciation, and as a consequence, he was attributed with something he declared his innocence from in this report we mentioned.[30]

Imām al-Bukhārī—may Allah have mercy upon him—said in *Khalq Af'āl al-'Ibād*:

> As for what the two parties from the school of Aḥmad have claimed as proof, each for their own respective position, much of what they relate is not established as authentic, and perhaps they did not understand the depth of his position. What is well known from Aḥmad and the people of knowledge is that the speech of Allah is uncreated and everything besides Him is created, and they hated delving into minute and obscure matters, and they shunned the people of speculative theology and they shunned debate and disputation unless it is found in Sacred Knowledge and explained by the Messenger of Allah ﷺ.

[30] *Al-Asmā' wal-Ṣifāt*, p. 266.

We are absolutely certain that they—may Allah have mercy upon them—did not say this without there being a need for it. Allah forbid that they should ever speak about a matter the Companions and followers were silent about. However, since they saw that the people flung this door wide open, discussed it, and spoke about it incorrectly, they were obliged to speak about it in order to clarify the truth and prevent the people from engaging in it.

ʿAllāma al-Kawtharī—may Allah have mercy upon him—said in his annotation of *Tabyīn Kadhib al-Muftarī*:

> As for Aḥmad's words against Ibn Kullāb and his companion [al-Muḥāsibī], it was due to his hatred of discussing theological rhetoric and his pious scrupulousness away from it. The truth of the matter is that it is obligatory to discuss it when there is a need—contrary to the view of Aḥmad.[31]

In summary, this is a minor issue, as described by al-Ḥāfiẓ al-Dhahabī. It is one in which the opinions of the Imāms differed; however, they were all in agreement that the Qurʾān—as an attribute of the Ever Merciful and His speech—is uncreated. In the course of this section, we have demonstrated that Ibn Kullāb was not alone in this particular question. Nay, many of the major scholars of the religion held his opinion. We have also demonstrated that he did not innovate or oppose the way of the *Salaf* or the Sunna. Nay, he is from the major figures of Ahl al-Sunna wal-Jamāʿa who treaded the path of the pious predecessors. Having established this, where does the idea of Imām al-Ashʿarīs retraction from his path originate? This question brings us to the third premise.

REFUTING THE THIRD PREMISE

The book *Al-Ibāna* is the ostensible proof and reference for those who believe that Imām al-Ashʿarī went through three stages in his life. Now, there is no doubt that in this book and in many other essays ascribed to him the Imām employed a unique style.

---

31 *Tabyīn Kadhib al-Muftarī*, p. 406.

Most of the time in this book, he would tread the path of the majority of the *Salaf* with respect to the ambiguous verses. What we mean is that he would follow the path of non-specific interpretation [*tafwīḍ*]. As a result of this style, some inferred that the Imām retracted from the path of Ibn Kullāb that he was upon, and returned to the path of the *Salaf*!

In our refutation of the second premise, we established that Ibn Kullāb did not oppose the *Salaf* and that he was in fact from the *Salaf* and upon their way and that he treaded the path of non-specific interpretation. We previously mentioned al-Ḥāfiẓ Ibn Ḥajar's refutation of Ibn Nadīm's statement regarding Ibn Kullāb: "He was from the *Ḥashawī* riff-raff." Ibn Ḥajar commented: "What he means is that [a *Ḥashawī* is] whoever is upon the way of the *Salaf* by abandoning figurative interpretation of the verses and Ḥadīth reports about the Divine attributes; they are also called the people of non-specific interpretation [*mufawwiḍa*]."[32]

In addition to that, the book *Al-Ibāna* is the reference point for those who make this claim and it is their proof of Imām al-Ash'arī's alleged retraction from the way of Ibn Kullāb. We say: the book itself contradicts the claim of al-Ash'arī's retraction from his path, for he authored it in the manner and method of Ibn Kullāb; how can he retract from the path of Ibn Kullāb and then author his final book based upon his way? Al-Ḥāfiẓ Ibn Ḥajar said: "In his book *Al-Ibāna*, al-Ash'arī traversed upon his [Ibn Kullāb's] path."[33]

This increases us in certainty upon certainty that Imām Ibn Kullāb was upon the path of the pious predecessors and one of their Imāms, because the [book] *Al-Ibāna* that al-Ash'arī wrote at the end of his life was based on the methodology of the *Salaf and* written according to the way of Ibn Kullāb. This clearly entails that the path of the *Salaf* and the path of Ibn Kullāb are in reality one path and that it was the path followed by Imām al-Ash'arī after his retraction from the doctrine of the Mu'tazila.

Imām al-Ash'arī did not go through three stages in his life. He went through two stages: the stage of following the doctrine of the Mu'tazila, and the stage in which he returned to the way

---

[32] *Lisān al-Mīzān*: 3:291.

[33] Ibid.

of the *Salaf* followed by Ibn Kullāb, al-Muḥāsibī, al-Qalānisī, al-Karābisī, al-Bukhārī, Muslim, Abū Thawr, al-Ṭabarī, and others. That is the stage in which he wrote his book *Al-Ibāna*.

It is related that when Imām al-Ash'arī wrote *Al-Ibāna*, it was rejected by some of the Ḥanbalīs[34] out of bigotry and they did not accept it from him.[35] Perhaps this also supports our assertion that *Al-Ibāna* was written in accordance to the way of Ibn Kullāb who was forsaken by the Ḥanbalī Imāms who chose to abandon him because of the question on pronunciation and his delving into speculative theology in order to refute the opponents from the Mu'tazila and others.

What we have mentioned here about *Al-Ibāna* is only with respect to the original work written by the Imām, *not* the version that is printed and widely available today. The current version we have today has faced interpolation, extraneous additions, and deletion.

'Allāma al-Kawtharī—may Allah have mercy upon him—said in his introduction to *Tabyīn Kadhib al-Muftarī*: "The edition of *Al-Ibāna* that was printed in India is full of typographical errors

---

[34] We say that it was rejected by some of the Ḥanbalīs because there has always been a large group among the Ḥanbalīs who allied themselves with Imām al-Ash'arī and who loved him and ascribed to him. In *Tabyīn Kadhib al-Muftarī*, al-Ḥāfiẓ Ibn 'Asākir refuted the author al-Ahwāzī who sought to use this incident as an affirmation of the Ḥanbalī's rejection of al-Ash'arī and his book *Al-Ibāna*. Ibn 'Asākir said in (p. 389): "If the matter was as he claimed, they would have cited it from their Shaykhs and made it well-known. I have not ceased hearing from those whom I deem reliable that the Imām was a friend of the Tamīmīs who were the predecessors of Abū Muḥammad Rizqullāh b. 'Abd al-Wahhāb b. 'Abd al-'Azīz b. al-Ḥārith, and I heard that they used to honour him. The effects of the blessings of that companionship has shown up in their progeny, so much so that their companion Abū al-Khaṭṭāb al-Kalwadhānī ascribed himself to him [al-Ash'arī]—and Aḥmad al-Ḥarbī, the student of Abū al-Khaṭṭāb, informs us of the truthfulness of what I mention. In addition to this, between them and his companion Abū 'Abdullāh b. Mujāhid and the companion of his companion Abū Bakr b. Ṭayyib al-Bāqillānī there was a connection, and they would eat with each other. This proves al-Ahwāzī's fabrication."

[35] See: *Siyar 'Alām al-Nubalā'*, 15:90, *Ṭabaqāt al-Ḥanābila*, 2:18, and *Al-Wāfī fī al-Wafiyāt*, 12:146.

and interpolations. Sinful people have gotten their hands on it so it must be reprinted based on a reliable source." He also said in his introduction to *Ishārāt al-Marām min 'Ibārāt al-Imām* of al-Bayḍāwī: "It is extremely rare to come across an authentic original copy of his written works despite their great number. The published version of *Al-Ibāna* was not from a reliable original copy, and regarding the *Maqālāt* that is available there is hesitation."

This was also the opinion held by Shaykh 'Abd al-Raḥmān Badawī. He supported the conclusion of al-Kawtharī: "And Shaykh al-Kawtharī duly noted that the edition published in India has been altered by sinful hands."[36]

Shaykh Wahbī al-Ghāwjī—may Allah have mercy upon him—has an essay on this subject titled *A Scientific Look at the Ascription of Al-Ibāna in its Entirety to Imām Abū al-Ḥasan* [*Naẓra 'Ilmiyya fī Nisba Kitāb Al-Ibāna Jamī'hi ilā al-Imām Abī al-Ḥasan*]. In this essay he presented solid evidence proving that are large portion of what is contained in the present day *Al-Ibāna* cannot be authentically attributed to Imām al-Ash'arī.

One edition of *Al-Ibāna* has been printed based on a comparison to four handwritten manuscripts. This edition was edited by Shaykh Fawqiyya Ḥusayn, and although it is better than the earlier editions, it still contains interpolations, deletions, and extraneous addition. Perhaps this confirms al-Kawtharī's opinion when he said: "It is extremely rare to come across an authentic original copy of his written works despite their great number."

Al-Ḥāfiẓ Ibn 'Asākir reproduced two chapters of *Al-Ibāna* in *Tabyīn Kadhb al-Muftarī*. Now, when we compare the published versions of *Al-Ibāna* and Shaykh Fawqiyya Ḥusayn's edition with the two chapters reproduced by Ibn 'Asākir in his *Tabyīn*, the full extent of interpolation this book has gone through becomes clear. Here are a few examples to illustrate this:

- In the published edition of *Al-Ibāna*, on page 17, it says the following: "And they denied that He [Allah] possesses two eyes ['*aynān*] even though He said: ﴾*Sailing under Our eyes.*﴿" Here you see it is mentioned in the dual form!

[36] *Madhāhib al-Islāmiyyīn*, 1:516.

- In the version reproduced by Ibn ʿAsākir on page 107 it says: "And they denied that He possesses an eye [ʿ*ayn*]." Here you see it is mentioned in the singular form.
- In the published edition on page 18 it mentions: "...and that He possesses two eyes [ʿ*aynayn*] without modality..."
- In the edition of Shaykh Fawqiyya Ḥusayn on page 22 it says: "And He, the Most High, possesses two eyes [ʿ*aynayn*] without modality." Here you see that in the published edition as well as Shaykh Fawqiyya's edition it is mentioned in the dual form!
- In the version reproduced by Ibn ʿAsākir on page 158 it says: "And He possesses an eye [ʿ*ayn*] without modality."

The singular form is in conformity with the Book, the Sunna, and the statements of the *Salaf.* This is a clear proof that the copies of this book have been altered. The wording "two eyes" [ʿ*aynān*] is not found in either the Qurʾān or the Sunna. Whoever uses the word "eye" [ʿ*ayn*] in the dual form has drawn a comparison between Allah and creation that is observed with the senses. Far exalted and free is Allah from that.

Al-Kawtharī—may Allah have mercy upon him—said in his annotation of al-Bayhaqī's *Al-Asmāʾ wal-Ṣifāt:*

> The dual form has not appeared in the Book or the Sunna. The narration of Abū al-Ḥasan al-Ashʿarī to that effect is interpolated into his books, considering what the bulk [of scholars] have quoted from him...
>
> Ibn Ḥazm said: "It is not permissible for anyone to describe Allah ﷻ as possessing two eyes because there is no Divine text stating that."

Ibn ʿAqīl said in his commentary on the Ḥadīth of the Dajjāl: "Some ignorant folk reckon that when he ﷺ negated blindness in one eye for Allah ﷻ he affirmed—via inference—that He possesses two eyes. This is farfetched; he only negated blindness in one eye as a negation of imperfections."

Ibn al-Jawzī refuted those who believe that Allah possesses two eyes: "I say: This is an innovation for which they have no proof. They only affirmed two eyes via inference from his ﷺ statement:

'Indeed Allah is not blind in one eye.' He only intended to negate imperfection from Him, the Exalted."

Another example of interpolation in *Al-Ibāna* is the attack against Imām al-Aʿẓam Abū Ḥanīfa ﷺ. In the published edition of *Al-Ibāna* on page 57 it says:

> Hārūn b. Isḥāq al-Ḥamadānī mentioned from Abū Nuʿaym, from Sulaymān b. ʿĪsā al-Qārī, from Sufyān al-Thawrī who said: "Ḥammād b. Abī Sulaymān said to me: 'Covey to Abū Ḥanīfa the idol-worshipper that I am most certainly innocent of him.'" Sulaymān then said: "That is because he used to believe that the Qurʾān is created."
>
> Sufyān b. Wakīʿ mentioned: "ʿUmar b. Ḥammād b. Abī Ḥanīfa said: 'My father informed me: "The speech for which Ibn Abī Laylā sought Abū Ḥanīfa's repentance was his statement: 'The Qurʾān is created.'" He then repented and it was announced to the people. My father said: "I asked him: 'What happened?' He replied: 'I was afraid he would stand against me so I practiced dissimulation [*tuqya*].'"'"
>
> Hārūn b. Isḥāq said: "I heard Ismāʿīl b. Abī al-Ḥakam mention from ʿUmar b. ʿUbayd al-Ṭanāfisī that Ḥammād [Ibn Abī Sulaymān] relayed to Abū Ḥanīfa: 'I am innocent of what you say unless you repent.' In [Ismāʿīl's presence] was Ibn Abī ʿUqba and he said: 'Your neighbour informed me that Abū Ḥanīfa invited him to that from which his repentance was sought.
>
> And it was mentioned from Abū Yūsuf that he said: "I debated Abū Ḥanīfa for two months until he retracted from his belief in the createdness of the Qurʾān."

Are we in any need of proving the falsehood of these reports or establishing that they are interpolated in the book of Imām Abū al-Ḥasan al-Ashʿarī? Is it not sufficient for us to merely quote these reports from the printed edition of *Al-Ibāna* to know that it has been subject to alteration and interpolation?

In Shaykh Fawqiyya Ḥusayn's edition of *Al-Ibāna* on pages 90 and 91, after the first report after Sufyān's statement, "That is because he used to believe that the Qurʾān is created," there appears: "Imām al-Aʿẓam, Abū Ḥanīfa ﷺ, is far removed from this belief! Nay, it is slander and falsehood; Abū Ḥanīfa was from the best of Ahl al-Sunna." After the statement of Ibn Abī 'Uqba there appears: "This is an unadulterated lie against Abū Ḥanīfa."

Al-Kawtharī—may Allah have mercy upon him—said in his annotation of the book *Al-Ikhtilāf fī al-Lafẓ* by Ibn Qutayba:

> One case of odd interpolation is that which has been falsely added to some editions of al-Ash'arī's *Al-Ibāna*—just as there are other false additions in it stating that Ḥammād b. Abī Sulaymān said: "Convey to Abū Ḥanīfa the idol-worshipper that I am most certainly innocent of his religion," and that he used to believe in the createdness of the Qur'ān. The statement of Ḥammād as found in al-Bukhārī's *Khalq Af'āl al-'Ibād* says: "Convey to Abū So-and-so;" not "Abū Ḥanīfa." Someone who did not fear Allah replaced "Abū So-and-so" with "Abū Ḥanīfa." Allah knows best who this Abū So-and-so was and what the issue was about...

In al-Bayhaqī's *'Itiqād* it mentions:

> We narrated from Muḥammad b. Sa'īd b. Sābiq that he stated: "I asked Abū Yūsuf: 'Did Abū Ḥanīfa used to say that the Qur'ān is created?' He replied: 'No! Allah's refuge is sought, and neither do I say it!' I then asked him: 'Did he hold the beliefs of Jahm [b. Ṣafwān]?' He replied: 'No! Allah's refuge is sought, and neither do I hold them.'" The narrators of this report are reliable.

The above narration contradicts the other report attributed to Abū Yūsuf in which he allegedly said: "I debated Abū Ḥanīfa for two months until he retracted from his belief in the createdness of the Qur'ān."

Shaykh Wahbī al-Ghāwjī—may Allah have mercy upon him—said:

> There is no harm if we say that if Imām al-Ash'arī—may Allah have mercy upon him—truly attributed this to the Imām [Abū Ḥanīfa], that he believed in the createdness of the Qur'ān, Imām al-Ash'arī would not have had a lofty

> status among the Ḥanafīs, the followers of Imām Abū Ḥanīfa—may Allah have mercy upon him. So, dear reader, do not glance at these quotes that are fragmentary and false in their chains of transmission. Have good thoughts about Imām al-Ashʿarī just as you have good thoughts toward the Imām of the jurists and the rest of the Umma—may Allah be pleased with them. Remember that many false things have been added to the Ḥadīth reports of the Messenger of Allah ﷺ and have been written with manufactured chains of transmission. In addition to this, do not forget that there are many extraneous expressions and statements gathered in the books of the scholars as well as many deletions—even during the lifetimes of those very authors.

Another example of this is found in the published editions of *Al-Ibāna* is regarding *istiwāʾ* (rising). On page 69 it says: "If someone asks: 'What do you say about *istiwāʾ*?' we say: Indeed Allah ﷻ is risen [*mustawin*] over His Throne as He said: ﴾*The Ever Merciful rose above the Throne*﴿..." In Shaykh Fawqiyya's edition on page 105 it says: "...we say: Indeed Allah ﷻ performed the act of *istiwāʾ* over His Throne—an *istiwāʾ* that befits Him and without indwelling or settlement..." So as you see, the ending statement is completely removed from the other published editions!

One page 73 of the published edition of *Al-Ibāna* it states: "All of that proves that He, the Exalted, is in/above [*fī*] the heavens: risen/established [*mustawin*] above His Throne. And by the consensus of the people the heaven is not the earth, so this proves that Allah, the Exalted, is Alone in His Divine Oneness and is risen/established [*mustawin*] above His Throne." In the Shaykh Fawqiyya's edition of the same passage (p. 113) it reads: "So this proves that He, the Exalted, is Alone in His Divine Oneness and risen/established above the Throne with an *istiwāʾ* that is transcendent above indwelling and union."

There are indeed tens of examples clearly proving that the book has been interpolated. This rules it impermissible to consider most of it truly representative of the doctrine of Imām al-Ashʿarī—except the parts that agree with the rest of the people of knowledge and those who cited from him.

If it is historically affirmed that the Imām was upon the way of the *Salaf* and Ahl al-Sunna after his retraction from the doctrine of the Muʿtazila, and if it is affirmed that Ibn Kullāb was from the Imāms of the *Salaf* and upon the way of the *Salaf*, and if it is affirmed that *Al-Ibāna*—which is the main source for the claim of the Imāms alleged retraction—was really written according to the way of Ibn Kullāb, then it is clearly established that the Imām did not go through three stages in his life. Rather, he went through two stages only: the stage in which he followed the doctrine of the Muʿtazila, and the stage in which he returned to the way of the *Salaf*.

We know of no other proof for those who repeat this claim except the style and method of *Al-Ibāna* and other essays. In *Al-Ibāna*, the Imām treaded the path of non-specific interpretation, which is the path of the majority of the *Salaf*. In reality, there is no contradiction between non-specific interpretation and specific figurative interpretation as long as the latter is performed with its proper conditions.

The Ashʿarīs believe in the entire content of *Al-Ibāna* (meaning the correct *Al-Ibāna* that was written by the Imām and not the altered version) and they grasp onto it firmly, for both non-specific interpretation and specific figurative interpretation are correct and there is no objection to either of them. There are examples of both that are reported from the Companions and the *Salaf* as we shall soon see.

Both parties agree upon Divine transcendence after affirming for Allah what He affirmed for Himself and both parties agree that the outwardly apparent meaning [of the attributes] that the creation is accustomed to in their world is incorrect.

Al-Ḥāfiẓ Ibn ʿAsākir—may Allah have mercy upon him—said:

> Nay, they [the Ashʿarīs] strongly believe in what is contained in it [*Al-Ibāna*] and they rely upon it. All praise is due to Allah, they are not Muʿtazila or Muʿaṭṭila (deniers) who negate Allah's attributes; they affirm for Him ﷻ the attributes He affirmed for Himself and they describe Him with what He described Himself with in the clear-cut verses, and with what His Prophet ﷺ described

> Him with in the rigorously authentic narrations. They declare Him exaltedly transcendent above imperfections and faults.[37]

Imām Ibn ʿAsākir's statement applies to the *Al-Ibāna* written by the Imām. As for the copy we have in our hands today, there is no confidence in it and in most cases it cannot be taken as a representation of the beliefs of the Imām or the Ashʿarīs unless it agrees with the views of the rest. He also said:

> The book *Al-Ibāna* has not ceased being seen as correct by the people of religion. I heard the ascetic jurist, Shaykh Abū Bakr Aḥmad b. Muḥammad b. Ismāʿīl b. Muḥammad b. Bashār al-Būshanjī—better known as al-Kharjirdī—relate from some of his Shaykhs that Imām Abū ʿUthmān Ismāʿīl b. ʿAbd al-Raḥmān b. Aḥmad al-Ṣābūnī al-Naysabūrī would not go out to his study circle except that the *Al-Ibāna* of Abū al-Ḥasan al-Ashʿarī would be in his hands. He would show amazement with it and say: "What is to be censured in this book in which he explained his doctrine?"[38] So this is the statement of Imām Abū ʿUthmān and he was one of the notable traditionalists of Khorasan.[39]

Look at the esteem the notables of the Umma gave to *Al-Ibāna* and its author. Here we have Shaykh al-Islām Abū ʿUthmān al-Ṣābūnī—may Allah have mercy upon him—who was known for his nobility, knowledge, and asceticism,[40] lavishing praise on both the Imām and his book *Al-Ibāna*. From this you can also infer that Shaykh al-Islām Abū ʿUthmān al-Ṣābūnī was upon the path of Imām al-Ashʿarī.

---

[37] *Tabyīn Kadhib al-Muftarī*, p. 388.

[38] This doctrine was the same as what Ibn Kullāb was upon, for *Al-Ibāna* was written according to his method. From this we can consider al-Ṣābūnī's praise of *Al-Ibāna* and Imām Abū al-Ḥasan as praise for Ibn Kullāb as well—so let this praise be added to the list of the other scholars who praised Ibn Kullāb.

[39] Ibid., 389.

[40] Al-Tāj al-Subkī said about him: "He has the nickname Shaykh al-Islām and that was given to him by the Sunnis of Khorasan. So when they use this term they do not intend anyone else besides him."

How could that not be the case when his education and training was under the tutelage of Imām Abū al-Ṭayyib Sahl b. Abī Sahl al-Ṣuʿlūkī who was from the companions of the companions of Imām al-Ashʿarī (the second rank)? The Imāms of that era used to attend the gatherings of Abū ʿUthmān such as Ustādh Abū Isḥāq al-Isfarāyīnī, Ustādh Abū Bakr b. Fūrak, and the rest of the Imāms. These notables from the Umma of Islam were from the esteemed Ashʿarīs; their praise of him and his praise of them prove that they were all upon a single path. May Allah have mercy upon all of them and be well pleased with them.[41]

Is it correct according to the scientific method of inquiry to ignore all of the historical, scientific, and rational proofs mentioned, and hold fast to contrived views that do not reach the level of conjecture and that are unsupported by either texts or rational thought? Even if we were to go out of our way and consider the source for this claim as a proof, it would still be impossible for us to accept it scientifically because whenever a proof carries other possibilities it is clothed in ambiguity and can no longer be used as evidence. This is established in the science of legal theory. If that is when a proof carries another possibility only, what will happen if this possibility is close to certainty—as is the case with the proofs that *Al-Ibāna* was altered?

Let us assume for argument's sake that edition of *Al-Ibāna* available to us is not altered and that it is correctly ascribed to Imām al-Ashʿarī and that he actually did retract from his belief in Divine transcendence: does that imply that the Umma must follow him in that? Whoever believes such a thing thinks ill of the intellects of over one thousand years' worth of scholars and Imāms and accuses them of blind conformism in matters of doctrine. This person is seemingly unaware that the Umma has ascribed itself to Imām al-Ashʿarī because he stood at the forefront carrying the banner of the Sunna upon the way of the *Salaf* in the face of the people of innovation and vain desires. They did not blindly follow him in his views if he retracted from his doctrine; so that does not mean they would retract if he retracted.

---

[41] See the biographical notice on Abū ʿUthmān al-Ṣābūnī in *Tārīkh Madīna Dimashq*, 9:3; *Siyar ʿAlām al-Nubalāʾ*, 18:40; and *Al-Ṭabaqāt al-Kubrā*, 4: 271.

Imām Tāj al-Dīn al-Subkī—may Allah have mercy upon him—said: "If these [Imāms] were gullible and he [al-Ashʿarī] fooled them, then there is no intelligence to be found after the Prophets and the Companions. O Allah! Save the Muslims!"[42]

So in reality, they are ascribed to the Messenger of Allah ﷺ and the pious predecessors. Imām al-Ashʿarī—may Allah have mercy upon him—and others among the Imāms were nothing more than guides upon the path. Those who propagate these false claims wish to say with the tongue of mute eloquence [*lisān al-ḥāl*], if not with the actual tongue of speech: "If this doctrine was really true, the Imām would not have retracted it!" According to such a person, the truth is known by the one who said it and adopted it and not by the proofs and evidence that support it! Has anyone fallen except as a result of exalting elders to the point where they are blinded to their elders' faults and they blindly follow their elders' errors whilst believing they are upon the truth that is untouched by falsehood?

May Allah bless Imām Ibn al-Jawzī. How truthful were his words when he said:

> Indeed, Imām Aḥmad b. Ḥanbal—may Allah have mercy upon him—said: "It is from the narrowness of a man's knowledge that he blindly follows men in his religion."
>
> It is not appropriate for you to hear anything regarding the tenets of belief from someone who is glorified in the souls and blindly follow him in it. If you hear one of them say something that does not agree with the correct beliefs, you should say: "This is from the narrator," for indeed it is established from the Imām [Aḥmad] that he did not say anything from his opinion.
>
> So even if we assume it is authentically reported from him, he is still not to be followed blindly in the fundamentals—and neither is Abū Bakr or ʿUmar ﷺ. This is a tremendous fundamental that must be built upon. Do not allow the mention of someone who is glorified in the souls intimidate you.[43]

---

[42] *Al-Ṭabaqāt al-Kubrā*, 6:145.
[43] *Ṣayd al-Khāṭir*, p. 187.

We have gone into enough detail refuting this claim. Were it not for the fact that some hold fast to it and consider it a given fact upon which they base their arguments we would not have dealt with it. In reality this issue is very minor. It would have sufficed us in this argument to quote the report: "The burden of proof is upon the claimant." There is no evidence—circumstantial or otherwise—for this claim.

No matter how esteemed the person who repeats this claim is, it will not change reality one iota. A claim must be according to proofs and evidence that are either confirmed —which demonstrates that the claim is real—or denied—which demonstrates that the claim is incorrect or folly that must be retracted. Anyone may have his statement accepted or rejected except the infallible one ﷺ. The truth has more right and is more valuable to be sought after by the Muslim.

After having learned this—may Allah grant you and us success—you should not look to who said something (for the truth is not known by men), but rather know the truth and you shall know its people. Stick to that which is true; returning to the truth is better than persisting upon falsehood.

REFUTING THE CLAIM THAT SOME OF THE IMĀMS RETRACTED FROM THE ASHʿARĪ DOCTRINE

A claim similar to the one made about Imām Abū al-Ḥasan al-Ashʿarī—may Allah have mercy upon him—is made regarding some of the Imāms such as Imām al-Juwaynī, al-Ghazālī, and al-Rāzī—may Allah have mercy upon all of them. It is claimed that they retracted from the Ashʿarī doctrine and repudiated it. Those who propagate these claims wish to say: "If the doctrine from which these Imāms retracted was really the truth, they would not have forsaken it!"

In response to this we say: The Ashʿarī doctrine that these Imāms allegedly retracted from is either the truth or it is falsehood. If it is the truth, then what harm shall befall the doctrine or those who subscribe to it if these Imāms repudiated it (assuming that is correct)? Did the Ashʿarī doctrine become the truth when they believed in it, but turned to falsehood once they left it? If the Ashʿarī doctrine which they allegedly retracted from was false, then woe unto the Umma of Islam that has adopted falsehood for all these generations while only three or four people discovered its falsehood! This is incorrect. The scholars of Islam are not a handful of blind following commoners who are swayed left and right by words here and there without insight and proof.

When the scholars saw that these two noble Imāms, Abū al-Ḥasan al-Ashʿarī and Abū al-Manṣūr al-Māturīdī—may Allah have mercy upon both of them—were erected as guides to the way of the pious predecessors, guarding their doctrine and defending the Book and the Sunna, they hastened to aid them, assist them, and disseminate their method of affirming the doctrine of the pious predecessors. For this reason and this reason alone the scholars ascribed themselves to these two Imāms. This is contrary to what some imagine, namely, that the scholars blindly followed them in their views. If we were to assume for argument's sake that the aforementioned Imāms actually did retract from the Ashʿarī doctrine, nay, if we were to assume that tens of others also retracted from Ashʿarism, that would not change the reality agreed upon by the Umma. The most that could be said is that those Imāms were mistaken.

Having said that, those Imāms did not retract from the Ashʿarī doctrine or declare their innocence from it. How could that be the case when it is the natural extension of what the *Salaf* were upon? The most that can be said is that those Imāms retracted from the position of giving figurative interpretations to the ambiguous verses and—after having declared Allah exaltedly transcendent above the literal meanings that seem to indicate resemblance to the creation—adopted the path of non-specific interpretation, which is the way of the majority of the pious predecessors. Both the way of non-specific interpretation and the way of figurative interpretation (with its proper conditions) are confirmed from the *Salaf* of this Umma, as we shall soon demonstrate. Both methods are valid according to the people of truth.

What is rejected both rationally and textually is ascribing the lexical realities of these words to Allah, the Exalted, and understanding the outward expressions according to their usage among creation. Clearly none of the Imāms who allegedly retracted from the Ashʿarī doctrine ever believed that. The opposite, however, is true: their statements and texts are explicit and clear regarding those who hold such beliefs—nay, their views regarding that are even found in the books wherein they allegedly made their retractions!

Take for instance Imām al-Juwaynī whom they claim retracted from the Ashʿarī doctrine. In his essay *Al-Niẓāmiyya*, he explicitly states that the people of truth were unanimous in their belief that Allah is exaltedly transcendent above the literal and outward meanings of the ambiguous [verses and reports]. He said: "According to the people of truth, it is impossible to believe its [outward] signification and relay it according to the dictates of what first appears in the understanding of the linguists concerning it..."[44]

Moreover, Imām al-Juwaynī wrote *Al-Niẓāmiyya* to the vizier Niẓām al-Mulk, which is why he called it *Al-Niẓāmiyya* in the first place, naming it after him. It is no secret that Niẓām al-Mulk was an Ashʿarī in doctrine. Al-Ḥāfiẓ al-Dhahabī said concerning him, after praising him exquisitely: "And he was a Shāfiʿī and Ashʿarī."[45] Do you think that Imām al-Juwaynī would gift the vizier with an essay that contradicts his doctrine?

Furthermore, there is nothing in *Al-Niẓāmiyya* that contradicts the doctrine of the Ashʿarīs one bit. The preference al-Juwaynī mentioned of non-specific interpretation over specific figurative interpretation is one of the two accepted views of the Ashʿarīs regarding the ambiguous texts and it is also recorded from the Imāms among the pious predecessors—as we shall soon demonstrate.

Imām Ibn al-Subkī—may Allah have mercy upon him—said:

> Moreover, I say: the Ashʿarīs have two well-known views regarding the affirmation of the Divine attributes: are they to be passed on in their outward wording while believing in Divine transcendence, or are they to be given specific figurative interpretation?
>
> The view stating that they are to be passed on in their outward wording while believing in Divine transcendence is attributed to the *Salaf*, and it was the preferred view of

---

[44] *Al-Niẓāmiyya*, p. 23.
[45] *Siyar ʿAlām al-Nubalāʾ*, 19:96.

> the Imām—meaning al-Juwaynī in his *Al-Niẓāmiyya* and in other places. So his retraction meant his return from the belief in figurative interpretation to non-specific interpretation; and there is no condemnation of either view.
>
> This—the issue of specific figurative interpretation or non-specific interpretation with the belief in Divine transcendence—is an issue of independent scholarly judgement [*ijtihād*]. The great calamity and tumult lies in relaying the outward meanings and believing that they are intended and that they are not [rationally] impossible for the Creator...

Anyone who peruses *Al-Niẓāmiyya* will know that it is in agreement with the doctrine of the Ashʿarīs—Ahl al-Sunna. An example of that is when Imām al-Juwaynī declared Allah Divinely transcendent above direction, place, spatial contact, letter, sound, the outward meanings of the ambiguous texts, and his severe rebuke of those who believed in the infinite regress of contingents in the past without a first, and other issues that clearly prove that he held firmly to the doctrine of the esteemed Ashʿarīs.

In addition to this, in Imām al-Ghazālī's *Iljām al-ʿAwām*—in which he allegedly retracted his belief in the Ashʿarī doctrine—there is in reality a solid foundation laid for the doctrine of the esteemed Ashʿarīs in declaring Allah Divinely transcendent above the traits of contingent beings, such as direction, place, letters, sounds, and the outward meanings of the ambiguous texts. Nay, in some places in his book, like his explanation of the fifth protocol that the laymen must observe when hearing anything from the ambiguous texts, he employed specific figurative interpretation. That spans over ten pages and is truly beneficial. We urge the reader to read the *Iljām al-ʿAwām* and refer to it, as there is no book quite like it in its genre. In it, *Ḥujja al-Islām* [Imām al-Ghazālī]—may Allah have mercy upon him—mentioned numerous points of benefit.

Anyone who reads the *Iljām al-ʿAwām* will know that Imām al-Ghazālī—may Allah have mercy upon him—did not abandon the doctrine of the Ashʿarīs or retract from it. All he did was prefer the way of non-specific interpretation over the way of specific figurative interpretation, and even still, his preference was not unrestricted and he did not declare those who employ specific figurative interpretation misguided. Allah forbid that, for he knew that both methods are sound, even if the preferred and best way according to him—when there is no need—is the way of non-specific interpretation, which was the way of the majority of the *Salaf*. Nay, one may go as far as to say that it is the preferred and best way according all of the Ash'arīs—and that is our belief.

The best way to follow is to stop where the *Salaf* stopped at after declaring Allah Divinely transcendent above what the outward meanings [of the ambiguous texts] seem to indicate. This method, as we mentioned, is when there is no need. There must be clarity when people dispute about the ambiguous texts. One type of clarity is specific figurative interpretation. In *Al-Iljām*, Imām al-Ghazālī did not bring anything that was opposed to what is found in his other writings.

Let it be noted that those who claim that these Imāms retracted from their beliefs and returned to the way of the *Salaf* are forced by implication to admit that the way of the *Salaf* is to declare Allah Divinely transcendent above the outward meanings of these [ambiguous] texts, because that is what is stated in these books where they allegedly returned to the way of the *Salaf*.

If these reports are true, we in no way censure those Imāms for returning to the way of the majority of the *Salaf*—which is the way of non-specific interpretation after declaring Allah Divinely transcendent above the outward meanings of the [ambiguous] texts.

What we do censure, and what is rejected by those very texts from the Imāms, is the claim that this way goes against the doctrine of the Ash'arīs. This claim is debunked in the books of these Imāms and in the books of all of the Ash'arīs and what is quoted from them, and they are the notables of this Umma in every science related to the Sacred Law.

Another example of this is cited regarding Imām al-Rāzī and it is no different from what we have mentioned. Nay, up until his last moments of life, Imām al-Rāzī advised others to read his books. In his final advice that he dictated on his death bed to one of his students he said: "Regarding the scientific books that I wrote in which I presented numerous inquiries into the views of the early ones, if anyone reads them and finds goodness in those inquiries, let him mention me in his good prayers as a favour and kindness. Otherwise, let him remove the bad statements, for my intention was only to increase in research and sharpen minds."[46]

Al-Rāzī is alleged to have said:

> I have contemplated the ways of speculative theology and the methods of the philosophers. I did not find them healing the afflicted or quenching the thirst. I saw the closest way to be that of the Qurʾān.
>
> For affirmation, you may read: ﴾*The All-Merciful rose above the Throne*﴿ and ﴾*Unto Him the good word ascends and the righteous action raises it.*﴿ For negation, you may read: ﴾*There is nothing like unto Him*﴿, ﴾*They do not encompass knowledge of Him*﴿ and ﴾*Do you know of any equal unto Him?*﴿ Whoever has experienced what I have experienced will know as I do...

In response, we say that even if this is authentically attributed to him, it does not indicate—explicitly or implicitly—that he abandoned the doctrine of the Ashʿarīs. The most this quote indicates is that he—may Allah have mercy upon him—believed that the closest way to affirm the attributes of the Lord ﷻ was the way of the Qurʾān. This is the truth in which there is no doubt and no one opposes that except a heretic.

The claim that Imām al-Rāzī retracted from the doctrine of the Ashʿarīs—if this quote is authentically attributed to him—amounts to nothing more than putting words in his mouth that he did not say and giving his words far-fetched interpretations that do no hold.

We have demonstrated here that the status of the Imāms of Islam is too great and noble to blindly follow anyone in matters related to the tenets of faith besides the Messenger of Allah ﷺ—even the Imām of Ahl al-Sunna wal-Jamāʿa, Abū al-Ḥasan al-Ashʿarī. The Umma's following of him is out of right guidance, not servile conformism.

---

[46] *Ṭabaqāt al-Aṭṭibāʾ*, p. 469.

For this reason, any attempt to sow doubts regarding doctrine of the Ash'arīs by claiming that Imām Abū al-Ḥasan or any other Imām retracted it will prove to be of no benefit and will not change the truth that the Umma and its scholars have concurred upon one bit.

The most that can be said regarding any claim of a scholar's retraction—if it is authentic to begin with—is that he was mistaken in his view and he is not to be followed blindly in that. Every person may have his statements accepted or rejected except the infallible one ﷺ.

CHAPTER FOUR

AHL AL-SUNNA WAL-JAMĀʿA

AHL AL-SUNNA WAL-JAMĀʿA is a technical term that appeared in order to indicate who was following the way of the pious predecessors in adherence to the Qurʾān, the Sunna, and the narrated reports from the Messenger of Allah ﷺ and his Companions ﷺ, in order to distinguish them from the doctrines of the innovators and people of vain desires. When this term is mentioned in the books of the scholars, it means the Ashʿarīs, the Māturīdīs, and the people of Ḥadīth,[47] because they followed the way of the Messenger of Allah ﷺ and did not alter or replace anything as others did among the people of heresy and blameworthy innovation.

The Messenger of Allah ﷺ described the saved group [*al-firqa al-nājiyya*] as the "great bulk" [*al-siwād al-ʿaẓam*] of the Umma. This description fits the Ashʿarīs, Māturīdīs, and people of Ḥadīth, for they are the majority of the Umma from whom gathering upon misguidance is negated by the text of the well-known Ḥadīth report: "My Umma shall not gather upon misguidance."[48]

Imām Tāj al-Dīn al-Subkī—may Allah have mercy upon him—said:

> Know that Ahl al-Sunna wal-Jamāʿa all agree upon one creedal doctrine regarding that which is necessary, possible, and impossible [for Allah and the Messengers],

---

[47] Some might gather from this division that the Ashʿarīs and Māturīdīs are distinct from the people of Ḥadīth, but in reality this is not the case. Most of the Ḥadīth scholars who came after Imām al-Ashʿarī and al-Māturīdī were themselves either Ashʿarīs or Māturīdīs, or in agreement with them. Imām Tāj al-Dīn al-Subkī—may Allah have mercy upon him—said: "And it [the doctrine of al-Ashʿarī] was the doctrine of the Ḥadīth scholars then and now." (*Al-Ṭabaqāt*, 4:32).

[48] Al-Ḥāfiẓ al-Sakhāwī said, after enumerating the routes of this Ḥadīth report and its respective chains: "In general it is a Ḥadīth whose text is well-known [*mashhūr*], possessing many chains and corroborating reports in the raised [*marfūʿ*] reports and in others." (*Al-Maqāṣid al-Ḥasana* §1288).

> even if they if differ concerning the methods and fundamentals that arrive unto that and the reasons why. By induction, they are three groups:
>
> **One**: the people of Ḥadīth. Their relied upon fundamentals are in the revelatory proofs—meaning the Book, the Sunna, and consensus.
>
> **Two**: the people of rational inquiry and thought. They are the Ashʿarīs and the Ḥanafīs [the Māturīdīs]. The Shaykh of the Ashʿarīs is Abū al-Ḥasan al-Ashʿarī and the Shaykh of the Ḥanafīs is Abū Manṣūr al-Māturīdī...
>
> **Three**: the people of ecstatic experience and spiritual unveiling. They are the Sufis. Their fundamentals in the beginning are the fundamentals of the people of rational inquiry and the people of Ḥadīth, and in the end [their fundamentals are] spiritual unveiling and inspiration.

Imām ʿAḍud al-Dīn al-Ījī—may Allah have mercy upon him—explained who the saved group is, after enumerating the destroyed groups: "As for the saved group that is excluded—regarding whom the Prophet ﷺ said: 'They are those who are upon my way and the way of my Companions'—they are the Ashʿarīs and the *Salaf* among the Ḥadīth scholars and Ahl al-Sunna wal-Jamāʿa; their way is free of the innovations of the former [the destroyed groups]."[49]

Imām al-Jalāl al-Dawānī—may Allah have mercy upon him—said:

> The saved group are the Ashʿarīs: those who follow Shaykh Abū al-Ḥasan in the tenets of faith... If you retort: "How has it been judged that the Ashʿarīs are the saved group, when all groups claim that they are saved?" I respond: the context of the Ḥadīth alludes to this, i.e., that they—the saved group—are those who believe in that which has been narrated from the Prophet ﷺ and his Companions, and that only applies to the Ashʿarīs, for in their doctrine they firmly adhere to the rigorously authentic Ḥadīth reports taken from him ﷺ and his Companions; they do not depart from the outward

[49] *Al-Mawāqif*, p. 430.

> meanings of those reports except in cases in which it is a necessity, and they do not over-rely on their intellects like the Muʿtazila.[50]

The reason why the Ashʿarīs are mentioned alone in the texts of the Imāms is because they are the majority of Ahl al-Sunna. It should not be understood that the other groups of Ahl al-Sunna are somehow excluded from the ranks of the saved group. Those who do not follow Imām al-Ashʿarī directly are at least in agreement with him.

The knower of Allah, Imām Aḥmad Ibn ʿAjība[51]—may Allah have mercy upon him—said: "As for Ahl al-Sunna, they are the Ashʿarīs and those who follow them in their correct doctrine, as is established in the books of Ahl al-Sunna."[52]

Imām Tāj al-Dīn al-Subkī—may Allah have mercy upon him—said:

> The Shaykh and Imām [his father, Taqī al-Dīn al-Subkī] said in his narration to us: "I stumbled across a written work by one of the Muʿtazila called *Ṭabaqāt al-Muʿtazila* [a collection of biographies], and he opened it by making mention of ʿAbdullāh b. Masʿūd ﵁, thinking that he—may Allah exonerate him from them—held their doctrine. This is extreme partisanship, for a person is only ascribed to the one whom he follows."
>
> I agreed with the Shaykh and Imām [Taqī al-Dīn]: if this was conceded to them, the Ashʿarīs would be able to claim Abū Bakr and ʿUmar ﵄ for themselves, because they [the Ashʿarīs] follow, call to, and defend their doctrine and the doctrine of the other Companions. It alone they aid and within its demarcation lines they abide. He [Taqī al-Dīn] smiled and then said: "The followers of an individual are those who adhere to his doctrine and say as he says out of

---

[50] *Sharḥ al-ʿAqīda al-ʿAḍudiyya*, 1:34.

[51] He is Abū al-ʿAbbās Aḥmad b. Muḥammad b. ʿAjība al-Ḥasanī al-Fāsī—the erudite scholar and upright Sufi who gathered between the sciences of the Sacred Law and the Spiritual Realities. He died in the year 1224 AH. (See: *Shajara al-Nūr al-Zakiyya* [*fī Ṭabaqāt al-Mālikiyya*], p. 400, and *Fahras al-Fahāris*, 2:854).

[52] *Al-Baḥr al-Madīd*, *Tafsīr Sūra al-Fātiḥa*, p. 608.

> a sense of adherence and holding fast that is more particular than just agreement. Between adherence and mere agreement there is a vast difference."[53]

Imām 'Abd al-Qādir al-Baghdādī—may Allah have mercy upon him—said:

> As for the seventy-third group, they are Ahl al-Sunna wal-Jamā'a from the people of analogy [*ahl al-ray'*] and the people of Ḥadīth [*ahl al-Ḥadīth*]—excluding those who purchase vain talk—and the jurists among these two groups as well as their reciters, Ḥadīth scholars, and the theologians of the people of Ḥadīth among them. All of them agree upon one central doctrine... They do not charge each other with misguidance and corruption on account of the things in which they differ. They are the saved group... Whoever believed according to what we have mentioned and did not mix his faith with anything from the innovations of the people of vain desires, he is from the general ranks of the saved group, provided that Allah causes him to die upon it. Included in this general [saved group] are the majority and great-bulk of the Umma among the companions of Mālik, al-Shāfi'ī, Abū Ḥanīfa, al-Awzā'ī, al-Thawrī, and the Ẓāhirīs...

After enumerating the Imāms of Ahl al-Sunna wal-Jamā'a among the theologians of the Companions, the followers, and their followers, he said:

> Then, after them comes the Shaykh of rational inquiry and the renowned Imām of debate and investigation: Abū al-Ḥasan 'Alī b. Ismā'īl al-Ash'arī, who became a thorn [*shajjan*] in the throats of the Qadariyya... The world is filled with his books. None of the theologians who came after him were provided what was given to him, because all of the people of Ḥadīth and all of the people of analogy who did not adopt the way of the Mu'tazila follow his doctrine.[54]

---

[53] *Ṭabaqāt al-Shāfi'iyya*, 3:365.

[54] *Al-Farq bayn al-Firaq*.

The Imām, ascetic, and exemplar, Abū ʿAmr al-Dānī[55]—may Allah have mercy upon him—said: "Know, may Allah assist you with His Divine granting of success and may He grant you His Divine succour and aid, that the belief of Ahl al-Sunna wal-Jamāʿa among the early and latter-day Muslims from the people of Ḥadīth, the jurists, and the theologians..."[56] He then went on to mention the doctrine of Ahl al-Sunna. By his statement: "the jurists, and the theologians" he meant the Ashʿarīs and Māturīdīs. His essay is overflowing with evidence for [Allah's] Divine transcendence, may Allah have mercy upon him. He was clearly influenced by his Shaykh and teacher, the Shaykh of Ahl al-Sunna: Qāḍī Abū Bakr al-Bāqillānī—may Allah have mercy upon him—and the method of Imām al-Ashʿarī is evident from his essay, and this is not lost on those who peruse al-Ashʿarī's works. Nay, some of the expressions and words used [in Abū ʿAmr's essay] are taken directly from some of al-Ashʿarī's books.

The Proof of the Theologians, Imām Abū al-Muẓaffar al-Isfarāyīnī—may Allah have mercy upon him—said after explaining the doctrine of Ahl al-Sunna: "And that you know that everyone who follows this religion that we have described from the creed of the saved group is upon the truth and the straight path; so whoever imputes him with blameworthy innovation

---

[55] Abū ʿAmr al-Dānī is too renowned for needing any introduction. Imām al-Dhahabī—may Allah have mercy upon him—said about him: "He is the Imām, the Ḥadīth master, the melodious reciter, and the sagacious scholar of Andalusia." He also said: "He is the ultimate reference regarding the final say on the canonical modes of recitation and Qurʾānic script, in addition to his sagacity in the science of Ḥadīth, Qurʾānic exegesis, grammar, and other sciences. He was known as Ibn al-Ṣayrafī for the longest. Ibn Bashkuwāl said about him: 'He was one of the Imāms in the science of the Qurʾān and its canonical narrations, as well as its exegesis, meanings, routes, and inflection [*ʿirāb*]...' He also possessed knowledge concerning the Ḥadīth reports, their routes of transmission, the names of their narrators and those who relayed them. He was assiduous in his scholarly precision and was among the people of intelligence, strong memory, and well-roundedness in knowledge. He was religiously observant, virtuous, scrupulous, and a Sunni." He died in the year 444 AH and was buried in the Dāniya cemetery. (*Siyar ʿAlām al-Nubalāʾ*, 18:77, *Al-Ṣila*, 2:405, and *Al-Dībāj*,2:84).

[56] *Al-Risāla al-Wāfiya fī Muʿtaqad Ahl al-Sunna wal-Jamāʿa*, p. 117.

is an innovator; whoever imputes him with misguidance is misguided; and whoever imputes him with disbelief is a disbeliever."[57]

See—may Allah look after you—how serious this matter is! If you understand this, you will realize the recklessness of those who malign the honour of the Ashʿarīs, defame them, and accuse their doctrine of misguidance! There is no might or power but through Allah!

Imām Abū Isḥāq al-Shīrāzī—may Allah have mercy upon him—said: "Abū al-Ḥasan al-Ashʿarī is the Imām of Ahl al-Sunna and the generality of al-Shāfiʿī's companions follow his doctrine; and his doctrine is the doctrine of the people of truth."[58] Let it suffice you to know Abū Isḥāq al-Shīrāzī's rank in knowledge, jurisprudence, piety, scrupulousness, and excellence in the religion.

Imām Ibn Ḥajar al-Haytamī—may Allah have mercy upon him—was asked about Imām Abū al-Ḥasan al-Ashʿarī, al-Bāqillānī, Ibn Fūrak, Imām al-Ḥaramayn [al-Juwaynī], al-Bājī, and others who followed the way of al-Ashʿarī. He responded:

> They are the Imāms of the religion and the sires among the scholars of the Muslims. It is obligatory to follow them because of their aid to the Sacred Law, their clarification of confusing matters, their refutations of the misconceptions of the people of heresy, and their explanations of what is obligatory in the realm of doctrine and religion. This is due to their knowledge of Allah and what is necessary for Him, impossible for Him, and possible...
>
> It is obligatory to attest to the virtue of the aforementioned Imāms as well as those who came before them, and to attest that they are included among those meant by the statement of the Prophet ﷺ: "This knowledge will be carried in each generation by the trustworthy ones who will negate from it the distortions of the extremists, the deviance of the deniers, and the false interpretations of the ignorant." Only an ignorant dolt or deviant innovator believes that they are

[57] *Al-Tabṣīr fī al-Dīn*, p. 111.
[58] *Ṭabaqāt al-Shāfiʿiyya*, 3:376.

> misguided, and no one but a corrupt sinner insults them. It is therefore a must that the ignorant person is made aware, that the corrupt sinner is reprimanded, and that repentance is sought from the innovator.[59]

The erudite Ḥanbalī scholar al-Safārīnī—may Allah have mercy upon him—said: "Ahl al-Sunna wal-Jamāʿa consists of three groups: the Atharīs—their Imām is Aḥmad b. Ḥanbal ﷺ, the Ashʿarīs—their Imām is Abū al-Ḥasan al-Ashʿarī—may Allah have mercy upon him, and the Māturīdīs—and their Imām is Abū al-Manṣūr al-Māturīdī—may Allah have mercy upon him."[60]

Imām al-Murtaḍā al-Zabīdī—may Allah have mercy upon him—said: "When the term *Ahl al-Sunna wal-Jamāʿa* is used, it means the Ashʿarīs and Māturīdīs."[61] Elsewhere he said: "What is meant by Ahl al-Sunna are the four groups: the Ḥadīth scholars, the Sufis,[62] the Ashʿarīs, and the Māturīdīs."[63]

One work that may be cited as proof here is the treatise of Abū Jaʿfar al-Ṭaḥāwī—may Allah have mercy upon him—on doctrine, called *Al-ʿAqīda al-Ṭaḥāwiyya*. In this work he summarized the doctrine of the *Salaf*—may Allah be pleased with all of them—and with which the Umma has met with acceptance. The contents of his work on doctrine contain the exact beliefs of the Ashʿarīs, baring a few minor points that do not entail accusations of misguidance or corruption. Imām Tāj al-Dīn al-Subkī—may Allah have mercy upon him—said:

> I heard the Shaykh and Imām [his father, Taqī al-Dīn]—may Allah have mercy upon him—say: "That which is contained in the doctrine of al-Ṭaḥāwī is what al-Ashʿarī believed; he did not differ with it except in three issues."

---

[59] *Al-Fatāwā al-Ḥadīthiyya*, p. 205.

[60] *Lawāmiʿ al-Anwār al-Bahiyya*, 1:73.

[61] *Itḥāf al-Sāda al-Muttaqīn*, 2:6.

[62] The Sufis intended here are those who followed the way of the people of truth, such as Imām al-Junayd, Maʿrūf al-Karkhī, Bishr al-Ḥāfī, Ibrāhīm b. Adham, and others who were guides unto Allah and who came after them and traversed their path of adherence to the Book and the Sunna.

[63] Ibid., 2:86.

> I have contemplated the doctrine of Abū Ja'far al-Ṭaḥāwī and I have found the matter to be as the Shaykh and Imām [Taqī al-Dīn] said. The creed of al-Ṭaḥāwī says that it is the doctrine followed by Abū Ḥanīfa, Abū Yūsuf, and Muḥammad [al-Shaybānī]. He did well in it. Afterwards, I perused the books of the Ḥanafīs and I found that the issues in which there is disagreement between us and them amount to thirteen issues: six issues among them are actual differences in meaning, and the remaining issues are differences in semantics. And those six issues do not necessitate—on either our part or theirs—accusations of disbelief or blameworthy innovation. This was explicitly stated by Ustādh Abū al-Manṣūr al-Baghdādī and others among our Imāms and theirs. It is, in fact, too obvious to warrant explicit declarations.[64]

Then al-Subkī quoted the words of al-Ḥāfiẓ Ibn 'Asākir (found in *Tabyīn*):

> "Our colleagues [*al-aṣḥāb*], despite their disagreements in some issues, are nevertheless united in their abandonment of mutual accusations of disbelief—contrary to others among the various groups and the rest of the sects..." I [al-Subkī] say: This is the truth. These issues are naught but similar to the many issues in which the Ash'arīs disagreed, even though all of them defend the grounds of Abū al-Ḥasan and fight with his sword. Do you see them declaring each other innovators?

Then al-Subkī went on to mention the issues in which there are disagreements between the Ash'arīs and Māturīdīs, and he followed them up with issues in which the Ash'arīs disagreed among themselves.

Having said this, anyone who peruses *Al-'Aqīda al-Ṭaḥāwiyya* will know its congruence with the way of the esteemed Ash'arīs, and he or she will know that all of them come from one single

---

[64] *Ṭabaqāt al-Shāfi'iyya al-Kubrā*, 3:378.

light-source. Take the following examples from the *Ṭaḥāwiyya* that illustrate this congruence.

Regarding the Qurʾān, al-Ṭaḥāwī—may Allah have mercy upon him—said: "The Qurʾān is Allah's speech having proceeded from Him without modality, as words [*qawlan*]. He sent it down upon His Messenger by way of revelation; and the believers had conviction in it that is truly as such." His statement: "having proceeded from Him" means that it manifested and does not mean that it began (as the opposite of ended)—Allah is exalted above that.

Al-Ghunaymī al-Maydānī said: "Without a modality that we can comprehend, such as letter or sound, or beginning or silence, ...and it [Allah's speech] is a pre-eternal attribute that subsists with His Exalted Entity; this negates silence or defect; and it is not letter or sound." Al-Bābartī said: "By negation of modality he meant to affirm its pre-eternality, as a refutation against the Muʿtazila and the Karrāmiyya; and he negated it being from the genus of letters and sounds."

After that, al-Ṭaḥāwī said: "[And they knew for certain that it was] Allah's speech in reality [*bil-ḥaqīqa*], not created speech like the speech of mankind."

Al-Ghunaymī said: "It is not created like the speech of mankind that is composed of letters that form sounds..."

Al-Bābartī commented on al-Ṭaḥāwī's words: "It does not resemble the words of man...," saying: "All of this is an emphasis on the negation of the contingency of His speech and its inclusion in the genus of letters and sound that resemble the speech of the creation. Whoever says that the Qurʾān is created and contingent and that it is from the genus of letters and sounds has qualified the Creator with the attributes of mankind."

Regarding the beatific vision of Allah in the Hereafter, Imām al-Ṭaḥāwī said: "The beatific vision is a reality for the people of Paradise without [there being any] encompassing or modality..."

Al-Bābartī said in his commentary:

> He wished to affirm that the beatific vision of Allah, the Exalted, with the eyes in the Abode of Settlement [*dār al-qarār*] for the pious is true. The pious shall see Him, although not in a place or direction or as a result of

> connections between rays of light or distance between them and the Most High. This is what is meant by his statement: "or modality." His intent is that one should believe in the beatific vision and not become preoccupied with [pondering] a modality. The only reason he said: "...without [there being any] encompassing..." is because encompassing—which is to grasp the sides of something—is impossible with respect to Allah because He is not a corporeal body that can possess sides and thus be grasped.

Al-Ghunaymī al-Maydānī said in his commentary:

> And we say: The beatific vision of the Exalted Being that is transcendent above encompassment and direction is true. In other words, it is affirmed for the people of Paradise without encompassing the sides or limits of the one seen, because He is exaltedly transcendent above boundaries and being qualified with sides and limits. There is no modality, such as directionality, place, conjunction of rays of light, and distance between the seer and the one seen; all of this is [affirmed] with respect to the vision of corporeal bodies, and Allah is not a body, therefore the vision of Him is not like the vision of bodies.

Al-Ṭaḥāwī—may Allah have mercy upon him—said: "For indeed, our Lord ﷻ is characterized by the attributes of Oneness and the qualities of uniqueness; none of creation is in any sense [*maʿnā*] like Him. Exalted is He above [having] limits, ends, limbs, organs, or instruments. The six directions do not contain Him as they do the rest of things that are formed." Al-Bābartī said:

> The Pre-eternal ﷻ is Divinely transcendent above all of these descriptions, because He negated that He is like anything: ﴾*There is nothing like unto Him.*﴿ With the affirmation of direction and boundaries comes the affirmation of similarity to corporeal bodies, and describing Him with directions is to say that He is encompassed by them, and the belief [that He is] in a direction is to affirm [that He is in] need of a place. All of that entails that He is necessarily contingent and that He is stripped of His pre-eternality.

With respect to the ambiguous texts, Imām al-Ṭaḥāwī took the view of the majority of the *Salaf*, namely the position of non-specific interpretation and relegating their meanings to Allah, the Exalted, and abstaining from delving into their interpretation. This is but one of the two methods of the Ashʿarīs and there is no harm in either of them.

His statement regarding the works of the servants [*afʿāl al-ʿibād*] is the exact belief of the Ashʿarīs, namely, that the works of the servants are Allah's creation and the servant's acquisition [*kasb*]. There are other examples that show the congruence and agreement between the two methods [that of al-Ṭaḥāwī and al-Ashʿarī].

The Imām and erudite scholar Aḥmad al-Dardīr—may Allah have mercy upon him—said in his commentary on his didactic poem on creed called *Al-Kharīda al-Bahiyya*:

> *And follow the path of the devout scholars*
>
> [*Scholars*] is the plural of scholar, and the scholar is the one who is knowledgeable regarding the rulings of the Sacred Law around which the validity of the religion revolves, be they related to matters of creed or matters of action. Those meant [here in this line] are the pious predecessors and those who followed them in righteousness. Their path is restricted to belief, knowledge, and action in accordance with [sound] knowledge.
>
> Those who came after them among the Umma's Imāms who must be followed were three different groups: a group that took it upon themselves to explain the practical rulings of the Sacred Law, and they are the four Imāms and others besides them among the diligent [*mujtahid*] scholars; however, none of the satisfying juridical schools remained in place besides the schools of the four Imāms. The second group are those who took it upon themselves to explain the doctrine followed by the *Salaf*, and they are al-Ashʿarī, al-Māturīdī, and those who follow them. The third group are those who took it upon themselves to engage in works and spiritual struggles in

> accordance to the way of the two aforementioned groups. This group includes Imām Abū al-Qāsim al-Junayd and those who follow him.
>
> These three groups represent the elite of the Muḥammadan ﷺ Umma. All other groups besides them are upon misguidance, and even if some of them are [still] judged with Islam [i.e., they are still Muslims], the one who is saved is the one whose creed is according to the way explained by Ahl al-Sunna.

The Imām and erudite scholar ʿAbdullāh b. ʿAlawī al-Ḥaddād—may Allah have mercy upon him—said:

> You should know that the doctrine of the Ashʿarīs in creed is that which the majority of the Umma of Islam and its scholars and notables were upon. Hence, those who ascribe themselves to them and those who traverse their way were the Imāms of the people of [religious] sciences one and all through the passing of days and years. They are the Imāms of the science of Divine Oneness and theology, Qurʾānic exegesis, canonical recitation, jurisprudence, legal theory, Ḥadīth and its ancillary sciences, Sufism, philology, and history.[65]

He also said:

> You must correct and protect your beliefs and conform to the way of the saved group, who are known from among the other Islamic factions as Ahl al-Sunna wal-Jamāʿa. They are those who firmly adhere to the way of Allah's Messenger ﷺ and his Companions.
>
> If you look with an upright understanding and sound heart into the source-texts relating to the sciences of faith found in the Book, the Sunna, and sayings of the pious predecessors, whether they were Companions or followers, you will know for certain that the truth is with the group called the Ashʿarīs, who were named after Shaykh Abū al-Ḥasan al-Ashʿarī—may Allah have mercy upon him—who codified the foundations of the creed of

[65] *Nayl al-Marām*, p. 8.

> the people of truth and recorded its evidence, these being the beliefs which the Companions and the best among the followers agreed upon.
>
> They constitute the doctrine of the people of truth in every time and place; it is the doctrine of the generality of the Sufis, as mentioned by Abū al-Qāsim al-Qushayrī in the beginning of his *Epistle*. Allah be praised, it is our doctrine, ...and the doctrine of our forefathers, ...from the Messenger of Allah ﷺ until today. And the Māturīdīs are the same as the Ashʿarīs in the above regard.[66]

The erudite scholar Ibn al-Shaṭṭī al-Ḥanbalī—may Allah have mercy upon him—said in his commentary on *Al-ʿAqīda al-Safārīniyya*: "Some scholars say that they, i.e., the saved group, are the people of Ḥadīth [*ahl al-Ḥadīth*], in other words the Atharīs, the Ashʿarīs, and the Māturīdīs."[67] He also said: "Benefit: Ahl al-Sunna wal-Jamāʿa consists of three groups: the Atharīs—their Imām is Aḥmad b. Ḥanbal ﷺ, the Ashʿarīs—their Imām is Abū al-Ḥasan al-Ashʿarī—may Allah have mercy upon him, and the Māturīdīs—and their Imām is Abū al-Manṣūr al-Māturīdī—may Allah have mercy upon him."[68]

The erudite scholar of Kuwait, Shaykh ʿAbdullāh b. Khalaf al-Duḥayān—may Allah have mercy upon him—said in his footnote regarding al-Safārīnī's division of Ahl al-Sunna into three groups:

> If you retort: "But the wording of the Ḥadīth indicates that it does not transcend a single group,[69] for he ﷺ said: 'My Umma shall split into over seventy groups; all of them shall be in the fire except for one group, and they are [the group] that are upon what I and my Companions are upon'"—the answer to this is as follows: These three groups are [in reality] one group, because they are all

---

[66] *Book of Assistance* [*Kitāb Risāla al-Muʿāwana*], pp. 67–68.

[67] *Tabṣīr al-Qāniʿ fī al-Jamiʿ bayn Sharḥayn Ibn Shaṭṭī wa-Ibn Māniʿ ʿalā al-ʿAqīda al-Safārīniyya*, p. 73.

[68] Ibid.

[69] In other words, the wording of the Ḥadīth indicates that salvation is restricted to only one group and that it does not apply to three groups.

> *ahl al-Ḥadīth*. The Ashʿarīs and Māturīdīs did not reject or neglect the Ḥadīth reports; they either took a position of non-specific interpretation [regarding their meanings], or they specifically interpreted them. All of them are *ahl al-Ḥadīth*. Hence, the three [groups] are in fact one, because they follow the reports and embrace the narrations, contrary to the other groups, for they gave precedence to reasoning and opposed the source-texts, and thus they are the people of innovation, misguidance, opposition, and gross ignorance. And Allah, the Exalted, knows best.[70]

The erudite Ḥanbalī Shaykh Muḥammad b. ʿAlī b. Salūm—may Allah have mercy upon him—stated similar words in his commentary on *Al-ʿAqīda al-Safārīniyya*.[71]

The erudite scholar al-Mawāhibī al-Ḥanbalī—may Allah have mercy upon him—said: "The factions of Ahl al-Sunna are three: the Ashʿarīs, the Ḥanbalīs, and the Māturīdīs. This is proven by the apposition of the Ḥanbalī scholars next to the Ashʿarīs within many books of theology, and in all of the books of the Ḥanbalīs."[72]

The Ḥadīth scholar Muḥammad b. Darwīsh al-Ḥūt al-Bayrūtī—may Allah have mercy upon him—said: "Benefit: the Imām of the Mālikīs and Shāfiʿīs is Abū al-Ḥasan al-Ashʿarī, from the family of Abū Mūsā al-Ashʿarī ﷺ. The Ḥanafīs are Māturīdīs and their Imām is Abū al-Manṣūr al-Māturīdī. They are the two Imāms of Ahl al-Sunna, and the Ḥanbalīs are the Atharīs."[73]

The Imām and erudite scholar Kamāl al-Dīn al-Bayāḍī—may Allah have mercy upon him—said:

> The saved group is the group of the many that cling to the clear-cut texts of the Book and the Sunna in matters of doctrine. This is in accordance to the way of the Messenger ﷺ and the way of the Companions. They do not go beyond the outward meaning [of the texts] unless [the outward meaning] of the text contradicts

---

[70] *Tabṣīr al-Qāniʿ*.

[71] *Sharḥ al-Durra al-Maḍiyya*, p. 58.

[72] *Al-ʿAyn wal-Athar*, p. 53.

[73] *Rasāʾil fī Bayān ʿAqāʾid Ahl al-Sunna wal-Jamāʿa*, p. 77.

> an unequivocal textual or rational proof. Indeed, the proofs of Allah strengthen each another and they do not mutually contradict each other.

Whoever looks with the eye of sound reasoning and objectivity in arriving at the truth will know with certainty that there is no group that fits this description besides the Ashʿarīs, the Māturīdīs, and *ahl al-Ḥadīth*. They are the ones who have filled each place and era and who are well-known the world across.

Imām ʿAbd al-Qādir al-Baghdādī—may Allah have mercy upon him—said:

> When the Prophet ﷺ mentioned the splitting of the Umma into seventy-three groups and informed that only one of those groups is the saved group, he was asked about that saved group and its qualities, so he indicated those who are upon his way and the way of his Companions. We do not find today any of the groups of this Umma that are in agreement with the Companions besides Ahl al-Sunna wal-Jamāʿa among the jurists of the Umma and the theologians of the *Ṣifātiyya* [those who affirm Allah's attributes].[74]

He went on to explain how the other groups are not saved and provided examples of their deviation from the way of the Messenger ﷺ and his Companions. After that he said:

> From this it becomes clear that those who follow the Companions are those who act in accordance to the authentic reports regarding their legal judgements and behaviour; that is the way [*sunna*] of Ahl al-Sunna, contrary to the way of the innovators. The soundness of what we have mentioned here establishes that they are in fact saved, due to the judgement of the Prophet ﷺ who stated that those who follow his Companions are saved. All praise is due to Allah for that.[75]

---

[74] *Al-Farq bayn al-Firaq*, p. 247.
[75] Ibid.

Imām Ibn Ḥajar al-Haytamī—may Allah have mercy upon him—said: "What is meant by *sunna* is that which the two Imāms of Ahl al-Sunna are upon: Shaykh Abū al-Ḥasan al-Ashʿarī and Abū al-Manṣūr al-Māturīdī...'"[76]

The erudite scholar, Ṭāshkopruzāde—may Allah have mercy upon him—said:

> You should then know that the heads of Ahl al-Sunna wal-Jamāʿa in the science of speculative theology—that is, doctrine—are two men: one is Ḥanafī and the other is Shāfiʿī.[77] The Ḥanafī is Abū al-Manṣūr Muḥammad b. Maḥmūd al-Māturīdī, the Imām of guidance...
>
> The Shāfiʿī is the Shaykh of the Sunna and the head of the group; the Imām of the theologians and champion of the Sunna of the best of the Messengers ﷺ; the defender of the religion and the one who struggled to preserve the doctrine of the Muslims: Abū al-Ḥasan al-Ashʿarī of Basra. He defended the noble Sacred Law from false accretions and stood up in defence of the religion of Islam and gave it a manifest victory.[78]

The statements of the scholars of Islam are unanimous that the Ashʿarīs and those who agreed with them in matters of doctrine from among the other groups of the people of truth are from the saved group. They are the ones intended by the Prophet's ﷺ statement: "...that which I and my Companions are upon."

They are the moderate group as opposed to the heretical sects. They have abandoned the people of deviance and distanced themselves from them to the utmost. Anyone who comes after them and seeks to somehow distance himself from misguidance more than them will inevitably fall into that [misguidance] or at least incline to it.

---

[76] *Al-Zawājir*, p. 82.

[77] The Mālikīs dispute this and include him in their biographical works. The correct view is that he was a Shāfiʿī. The Shaykh of the Ashʿarīs, Imām Abū Bakr b. al-Bāqillānī, was a Mālikī. See: *Ṭabaqāt al-Shāfiʿiyya al-Kubrā*, 3:352.

[78] *Miftāḥ al-Saʿāda*, 2:33.

CHAPTER FIVE

THE STATEMENTS OF SOME CONTEMPORARY SCHOLARS REGARDING THE ASHʿARĪS

WE HAVE MENTIONED the statements of the early and latter-day scholars in which the term *Ahl al-Sunna* is applied exclusively to the Ashʿarīs, Māturīdīs, and *ahl al-Ḥadīth*. Here we present the statements of some of the contemporary Sunni scholars who also mention their virtue.

The Shaykh and caller Ḥasan Ayūb—may Allah have mercy upon him—said:

> Ahl al-Sunna are: Abū al-Ḥasan al-Ashʿarī, Abū al-Manṣūr al-Māturīdī, and those who follow their path. They traversed the path of the pious predecessors in their understanding of doctrine. They took the Holy Qurʾān as their sweet-spring to which they held fast in gaining knowledge of their doctrine. They would understand the points of doctrine from the Qurʾānic verses, and whatever was unclear to them, they would attempt to understand in light of the rhetorical devices found in the [Arabic] language and that which wasn't rationally negated. If they were unable [to arrive at a conclusion after that] they would stop and take a position of non-specific interpretation. The followers of Abū al-Ḥasan al-Ashʿarī are called Ashʿarīs, and [the followers of] Abū al-Manṣūr al-Māturīdī are called Māturīdīs.[79]

The Ustādh and caller Saʿīd Ḥawwā—may Allah have mercy upon him—said:

> Historically the Muslims have had their Imāms in doctrine, Imāms in jurisprudence, and Imāms in Sufism and spiritual wayfaring to Allah, the Exalted. Their Imāms in doctrine include Abū al-Ḥasan al-Ashʿarī and Abū al-Manṣūr al-Māturīdī...

[79] *Tabṣīṭ al-ʿAqāʾid al-Islāmiyya*, p. 299.

> These and their likes are specialists in their respective fields; what is recorded from them establishes that they put forth the clearest understanding of the Book and the Sunna. Moreover, the Umma unanimously concurred that their statements are relied upon and accepted in the face of the innumerable viewpoints and false beliefs—some of which have died out and some of which remain.[80]

In this book and in most of his other books Shaykh Saʿīd Ḥawwā cited the opinion of the Imām and martyr, Ḥasan al-Bannā—may Allah have mercy upon him. He was in agreement with the way of the *Salaf* and those after them regarding Allah's Divine transcendence above all that does not befit Him.

He also said—may Allah have mercy upon him: "Just as there are authors and books on jurisprudence, and just as there are Imāms in jurisprudence that the Umma unanimously accepted, similarly in the realm of doctrine there are Imāms whose Imāmate the Umma has concurred upon, such as Abū al-Ḥasan al-Ashʿarī and Abū al-Manṣūr al-Māturīdī."[81]

Another contemporary scholar who mentioned the virtue of the Ashʿarīs was the Shaykh and caller Abū al-Ḥasan al-Nadwī: "The Islamic world—in all of its reaches—submitted to their knowledge and influence... By virtue of them, the intellectual leadership and direction of the Islamic world transferred from the Muʿtazila to Ahl al-Sunna."[82]

He also said:

> Al-Ashʿarī travelled his path as a *mujāhid* (one who struggles), a resister, and person of productivity... He did not care about what others said about him, for he believed that it was the path that would benefit the religion in his time and return the Sacred Law to its sanctity and honour and safeguard the coming generations in their religion and creed. By his constant efforts, strong personality, expansive intellect, and rare sincerity, he was able to hold back the floods of extreme rationalism [*ʿitizāl*] and

---

[80] *Jawalāt fī al-Fiqhayn; Al-Kabīr wal-Akbar*, p. 22.
[81] Ibid.
[82] *Rijāl al-Fikr wal-Daʿwa fī al-Islām*, p. 137.

> philosophy that threatened the religion. He was able to make firm many of those whose feet had slipped and whose minds and beliefs became confused, and he was able to inspire within Ahl al-Sunna a new-found confidence in their doctrine.[83]

Shaykh Wahbī al-Ghāwjī—may Allah have mercy upon him—said:

> The first person to write about the fundamental tenets of faith and refute the obfuscations of the people of heresy in matters of doctrine was the greatest Imām, Abū Ḥanīfa—may Allah have mercy upon him. [He refuted them] textually and rationally. This was followed up by those who wrote about the fundamental tenets of faith, up until its principles were codified by the two illustrious Imāms: Abū al-Manṣūr al-Māturīdī and Abū al-Ḥasan al-Ash'arī—may Allah have mercy upon both of them.[84]

This is the rank and esteem the Ash'arīs are held in among the early and latter-day scholars. This is their status in history. Only an arrogant person can deny their virtue and struggle. No matter how much some people exaggerate in detracting from them, and no matter how much they deny their virtue, they are still indebted to their sciences. There is not a single student or teacher except that he owes a debt of gratitude to the fruits of their sagacity and intelligence and what their hands wrote. Can any scholar or student of Sacred Knowledge do without, for example, Ibn Ḥajar al-'Asqalānī's *Fatḥ al-Bārī* or Imām al-Nawawī's commentary on *Ṣaḥīḥ Muslim*?

It is now evidently clear from the citations and quotes taken from the early and latter-day scholars, as well as contemporary scholars, who is meant by the term *Ahl al-Sunna wal-Jamā'a*, and who is the saved group that is mentioned in the texts and uniquely chosen for salvation and guidance to the exclusion of the rest. How, then, can any fair-minded person justify excluding the Ash'arīs and Māturīdīs from Ahl al-Sunna wal-Jamā'a?

---

[83] Ibid.

[84] *Arkān al-Imān*, p. 7.

THE AMBIGUOUS VERSES ACCORDING TO THE EARLY AND LATTER-DAY SCHOLARS

Some people insist on imputing the Ash'arīs and Māturīdīs with misguidance because the majority of them permitted figurative interpretation (with its prerequisites) of the ambiguous texts that speak of Allah's attributes. They seem to forget however, that most of the Umma adhere to the position of figurative interpretation and that groups among the *Salaf* also held this view.

Imām al-Zarkashī—may Allah have mercy upon him—explained the three positions regarding the ambiguous verses: "The third position is that they are given figurative interpretation, and they [those who held this view] interpreted them according to what befits Him [Allah]. The first position [the position of taking them literally] is false, and the other two positions are recorded from the Companions... Those who have been reported using figurative interpretation include 'Alī, Ibn Mas'ūd, Ibn 'Abbās, and others."[85]

Imām al-Nawawī—may Allah have mercy upon him—said regarding the position of figurative interpretation: "It is the position of most of the theologians, some groups among the *Salaf*, and it is related from Mālik and al-Awzā'ī."[86]

THE CORRECT UNDERSTANDING OF THE AMBIGUOUS VERSES

The Exalted said: ﴾*It is He Who has revealed unto you the Book, wherein are plain verses, which are the foundation of the Book; others are ambiguous.*﴿ [Āl-'Imrān: 6]

The term "ambiguous" [*mutashābih*] primarily refers to that which humans have no way of understanding. Here it refers to what has come in the Qur'ān and well-known authentic Sunna of texts that, in their outward form, seem to allude to resemblance between Allah and His creation.

Al-Rāghib al-Iṣfahānī—may Allah have mercy upon him—said: "Those things that are ambiguous in their meanings are the descriptions of Allah, the Exalted, and the descriptions of the Day of Resurrection. These qualities are inconceivable for us

---

[85] *Al-Burhān fī 'Ulūm al-Qur'ān*, 2:207.

[86] *Sharḥ Ṣaḥīḥ Muslim*, 6:36.

[*la tutaṣawwar lanā*], for we cannot conceive in ourselves the image of that which we have not sensed, or [the image] of that which is not in the genus of what we sense."[87]

Examples of ambiguous verses in the Qurʾān include: ﴾*The All-Merciful rose above the Throne*﴿, ﴾*Allah's hand is above their hands*﴿, ﴾*For indeed you are under Our eyes*﴿, ﴾*And let it be made under Our eyes*﴿ and ﴾*For the one I created with My two hands.*﴿ Examples of ambiguous texts in the Sunna include his ﷺ statements: "Our Lord descends at the last third of the night...," "Tonight, Allah has laughed at what you two did," and "Verily Allah created Ādam with his image."

The ruling these ambiguous texts take is that we should have faith in them according to Allah's intended meaning, and unequivocally believe that they have a mighty and noble meaning with Allah, the Exalted—after we have declared Allah's Divine transcendence above the outward meaning that is impossible for Him, the Exalted. This is the general agreement of the scholars in their ruling on the ambiguous texts. Beyond this, however, they disagreed.

The source of their disagreement was in their understanding of the verse pertaining to the ambiguous verses and their difference of opinion regarding the proper stopping point [*waqf*] in Allah's words: ﴾*...yet none know its explanation save Allah, and those who are of sound knowledge say: "We believe in it. All of it is from our Lord."*﴿ [Āl-ʿImrān: 6]

The majority of the *Salaf* posited that one must stop at the Divine Name. Based on that view, the word "and" found in Allah's words: ﴾*...and those who are of sound knowledge...*﴿ marks the start of a new sentence. That would cause the verse to mean that no one but Allah knows the explanation of the ambiguous verses; and the knowledge of their explanation is entrusted to Allah, for He knows best what they mean; thus, we should not occupy ourselves with interpreting any of it—after stating in unequivocal terms that the outward meaning is impossible for Allah and is not intended by either Him, the Exalted, or His Messenger ﷺ.

[87] *Mufradāt al-Qurʾān: sh-b-h.*

The latter-day scholars posited that the word "and" found in Allah's words: ﴾*...and those who are of sound knowledge...*﴿ is a conjunction that is linked with the Divine Name. That would cause the verse to mean those who are of sound knowledge *also* know the explanation of the ambiguous verses. No matter the case, neither of the two groups accuses the other of misguidance. How could that be when both positions have been narrated from the *Salaf* of this Umma, from the Companions, the followers, and their followers?

Ḥujja al-Islam, al-Ghazālī, summarized the obligation a Muslim is faced with when he or she hears these texts. He said:

> Know that the unequivocal truth, over which there is no dispute among those possessed of inner discernment, is the way of the early generations, meaning the way of the Companions and the Followers who came after them. Here I shall explain that along with its proofs. I say:
>
> The reality of the way of the *Salaf*—which is the truth in our view—is that any layman to whom one of these reports reaches is obliged to uphold seven matters: [1] exoneration, [2] affirmation, [3] acknowledgement of one's inability, [4] silence, [5] abstinence, [6] restraint, and then [7] acquiescing to the people of knowledge.
>
> *As for exoneration*, by this I mean one must declare the Lord, Exalted is He, transcendent above corporeality and its corollaries.
>
> *As for affirmation*, it is to believe in what the Prophet ﷺ said, that what he mentioned is truth, that he is truthful in whatever he says, and that it is truth in accord with what he said and intended.
>
> *As for acknowledging one's inability*, it is for one to acknowledge that knowing the intended meaning is beyond his capacity, and that such a thing is not his concern or area of expertise.
>
> *As for silence*, it is to refrain from asking about its meaning, to refrain from delving into it, and to know that asking about it is a reprehensible innovation, and to know that by delving into he puts his faith at risk, and that he is liable to fall into disbelief without knowing.

As for abstinence, it is for him not to alter or replace those expressions with another language, not to add or subtract from them, or to combine and separate words. Instead, he is only to utter that expression in the manner of its mention, inflection, morphological pattern, and wording.

As for restraint, it is to keep one's heart from searching for it and pondering over it.

As for yielding to its specialists, it is for one to not to believe that simply because it is hidden to him due to his inability, that it was also hidden to the Messenger of Allah ﷺ or hidden to the Prophet or to the veracious and the saints.

These, then, are seven conventions that all of the *Salaf* believed to be an obligation upon laypeople. It should not be thought that the *Salaf* differed over any of these.[88]

The erudite scholar, Shaykh Maḥmūd Khaṭṭāb al-Subkī—may Allah have mercy upon him—said:

> What is meant by them [the ambiguous texts] here are all the things cited in the Book or the authentic Sunna that seem to allude—in any sense—to resemblance between Him, the Exalted, and contingent beings. Unequivocal evidence has been established proving that the outward meanings of these texts cannot apply to Allah, and it is for this reason the early and latter-day scholars unanimously agreed that they should be given a non-specific interpretation in which the word is not used in its outward sense, as that is impossible for Allah due to the establishment of unequivocal proofs that there is nothing like unto Him.
>
> After that, the *Salaf* would not specify the intended meaning of that text; rather, they would entrust its meaning to Allah, the Exalted, considering that the stopping point is at His statement: ﴾*...yet none know its explanation save Allah.*﴿ The latter-day scholars, on the other hand, would give [the ambiguous texts] a detailed explanation and they would specify the intended

---

[88] *Iljām al-ʿAwām ʿan ʿIlm al-Kalām*, p.4.

> meanings thereof. This was due to the mitigating circumstances they were in and their need to refute the innovators who had increased in numbers during their time. The latter-day scholars considered the stopping point in the verse to be at His statement: ﴾*...and those who are of sound knowledge...*﴿[89]

Shaykh ʿAlī al-Ṭanṭāwī—may Allah have mercy upon him—said:

> In the Qurʾān, Allah explained that it contains plain verses that are clear in their meaning and explicit in their expression, as well as ambiguous verses that are not completely clear in their meaning. He explained that the duty of the believer is that he does not delve into their meanings or gather them all together, lest he subject people to tribulation by searching them out. Among the ambiguous verses are the verses pertaining to the Divine attributes.[90]

In his own footnote the Shaykh said: "Whoever gathers them together and presents them to students has not followed the way of the *Salaf*, especially if he adds to them singular Ḥadīth reports on the same subject that are not considered unequivocal proofs in matters of doctrine." He then explained the position a Muslim should take in all this:

> The early Muslims—the *Salaf* of this Umma and its best and most virtuous—did not speak about these [attributes] or attempt to explain them. Nay, they believed in them as they came from Allah, and as intended by Allah. When speculative theology grew and doubts and obfuscations were spread about the doctrine of Islam, a new generation of scholars appeared who were dedicated to refuting these doubts. These scholars spoke about the verses pertaining to the Divine attributes and understood them according to the way of the Arabs, using figurative interpretation.

---

[89] *Itḥāf al-Kāʾināt bi-Bayān Madhhab al-Salaf wal-Khalaf fī al-Mutashābihāt*, p. 167.

[90] *Taʿrīf ʿĀm bi-Dīn al-Islām*, p. 84.

> Regarding this, it has been said: "*The way of the Salaf is safer, and the way of the latter-day scholars is more precise.*" All of them were in agreement that these verses were revealed by Allah and that whoever denies anything from them is a disbeliever, and that whoever completely negates them, believing that they are expressions without meanings, is also a disbeliever. They also agreed that whoever understood them according to their human meaning and applied that to Allah—making the Creator like the creation—has disbelieved. The path is dangerous and the desert is treacherous; safety lies in avoiding delving into this matter.[91]

What the Shaykh stated—may Allah have mercy upon him—is good and well-said. The path is exceedingly dangerous and safety lies in abstaining from it completely. It is certainly unwise to present these texts to the common folk and expose them to this tribulation. There are numerous reports establishing that this is unlawful.

One such report was narrated by Muslim in the introduction to his *Ṣaḥīḥ* collection, from Ibn Mas'ūd ﵁ who said: "You do not narrate anything to a people that is not comprehended by their minds except that it is a trial for some."

Another report is found in al-Bukhārī's collection, in the *Book of Knowledge*, under the chapter heading: *Regarding the One who Selects Some People with Knowledge to the Exclusion of Others, for Fear of Them not Understanding.* 'Alī said [in a *marfū'* report]: "Speak to the people with what they know; would you like for them to belie Allah and His Messenger?"

Al-Ḥāfiẓ Ibn Ḥajar—may Allah have mercy upon him—said: "This contains proof that the ambiguous texts should not be mentioned in front of the common people... The guideline [*ḍābiṭ*] for that is if speaking about it will strengthen blameworthy innovation, and if the outward meaning of it is not intended; in that case, what is sought after is abstaining from it in the presence of one whom it is feared will take its outward meaning."[92]

---

[91] Ibid.

[92] *Fatḥ al-Bārī*, 1:272.

Imām Mālik forbade discussing things that would confuse the people. This was related by Imām Ibn Abī Zayd—may Allah have mercy upon him—in *Al-Nawādir wal-Ziyādāt*: "It is not appropriate for anyone to describe Allah, the Exalted, except with what He described Himself. Similarly, he should not give Him a resemblance to anything. Rather let it be said: He, the Exalted, has "two hands" as He described Himself; He has a face as He described Himself. Let one stop at what is in the Book [the Qur'ān], because Allah, the Glorified, has no likeness or resemblance or equal to Him. No one should narrate the likes of these Ḥadīth, such as [the report] 'Verily Allah created Ādam with his image' and other Ḥadīth. Mālik considered it egregious [*'aẓama*] that someone speak about or repeat the likes of these Ḥadīth reports.[93]

These are clear texts that speak about the prohibition of discussing the ambiguous verses. From this we can see the utter recklessness of those who delve into these texts and present them to the common people as if they are matters in which no one is allowed to be ignorant. What makes it even worse is that these same people relay these reports with the outward meanings that first come to people's minds and they impute misguidance upon those who give them a meaning that goes against the outward and impossible meaning—a meaning that was clearly not the intention of the Messenger of Allah ﷺ, nor was it understood by the Companions—may Allah be pleased with all of them.

Shaykh [Muḥammad Sa'īd] Ramaḍān al-Būṭī—may Allah have mercy upon him—said:

> There are certain verses in the Book of Allah that are outwardly problematic, as well as certain sound Ḥadīth narrations from the Messenger of Allah ﷺ that in their outward meanings and expressions seem to affirm certain imperfections or faults that we negate from Allah's Exalted Being, such as direction, corporeality, bodily limbs, parts, and being limited by space.

---

[93] See also *Al-Bayān wal-Taḥṣīl*, 18:504, *Al-Siyar*, 8:104, *Al-Muwāfaqāt*, 4:549, *Fatḥ al-Bārī*, 1:272, and *Al-Tamhīd*, 7:150.

Take for instance Allah's words: ﴾*And your Lord and the Angels come row by row*﴿, ﴾*Allah's hand is above their hand*﴿, ﴾*Nay, His hands are outstretched, He spends how He wills*﴿ and ﴾*The All-Merciful rose above the Throne.*﴿ Take also the statements of the Prophet ﷺ: "Verily the hearts of the children of Ādam are between two fingers of the fingers of the All-Merciful," and "Verily Allah created Ādam with his image."

These Qur'ānic texts are from a type of ambiguous verses that Allah mentions in His Book, saying that some verses are from it. What is meant by *ambiguous* is every text that entertains many possibilities regarding its intended meaning, and that indicates—in its outward meaning—that which sound proofs negate.

Having said that, there are verses pertaining to Allah's attributes that are plain, i.e., unequivocal in their indications, and that do not carry any possible interpretation beyond their clear and explicit meaning, such as the words of Allah ﷻ: ﴾*There is nothing like unto Him*﴿ and ﴾*Say: "He is Allah, the One. Allah, the Eternal Refuge. He neither begets, nor is He begotten. And there is not any equivalent to Him."*﴿

Allah mentioned in the clearest of terms within His Book that the believer must follow the clear-cut and plain verses in it, and that he must base his belief in Allah accordingly, and that he must place the ambiguous texts in the background in terms of their understanding and arriving at their intended meaning...

Based upon this, all of the Muslims are in unanimous agreement that Allah is Divinely transcendent above the attributes that negate His perfection and godhood and that are ostensibly indicated in the outward meanings of those Qur'ānic texts and Prophetic Ḥadīth reports...

After agreeing on this much—which is the minimum that a Muslim must believe—they disagreed in their stances regarding the ambiguous texts and they held two views: the first view was held by the *Salaf* who are followed, and the second view was held by the latter-day scholars after them.[94]

[94] *Kubrā al-Yaqīniyāt al-Kawniyya*, p. 137.

These two viewpoints are the only views reported from the scholars of the Umma: the way of non-specific interpretation—which is the way of most of the *Salaf*—and the way of specific figurative interpretation—which is the way of the latter-day scholars and groups among the *Salaf*. No consideration should be given to the one who says that we should take the outward meanings of the ambiguous texts, because that is a clear contradiction of the reports that have been cited on this and it goes against common sense.

Al-Ḥāfiẓ al-Bayhaqī—may Allah have mercy upon him—said after narrating the Ḥadīth of "descent" [*nuzūl*]:

> This is a rigorously authentic Ḥadīth narrated by a group of the Companions from the Prophet ﷺ. Regarding the likes of this report mentioned in the Book and the Sunna, and the meaning of which none of the Companions and followers spoke about, the companions of Ḥadīth are two groups: some of them accepted it and believed in it without interpreting it, and they entrusted the knowledge of it to Allah and negated resemblance and modality. Some of them accepted it and believed in it and interpreted it in a manner that conforms to its usage in the [Arabic] language and that does not contradict Divine Oneness...
>
> In general, it must be known that Allah's rising [*istiwā'*] is not a rising [that entails] straightening up after being bent, nor it is settlement in a place or with contact with anything of His creation. Rather, He is risen above His Throne as He informed and without modality, ...without "where;" He is distinct from all of His creation. It must also be known that His "coming" is not the coming from one place to another place. It must be known that His approaching is not a movement, His descent is not by displacement, His Self is not a corporeal body, His face is not an image, His hand is not a limb, and His eyes are not pupils. These descriptions are Divinely inspired, and thus we believe in them and negate modality from them, for Allah, the Exalted, said: ﴾*Do you know any equal to Him?*﴿[95]

[95] *Al-'Itiqād*, p. 92.

Imām al-Nawawī—may Allah have mercy upon him—said in his explanation of one of the Ḥadīth mentioning Divine attributes:

> This Ḥadīth is from the Ḥadīth reports pertaining to the Divine attributes, and there are two well-known positions the scholars take concerning it that were explained in the *Book of Faith*.
>
> In summary, the first position, which is the position of the majority of the *Salaf* and some of the theologians, is to believe that it is the truth as it befits Allah, the Exalted, and that its outward meaning which is customarily known among us is not intended, and that it should not be given figurative interpretation, while at the same time believing that Allah is Divinely transcendent above the qualities of the creation, displacement, movement, and the rest of the traits of creation.
>
> The second position, which is the position of most of the theologians, some groups among the *Salaf*, and it is related from Mālik and al-Awzā'ī, is that these reports are to be given specific figurative interpretation according to what is appropriate for them according to their context.[96]

He—may Allah have mercy upon him—mentioned only these two positions and stated that the position of specific figurative interpretation is also narrated from the *Salaf* ﷺ. This is in order to make it known to the naysayers that, when they cast blame on the Ash'arīs and Māturīdīs and describe them with misguidance due to their allowance of figurative interpretation with its prerequisites, they are in fact only condemning and detracting from the *Salaf*.

Al-Ḥāfiẓ Ibn Ḥajar—may Allah have mercy upon him—said about the texts mentioning the attributes: "There is to be either non-specific interpretation or specific figurative interpretation [of them]."[97]

He mentioned something similar when he refuted Abū Ismā'īl al-Harawī, when the latter objected to the one who gave the Ḥadīth of "descent" a figurative interpretation.

---

[96] *Sharḥ Ṣaḥīḥ Muslim*, 6:36.

[97] *Fatḥ al-Bārī*, 13:466.

Al-Harawī mentioned several Ḥadīth reports that mentioned "rising" and claimed that these reports do not accept [the possibility of] figurative interpretation. Al-Ḥāfiẓ [Ibn Ḥajar] refuted his claim, after stating that al-Harawī had exaggerated in affirmation [of the Divine attributes]. He then quoted the attacks that some levelled against him on account of his position.

He [Ibn Ḥajar] said: "All of these routes [of the Ḥadīth on 'rising'] are weak, and even if they were assumed to be established, his statement 'They do not accept [the possibility of] figurative interpretation' is unacceptable. What is taken from these reports is the mention of 'rising' after 'descent;' so just as 'descent' accepts figurative interpretation, there is nothing to prevent 'rising' from accepting figurative interpretation either—and submission is safer."[98]

Imām al-Kirmānī—may Allah have mercy upon him—said about one of the Ḥadīth pertaining to the attributes: "The same ruling is given to all of the ambiguous texts: either non-specific interpretation or specific figurative interpretation."[99] He also said: "This Ḥadīth is from the ambiguous texts, so there is either non-specific interpretation or specific figurative interpretation."

Imām Badr al-Dīn b. Jamāʿa—may Allah have mercy upon him—said regarding "rising" [*istiwāʾ*]: "The *Salaf* and the people of figurative interpretation both agreed that things that do not befit the Majesty of the Lord, Exalted is He, such as sitting and being upright [in a seat] are not intended... The *Salaf* remained silent without specifying what was meant, and the people of figurative interpretation interpreted it."[100]

Imām Abū ʿAbdullāh al-Ubbī said in his commentary upon *Ṣaḥīḥ Muslim*, explaining the Ḥadīth of "descent":

> The way of the people of truth concerning all of this is to carry the expression in a way that is different from the outward meaning which is [an] impossible [meaning].
>
> After that the question remains: is figurative interpretation given precedence or not, for example, by believing in the expression in a way that befits [Allah]

---

[98] Ibid.

[99] *Al-Fatḥ*, 13:13.

[100] *Īḍāḥ al-Dalīl fī Qaṭiʿ Ḥujaj Ahl al-Taʿṭīl*, p. 103.

> while at the same time entrusting the reality of that to Allah ﷻ...? The most apparent view among the people of truth is that of figurative interpretation.[101]

The erudite scholar and Imām, Mullā ʿAlī al-Qārī—may Allah have mercy upon him—said after quoting Imām al-Nawawī's comments that we mentioned earlier:

> From his words and the words of the lordly Shaykh Abū Isḥāq al-Shīrāzī, Imām al-Ḥaramayn, al-Ghazālī, and others among our Imāms and others, it is known that both positions are in agreement regarding carrying the outward expressions of these texts—such as coming, image, form, leg, foot, hand, face, anger, mercy, rising above the Throne, and being above the heavens—in a way that is different from what is understood from them literally, due to what that would necessitate of impossibilities that are clearly false and things that are judged as disbelief by scholarly consensus. This obliged all of the latter-day scholars and the *Salaf* to carry these expressions in a way that is different from their outward meanings.
>
> They only disagreed about whether we should carry these expressions away from their outward meanings while believing that He, the Glorified, is described with that which befits His Majesty and Grandeur and without interpreting them figuratively with anything else—which is the position of most of the *Salaf* and is a non-specific interpretation—or, alternatively, whether we should give them figurative interpretation—which is the position of most of the latter-day scholars and is specific interpretation. In that they did not intend to oppose the pious predecessors.
>
> Allah forbid that such a thing be thought regarding them! It was only the mitigating circumstances of their times that called for it, due to the large numbers of anthropomorphists, Jahmīs, and other sects of misguidance, and their influence on the common folk. They [the scholars] intended by that to refute and

[101] *Sharḥ Ṣaḥīḥ Muslim* 2:385.

> repudiate their [the sects'] false beliefs. Moreover, many of them excused themselves and said: "If we were in the same circumstances as the pious predecessors, with pure beliefs and no heretics, we would have abstained from delving into any figurative interpretation."[102]

Imām al-Zarkashī—may Allah have mercy upon him—said:

> The people differ regarding what is cited from them [the ambiguous texts] in the verses and Ḥadīth reports, and they are three groups:
>
> 1- [Those who believe that] there is no room for figurative interpretation of them, rather [they posit], they should be relayed according to their outward meanings and nothing of them should be interpreted. They are the anthropomorphists.
> 2- [Those who believe that] the [ambiguous texts] do have an interpretation, however, we are to refrain from that, while at the same time not believing in any resemblance or outright denial. [According to this view] we are to say: ﴾*None know its interpretation except Allah.*﴿ This is the view of the *Salaf*.
> 3- [Those who believe that] they are interpreted. They interpreted them according to what befits Him. The first position is false, and the other two positions are recorded from the Companions, ...and those who have been reported using figurative interpretation include ʿAlī, Ibn Masʿūd, Ibn ʿAbbās, and others.[103]

The erudite scholar Muḥammad Zakariyyā al-Kāndahlawī—may Allah have mercy upon him—said in his explanation of the Ḥadīth of "descent" in his commentary upon the *Muwaṭṭā'*: "Regarding that, the scholars are two categories: the people of non-specific interpretation, ...and the people of specific figurative interpretation."[104]

---

[102] *Mirqāt al-Mafātīḥ*, 2:136.
[103] *Al-Burhān fī ʿUlūm al-Qur'ān*, 2:207.
[104] *Awjaz al-Masālik*, 4:334.

After all this, the truth is clear to all who possess eyes. It is established that non-specific interpretation and specific figurative interpretation are the two correct positions taken with regards to the ambiguous texts about the Divine attributes. What remains is for us to explain the reason why such expressions were revealed in the Book and Sunna in the first place even though they are the source of disagreement and slipping.

We say: it is not farfetched that the revelation of these expressions is a trial and test for the people,[105] in order to make clear those who stay within the proper boundaries and those who follow the ambiguous verses, seeking mischief and seeking to lead creation astray.

The Exalted said: ﴾*It is He Who has revealed unto you the Book, wherein are plain verses, which are the foundation of the Book; others are ambiguous. As for those in whose hearts is deviation: they seek out that which is unclear of it, seeking mischief, and seeking its explanation—yet none know its explanation save Allah, and those who are of sound knowledge say: "We believe in it. All of it is from our Lord." And none take the reminder except those of understanding.*﴿ [Āl-ʿImrān: 6][106]

From this we learn that whoever believes in the outward meanings of these texts has opposed both the *Salaf* and the latter-day scholars, and has innovated a belief that has no portion of truth. In this issue there is nothing but the position of non-specific interpretation or specific figurative interpretation.

Furthermore, it is known that specific figurative interpretation is not a blameworthy innovation in the religion, as some like to ignorantly propagate to the masses. Nay, the position of specific figurative interpretation is a true position that is affirmed from the *Salaf* of this Umma and in accordance with the language of the Arabs.

---

105 See: *Al-Muwāfaqāt*, 4:123–126 and *Iljām al-ʿAwām*.

106 Alternatively, based on the other position regarding the stopping point in this verse, it reads: ﴾*...yet none know its explanation save Allah and those who are of sound knowledge.* [They] *say: "We believe in it. All of it is from our Lord."*﴿ [t]

AHL AL-SUNNA: THE ASHʿARĪS

The Testimony and Proofs of the Scholars

Chapter Six

Disagreements in Matters of Doctrine

Is it true that every disagreement in matters of doctrine—be it in the fundamental tenets or in subsidiary issues—results in disbelief or misguidance, or charges of blameworthy innovation and corruption? Did the Companions or scholars from the pious predecessors ever disagree about matters of doctrine? Did any of their disagreements in that lead to charges of misguidance and corruption?

In answering these questions we will make clear the mistake of those who are reckless in their accusations of misguidance against the Ashʿarīs, Māturīdīs, and the scholars and notables of this Umma, in addition to all who oppose them without sound knowledge or narration.

Considering the state of the Umma and its suffering and division that breaks the heart of every jealously protective person, it would have been more fitting for them to consider these disagreements—if any are found—in the best possible light, and in a manner commensurate with the expansive breast of this religion. It is more fitting that excuses are found as much as possible, so as not to increase the splitting and disunity of the Umma and assist its enemies against it—such as the one who lost his strength after having it.

Creed as such is divided into two categories: fundamental tenets and subsidiary issues. The fundamental tenets are further divided into the fundamentals of the religion and the fundamentals of the way of Ahl al-Sunna wal-Jamāʿa. The fundamentals of the religion include belief in Allah's existence, His Oneness, His everlastingness, His pre-eternality, belief in the contingency of the universe (which is everything besides Allah among existents), the veracity of the Messengers and Prophets, and so on. There is no disagreement that whoever goes against these matters has left the religion, because these [matters] represent the foundations upon which the religion is built. Those who go against these beliefs include the adherents to other religions and ways, such as the Jews, the Christians, and Zoroastrians, the Buddhists, etc.

In *Rawḍa al-Ṭālibīn*, Imām al-Nawawī—may Allah have mercy upon him—quoted Imām al-Mutawallī as saying:

> Whoever believes in the eternality of the world or the contingency of the Maker [Allah], or negates what is affirmed for the Pre-eternal [Allah] by consensus, such as Him being All-Knowing and All-Powerful, or affirms for Him what is negated by consensus, such as colours, or affirms that He is connected or disconnected—then he is a disbeliever. Similarly, whoever denies the [rational] possibility of Messengers being sent, or rejects the Prophethood of a particular Prophet among the Prophets —may prayers and salutations be upon them—or belies him, or rejects a single verse from the Qur'ān that is [considered a verse] by consensus, or adds a single word to the Qur'ān or believes that it is from it, or insults a Prophet or belittles him, or who declares licit that which is unlawful by consensus, such as alcohol, fornication, homosexuality, or who declares unlawful that which is lawful by consensus, or denies the obligation of that which is obligatory by consensus, such as a single unit from the five obligatory prayers, or believes in the obligation of something that is not an obligation by consensus, such as a sixth [obligatory] prayer or fasting in [the month of] *Shawwāl*, or who ascribes vileness [adultery] to ʿĀ'isha ﷺ or makes a claim to Prophecy after our Prophet ﷺ or believes in someone who makes that false-claim, or if he glorifies an idol by prostrating to it or seeks to draw close to it by sacrificing [an animal] in its name—all of this is disbelief.[107]

Before we move on and discuss the fundamentals of the way of Ahl al-Sunna wal-Jamāʿa, we must mention an issue that is extremely dangerous, namely the statement of Imām al-Mutawallī: "...or affirms that He is connected or disconnected." Here, he made the affirmation of connection or disconnection one of the issues that entails disbelief, and Imām al-Nawawī agreed with him.

---

[107] *Rawḍa al-Ṭālibīn*, 1:64.

Connection and disconnection are the qualities of being either inside or outside [of something]. Ahl al-Sunna declare Allah transcendent above being qualified by either of the two. No consideration should be given to anyone who opposes this belief, basing his view on ignorance of the necessary implications [of the belief in Allah being either inside or outside of the universe] or his lack of submission to its implications.

This issue is of dire importance and seriousness. Were it not for our knowledge that those who object to the Ashʿarīs do not understand this issue correctly, we would not have brought it up here (because of its detail). However, with that we will try to avoid going into its finer points and we will suffice with a general explanation and cite the statements of the scholars who have warned against describing Allah with either of these two descriptions. Whoever wishes to learn more about this may refer to the appropriate books of doctrine that discuss it.

We often read or hear people describe Allah, the Exalted, saying: "He is separate from His creation with His Essence." If what is meant by separation here is a distinction and negation of indwelling [*ḥulūl*] and union [*ittiḥād*], then it is undoubtedly true and it is also the doctrine of Ahl al-Sunna wal-Jamāʿa from the *Salaf* and the latter-day scholars—and this is what is meant by the expression when it is reported from any of them. On the other hand, if what is meant by this statement is actual [physical] separation, then the one who says this has fallen into an enormity. Separation with this meaning implies that the one described with it accepts a locus and direction, and Allah, the Exalted, is transcendent above that. Furthermore, the wording "with His Essence" is not recorded in either the Book, the Sunna, or upon the tongue of any of the Companions or followers!

Those sayings attributed to some of the *Salaf* in which they said: "He is distinct with His Essence" and "He is distinct from His creation" are understood as an affirmation of distinction and a negation of mixing [with the creation]. This meaning is correct, but one must be aware that each word takes on a different meaning when co-joined with another word.

For instance, when the phrase "with His Essence" is mentioned along with separation/distinction, two meanings are understood: the first meaning, which is permissible to say regarding Allah, the

Exalted, is distinction and negation of admixture and indwelling. The second meaning, which is forbidden to say unrestrictedly regarding Allah, the Exalted, is disconnectedness and "being outside."

The same cannot be said regarding "rising" [*istiwāʾ*], "descent" [*nuzūl*], "coming" [*ityān*], and so on, because when the phrase "with His Essence" is mentioned alongside these or similar expressions, their meanings are then restricted to a corporeal or sense-perception meaning [*ḥissī jismānī*]. So for instance, it should not be said that He rose with His Essence, descends with His Essence, or comes with His Essence, and then conclude it with the disclaimer: "Not like our rising, descent, or coming," as that is a clear contradiction.

Ibn al-Jawzī—may Allah have mercy upon him—said: "Whoever says 'He rose with His Essence' has made Him [Allah] the object of sense perception."[108]

Al-Ḥāfiẓ al-Dhahabī—may Allah have mercy upon him—said in his biographical notice on Ibn al-Zāghūnī: "We have previously mentioned that the phrase 'with His Essence' is superfluous and it troubles the souls. Leaving it is more fitting, and Allah knows best."[109]

Al-Ḥāfiẓ Ibn Ḥajar al-ʿAsqalānī—may Allah have mercy upon him—said in his commentary on the Ḥadīth "When one of you stands up to pray, he is in intimate conversation with his Lord [or alternatively], ...his Lord is between him and the *qibla*...": "This contains a refutation against the one who claims that He [Allah] is above the Throne with His Essence."[110]

Al-Ḥāfiẓ al-Dhahabī said in his book *Al-ʿUluw*, after citing the statement of Yaḥyā b. ʿAmmār: "Nay, we say that He is, with His Essence, above the Throne and His knowledge encompasses everything": "Your statement 'with His Essence' is from your own bag."[111] He also said in his biographical entry on al-Ḥāfiẓ Abū al-Qāsim Ismāʿīl b. Muḥammad al-Taymī: "I say: the correct position is to withhold from expressing such things, for there is

---

[108] *Dafaʿ Shubh al-Tashbīh*, p. 102.
[109] *Siyar ʿAlām al-Nubalāʾ*, 19:607.
[110] *Fatḥ al-Bārī*, 1:598.
[111] *Al-ʿUluw*, p. 263.

no Divine text mentioning it. And even if we assume that its meaning is correct, it is not for us to utter anything that Allah has not given permission for—out of fear that something of blameworthy innovation will enter the heart. O Allah! Safeguard our faith for us!"[112]

Imām al-Dhahabī's statement about assuming its meaning is correct is understood in light of the correct meaning of the phrase "with His Essence" that was used by Yaḥyā b. ʿAmmār—not the outwardly apparent meaning of it that first appears to the mind.

Imām Badr al-Dīn b. Jamāʿa—may Allah have mercy upon him—said:

> Whoever believes that the "rising" [*istiwā*ʾ] with respect to Him [Allah], the Exalted, is understood like the qualities of the contingent beings and says: "He rose with His Essence" or says: "He rose in reality [*ḥaqīqatan*]," then he has innovated this extraneous expression that is neither affirmed in the Sunna nor reported from any of the Imāms that are followed.[113]

Al-Ḥāfiẓ al-Dhahabī said in *Al-ʿUluw*: "They criticized him [Ibn Abī Zayd al-Qayrawānī] for his statement: "with His Essence" so would that he had left it out."[114]

Now we are most certain that Imām Ibn Abī Zayd al-Qayrawānī did not intend by this phrase—if it is authentically from him[115]—the meaning that some intend, and this is evident from the statements of those who wrote commentaries on his book.

---

[112] *Siyar ʿAlām al-Nubalā*ʾ, 20:86.

[113] *Īḍāḥ al-Dalīl*, p. 107.

[114] *Al-ʿUluw*, p. 256.

[115] The erudite al-Kawtharī—may Allah have mercy upon him—said in his footnote to *Tabyīn Kadhib al-Muftarī* (p. 123): "The commentators on his *Risāla* concur that this phrase is either interpolated or understood as a nominative phrase [*rafa*ʿ], in other words: '...upon the Throne, Glorious in His Essence [*...al-ʿArshi, al-Majīd bi-Dhātihi*]'" (as opposed to describing the Throne as glorious and affirming that He is above it with His Essence: "*al-ʿArshi al-Majīd bi-Dhātihi.*") [t]

He was an Ash'arī and he loved Imām Abū al-Ḥasan, as is clear from his response to someone who criticized him for his love for him. He said: "Al-Ash'arī is no more than a man who is well-known for refuting the people of innovation and the Qadariyya and the Jahmīs, and who holds firm to the Sunna." Al-Tāj al-Subkī mentioned him among the second tier of Ash'arīs that went unmentioned in al-Ḥāfiẓ Ibn 'Asākir's book *Tabyīn Kadhib al-Muftarī*.[116]

Imām Ibn 'Abd al-Barr—may Allah have mercy upon him—said: "And a group ascribed to the Sunna said that He, the Exalted, descends with His Essence! This statement is rejected, because He, Exalted is His mention, is not a locus for movement and He has nothing from the signs (characteristics) of the creation."[117]

He also said in his refutation against someone who said that He descends with His Essence: "This is rejected [*laysa bi-shay'in*] according to the people of understanding among Ahl al-Sunna because it is a modality [*kayfiyya*], and they flee from that because it is only suitable for something that is directly encompassed, and Allah, the Exalted, is transcendent above that."[118]

Al-Ḥāfiẓ al-Dhahabī said in his biographical entry of Kūtāh: "...Also His statement: ﴿*And your Lord comes...*﴾ and its likes. We say: He comes and He descends, without saying "He descends with His Essence" just as we do not say "He descends with His knowledge." Nay, we remain silent and do not seek to be more eloquent than the Messenger of Allah ﷺ using innovated expressions. And Allah knows best."

All of this shows that the phrase "with His Essence" is not established from the pious predecessors of this Umma and that it is rejected by both the intellect and the Divine texts. What stronger proof can there be as the statements of the Imāms only carry one possible meaning?

Abū al-Ḥasan Ibn al-Munādī—may Allah have mercy upon him—said: "We do not disagree that nothing of His creation can be over the Compeller [al-Jabbār] under any circumstance, and

---

[116] See: *Tabyīn Kadhib al-Muftarī* (p. 123) and *Ṭabaqāt al-Shāfi'iyya al-Kubrā*, 3:368.

[117] *Al-Istidhkār*, 8:153.

[118] *Al-Tamhīd*, 7:143.

[we do not disagree] that He does not indwell with anything with His Being remaining inseparable therefrom, because if He were to indwell in it He would be from it..."[119]

Ibn al-Munādī's statement: "...and [we do not disagree] that He does not indwell with anything with His Being remaining inseparable therefrom" is exactly what the scholars mean when they say that Allah, the Exalted, is not described with connection or disconnection or being inside or outside.

Ibn Munādī is Imām Aḥmad b. Ja'far, the reciter and Ḥadīth master. Imām al-Dhahabī said: "Al-Dānī said concerning him: 'A noble reciter, a master to the utmost. He was eloquent in speech and knowledgeable about the reports. He was a reliable reference in the knowledge of Arabic, and he was a Sunni, reliable and trustworthy.'"[120] The erudite scholar Ibn Khaldūn—may Allah have mercy upon him—said in his *Muqaddima*:

> There often occurs in the words of the people of doctrine from the scholars of Ḥadīth and jurisprudence that Allah, the Exalted, is separate from His creation; and there often occurs in the words of the scholastic theologians that He is neither separate nor connected [to the world]; and there often occurs in the words of the philosophers that He is neither inside of the universe nor outside of it...
>
> Here, we shall clarify the details of these positions and explain the reality of each one so their meanings become clear. [The word] separation [*mubāyana*] contains two meanings: separation in a direction and boundary, and it stands opposite of connection [*ittiṣāl*]. This juxtaposition is sensed when it [separation] is restricted to a place, either explicitly, which is anthropomorphism [*tajsīm*], or implicitly, which is resemblance [*tashbīh*] on account of the belief in a direction [for Allah].
>
> The likes of that have been transmitted from some of the scholars of the *Salaf*, in which "separation" is explicitly mentioned; however, it carries a different meaning than this. It is for this reason the scholastic theologians denied this "separation." They said: "It should

[119] *Dafa' Shubh al-Tashbīh*, p. 192.
[120] *Siyar 'Alām al-Nubalā'*, 15:361.

> not be said that the Creator is separate from His creation or connected to them, because that only applies to things restricted by spatial boundaries." As for the statement that a locus is either described with something or its opposite [its contradictory], that is first conditioned upon that thing accepting that quality. But when that is [rationally] impossible, it is not the case, nay, it is possible for [that thing] to be free of that thing and its opposite, just as it is said regarding a solid inanimate object: it is neither knowing nor ignorant; neither powerful nor incapable; and neither literate nor illiterate. For this description of "separation" to apply, that which is described with it must be in a direction, according to what is implied in its indication, and the Creator is Divinely transcendent above that. This was mentioned by Ibn al-Tilmisānī in his commentary on Imām al-Ḥaramayn's *Al-Luma'*. He said: "It should not be said that the Creator is separate from the universe or connected to it, and neither should it be said that He is inside of it or outside of it..."
>
> The second meaning of separation is distinction and dissimilarity. It is said that the Creator is distinct in His Essence, His Being, His existence, and His attributes. Distinction here stands opposite of union, admixture, and blending. This [belief in] distinction is the doctrine of the people of truth entirely, from the majority of the *Salaf*, the scholars of the Sacred Laws, the theologians, and the early Sufis, such as those mentioned in the *Epistle* [of Imām al-Qushayrī] and those who followed their way.[121]

Ibn al-Jawzī—may Allah have mercy upon him—said:

> That is because proximity and separation are from the necessary qualities of that which is contained within boundaries, and it is established that gathering and separation are from the necessary qualities of what is contained in a boundary. But the Real سبحانه وتعالى cannot be described with having boundaries... Likewise, it should be said that He is neither inside nor outside of the world, because being inside or outside of something is one of the

[121] *Al-Muqaddima*, p. 868.

> necessary qualities of something contained within boundaries. Likewise with movement and quiescence, and all other accidental qualities that are particular to substances... The words of these people [the anthropomorphists] are based upon the sensory, and the sensory has caused them to succumb to corporealism and confusion.[122]

Based on their belief that Allah is separate from His creation with His Essence—which is a physical-sensory separation—they affirmed a limit for Him ﷻ. And based upon that, they affirmed a direction for Him, i.e., that Allah is physically above and that He can be physically pointed at upwards, and they also affirmed a place for Him.

STATEMENTS FROM THE RELIABLE IMĀMS NEGATING DIRECTION FROM ALLAH, THE EXALTED, AND DECLARING HIM TRANSCENDENT ABOVE PLACE

Imām Mālik ؓ

The chief judge and Imām, Nāṣir al-Dīn b. al-Munīr al-Sakandarī al-Mālikī mentioned in his book *Al-Muntaqā fī Sharaf al-Muṣṭafā* ﷺ, after speaking about direction and negating it [from Allah]:

> And for this reason Imām Mālik—may Allah have mercy upon him—indicated that [after mentioning the Ḥadīth]: "Do not declare me superior to Yūnus b. Mattā." Mālik said: "He only made special mention of Yūnus for the sake of [declaring Allah's] transcendence, because he [the Prophet Muḥammad ﷺ] ascended to the Throne and Yūnus ؑ was taken to the bottom of the ocean—even though they were both linked to the Real [Allah] with one linkage, despite their different directions. If superiority was due to physical place, he [the Prophet Muḥammad] would be closer and superior than Yūnus b. Mattā and he would not have forbidden that."

[122] Dafaʿ *Shubha al-Tashbīh*, p. 130.

Imām Nāṣir al-Dīn went on to explain that the superiority was because of rank [*makāna*] and not place [*makān*], because the Throne is in the higher assembly and is superior to the lower level [on earth].[123]

Imām Mālik ﷺ said in his figurative interpretation of "descent" [*nuzūl*] mentioned in the Ḥadīth: "His command descends each night." He said: "As for Him ﷻ, He is Permanent and does not pass or displace Himself—there is no god but He."[124]

Imām Ibn ʿAbd al-Barr said after quoting the statement of Mālik: "It is possible that it is as Mālik—may Allah have mercy upon him—said regarding its meaning, i.e., that it is His mercy and pre-ordained pardon and response."

Then he said after mentioning the view of those who held that He [Allah] descends with His Essence: "This is rejected [*laysa bi-shayʾin*] according to the people of understanding among Ahl al-Sunna because it is a modality [*kayfiyya*], and they flee from that because it is only suitable for something that is directly encompassed, and Allah, the Exalted, is transcendent above that."[125]

This figurative interpretation—if it is authentically attributed to Mālik[126]—indicates a negation of direction and physical "aboveness."

---

[123] See: *Al-Sayf al-Ṣaqīl*, p. 40. It is mentioned that Imām al-Juwaynī said something similar in a story reported from him. This was mentioned by al-Kawtharī in his footnote and he attributed that narration to al-Qāḍī Ibn al-ʿArabī on the authority of many of Imām [Mālik's] companions, as is mentioned in al-Qurṭubī's *Al-Tadhkira*. See also: *Itḥāf al-Sāda al-Muttaqīn*, 2:105.

[124] See: *Al-Tamhīd*, 7:143, Imām al-Nawawī's commentary on *Ṣaḥīḥ Muslim*, 6:37, *Siyar ʿAlām al-Nubalāʾ*, 8:105, and *Al-Inṣāf* of Ibn al-Sayyid al-Baṭlayūsī, p. 81.

[125] *Al-Tamhīd*, 7:143.

[126] This particular interpretation is well-known from Imām Mālik among the Mālikī Imāms and others, such as Ibn ʿAbd al-Barr and Abū ʿAmr al-Dānī, as found in *Al-Risāla al-Wāfiya* (pp. 135–137), wherein it states: "And some of our colleagues said that [it means] His command, Exalted is He, descends, and this is proven by His ﷻ words: ﴾*He Who created the seven heavens and from the earth like them; the affair descends between them.*﴿ ...Moreover, Ḥabīb narrated from Mālik b. Anas—may Allah have mercy upon him..."

Imām al-Ṭabarī and his negation of physical loftiness [ʿ*uluw*]

Imām Ibn Jarīr al-Ṭabarī—may Allah have mercy upon him—said in his exegesis, concerning Allah's words: ﴿*And He is the Irresistible, above His servants*﴾: "He is above them with His irresistible dominance over them and they are under [less than] Him."[127]

Here we see that the Imām—may Allah have mercy upon him—stated that Allah's "aboveness" over His servants is one of irresistible dominance, and that His servants are under Him in this sense.

He gave a figurative interpretation to Allah's loftiness above His Throne and negated settlement and boundaries: "He is lofty above it with a loftiness of ownership and authority, not a loftiness [entailing] displacement and passage."[128]

Qāḍī ʿIyāḍ

Qāḍī ʿIyāḍ—may Allah have mercy upon him—said (as quoted by Imām al-Nawawī in his commentary on *Ṣaḥīḥ Muslim*): "There is no disagreement among the Muslims whatsoever—not between their jurists, Ḥadīth scholars, theologians, investigators, and common folk—that the outward meaning of the texts that mention Allah, the Exalted, being in the heavens, such as His statement: ﴿*Do you feel secure from He Who is in the heavens that he would not cause the earth to swallow you?*﴾ And its likes are not to be taken upon their outward meaning, nay, they are interpreted according to all."[129]

After that, he mentioned the statement of al-Awzāʿī when he was asked about the "descent": "Allah does what He wills." Abū ʿAmr said: "[This is with the] narration of Ḥabīb, Mālik's scribe, and they weakened him, nay, they accused him of forgery. The other route is not connected to Mālik and it also contains unknown narrators—however, the authorities [*aṣḥāb*] of the legal school [the Mālikīs] are better acquainted with the statements of their Imām than others, especially if we consider that the statement is wide-spread and well-known among them."

[127] *Tafsīr al-Ṭabarī*, 7:103.

[128] Ibid., 1:192.

[129] *Rawḍa al-Ṭālibīn*, 10:85.

Imām al-Nawawī

He—may Allah have mercy upon him—said: "And if he [the disbeliever] said: 'There is no god but He Who resides in the heavens' he will not be a believer. Similarly, if he said: 'There is no god but Allah, the One Who resides in the heavens' [he will not be a believer], because quiescence is impossible for Allah." He also said in his commentary on the Ḥadīth of the servant girl:

> This Ḥadīth is among the Ḥadīth reports pertaining to the Divine attributes. There are two positions concerning it. The first position is to have faith in it without delving into its meaning, while at the same time believing that there is nothing like unto Allah, the Exalted, and declaring Him Divinely transcendent above the traits of the creation.
>
> The second position is to interpret it in a fitting manner. The one who takes this latter position says: 'Perhaps what was intended here was to test the servant girl in order to see if she believed [in Allah's] Oneness and admitted that the Creator, Disposer of affairs, and Doer is Allah alone; the One who, when the supplicant calls, he faces the heavens, just as when a person prays he faces the Kaʿba. That is not because He is restricted to the heavens [in the case of the former], just as He is not restricted to the direction of the Kaʿba [in the case of the latter]. Nay, it is because the heavens are the *qibla* for the supplicants just as the Kaʿba is the *qibla* for those who pray. Or [alternatively], she was an idol worshipper and among them, so when she said: "In the heavens" it was understood that she was a believer in Divine Oneness and not an idol worshipper.[130]

Imām al-Shāṭibī

Imām al-Shāṭibī—may Allah have mercy upon him—said:

> From that [i.e., from the things that must be known in the science of the Qurʾān] is knowledge of the customs of the Arabs in their statements, actions, and states during the advent of Divine revelation—even if there is no specific

[130] *Sharḥ Ṣaḥīḥ Muslim*, 5:24.

> cause [for revelation]. Whoever desires to delve into the sciences of the Qur'ān must have this; otherwise he will fall into obfuscations and problems that he is not apt to come out of without it...
>
> Three [the third example of that]: The statements of the Exalted: ﴾*They fear their Lord above them*﴿ and ﴾*Do you feel safe from He Who is in the heavens...*﴿ and their likes; they [the pagan Arabs] were accustomed to taking deities on the earth, even if they believed in the godhood of the Real and One [Allah]. These verses mentioned above were specifically to bring to their attention the negation of what they claimed on the earth. There is no proof within them for the affirmation of direction whatsoever. For that reason, the Exalted said: ﴾*The ceiling fell from over them.*﴿ Ponder this and adopt this method for all of the verses and Ḥadīth reports.[131]

Al-Ḥāfiẓ Ibn Ḥajar al-ʿAsqalānī

Ibn Ḥajar—may Allah have mercy upon him—said: "That the direction of above and below are both impossible for Allah does not imply that He is not described with loftiness, because the description of loftiness is in meaning [alone]; what is impossible is for it to be in the physical sense."[132]

He also said in his comments on the Ḥadīth: "When one of you stands up to pray, he is in intimate conversation with his Lord [or alternatively], ...his Lord is between him and the *qibla*...": "This contains a refutation against the one who claims that He [Allah] is above the Throne with His Essence."[133] He also said in his commentary on the Ḥadīth: "There is no one [*shakhṣ*] more jealously protective than Allah":

> It is as if the expression "no one" was used for hyperbole in affirming the faith of someone who finds it difficult to grasp an existent that does not resemble anything of the existent beings, lest that lead him to negation and denial. This is similar to his ﷺ statement to the servant girl:

---

[131] *Al-Muwāfaqāt*, 3:351.
[132] *Fatḥ al-Bārī*, 6:158.
[133] Ibid., 1:598.

> "Where is Allah?" She answered: "In the heavens." He affirmed her faith, fearing lest she fall into denial because of her limited understanding that He [Allah] should be transcendently above things that entail resemblance [*tashbīh*]—and Allah is exalted and above that.

He also quoted Ibn Baṭṭāl who said: "And Allah is transcendent above indwelling in places, because indwelling is a passing, incidental state, and thus it is contingent, and a contingent does not befit Allah."[134]

He said in his commentary on the Ḥadīth of "descent" [*nuzūl*]:

> The one who affirms direction [for Allah] used this as proof and said: "It is the direction of above." This was negated by the majority, because belief in that leads to [belief in] boundaries—and Allah is exalted above boundaries.
>
> There are different opinions concerning the meaning of "descent." Some of them carried it upon its outward meaning and literal sense. They are the Mujassima (anthropomorphists)—exalted be Allah from their belief!
>
> Some denied the authenticity of the Ḥadīth altogether, and they are the Khawārij and the Muʿtazila—and that is simply stubbornness.
>
> Some passed it on as it was related, believing in it in a general sense and declaring Allah transcendent above modality and resemblance. They are the majority of the *Salaf*. Al-Bayhaqī and others related this positon from the four Imāms, the two Sufyāns, the two Ḥammāds, al-Awzāʿī, al-Layth, and others.
>
> Some of them interpreted it in a befitting manner that is employed in the language of the Arabs, ...and some of them differentiated between an approximate interpretation employed in the language of the Arabs and an interpretation that is farfetched and rejected. So [the one who took this position] gave a specific figurative interpretation sometimes, and took a stance of non-

---

[134] Ibid., 13:397.

> specific interpretation at other times. This is cited from Mālik,[135] and among those of the latter-day scholars who held this position was Ibn Daqīq al-ʿĪd.[136]

In this he refuted the one who affirmed a direction for Allah and who claimed that it is inconceivable that anything can exist that is not in a direction. According to the claimant, direction is an existing thing and is not in a direction unto itself, for if that were the case there would be a never-ending chain, and that is false. It follows then that direction is affirmed without a direction, and this demolishes the claim that it is inconceivable that anything can exist that is not in a direction.

It is clear that the default position regarding the ambiguous source texts is non-specific interpretation as long as there is no need for specific figurative interpretation. This was the position of the pious predecessors, as we shall soon demonstrate. If the *Salaf* found in their times what had occurred after them, they would have openly employed specific figurative interpretation, especially considering that it is affirmed that some groups of them did employ it.

Imām al-Qushayrī—may Allah have mercy upon him

Imām al-Qushayrī—may Allah have mercy upon him—said: "The Lord is qualified with the loftiness and highness of rank and tremendousness, and He is transcendent above being in a place or having spatial contact."

Qāḍī al-Quḍāt Ibn al-Munīr

Al-Ḥāfiẓ Ibn Ḥajar quoted the words of Ibn al-Munīr in which he declared Allah transcendent above place and direction:

> Ibn al-Munīr said: "His statement: '...the Lord of the Throne'—here he [al-Bukhārī] alluded to the falsehood of the statement of one who affirms a direction [for Allah], deducing it from his statement: '...the Possessor of the ways of ascent' he [the one who affirmed a direction for

[135] His statement here strengthens what was mentioned regarding Mālik's figurative interpretation of "descent."
[136] *Fatḥ al-Bārī*, 3:37.

> Allah] understood that physical highness is ascribed to Allah, the Exalted, so the author [al-Bukhārī] clarified that both the direction that is the heavens and the direction that is the Throne are created, cared for [*marbūb*], and contingent, and Allah was most certainly before that and other things. These places came into being and His quality of pre-eternality precludes Him being qualified with being bounded inside of them [these places], and Allah knows best."[137]

Here we see that al-Bukhārī, Ibn al-Munīr, and Ibn Ḥajar all agreed about this text and that Allah is transcendent above place and direction—and this is the belief of all people of transcendence.

Imām al-Bayḍāwī

Imām al-Bayḍāwī—may Allah have mercy upon him—said:

> Since it was affirmed in unequivocal [texts] that He, the Glorified, is transcendent above corporeality and boundaries, it is impossible that "descent"—with the meaning of displacement from one place to a place lower than it—applies to Him. What is meant [by "descent"] is the light of His mercy; in other words, it moves from the quality of Divine Majesty [*Jalāl*] that entails anger and vengeance to the quality of honour that entails pity and mercy.[138]

Imām al-Qurṭubī

Imām al-Qurṭubī—may Allah have mercy upon him—says in his exegesis of Allah's words: ﴾*And He is the Irresistible, above His servants*﴿: "[The statement:] ﴾*above His servants*﴿ means the 'aboveness' of exaltedness by domination and overmastery of them. In other words, they are under His Divine direction [*taskhīr*]; not an 'aboveness' of place."[139]

---

[137] Ibid., 13:429.
[138] Ibid., 3:37.
[139] *Tafsīr al-Qurṭubī*, 6:399.

In conclusion, the belief that Allah, the Exalted resides in the heavens, or that He is upon the Throne with His Essence, or that He descends with His Essence, or that He rose above the Throne with His Essence, or that He rose in a literal, physical sense, or that He, the Exalted, is physically separate from His Creation with His Essence—all of this is rationally and textually impossible for Allah. The passages we cited are clear in declaring Allah's transcendence above place, direction, boundary, connection, disconnection, being inside, and being outside, and these passages clearly rule that the one who affirms such things for Allah is guilty of giving resemblance [*tashbīh*].

It should not be understood from the statement of the people of truth that "Allah is neither inside of the universe nor outside of it" that they describe Him with non-existence [*'adam*]—Allah forbid! Rather, what they mean is that it is impermissible to describe Allah in such a way [that he is either inside or outside of the universe], for He is transcendent above it. At the same time, they agree that Allah, the Exalted, is neither dwelling in the universe nor is anything of the universe dwelling within Him. As for the terms "inside" and "outside" and "connection" and "disconnection," it is impermissible to ascribe any of these to Allah, the Exalted, because they are from the qualities of corporeal bodies.

With regard to the expressions found in the Book and the Sunna that seem to affirm direction and place for Allah, the Exalted, their outward meanings are disregarded, as agreed upon by the *Salaf* and the latter-day scholars. There is no difference of opinion among the Muslims regarding this, as was mentioned by Imām al-Nawawī who quoted from Qāḍī 'Iyāḍ.

The proper place for this discussion is found in the books of theology and creed; however, what can be done when this dangerous topic has become mere table-talk and the conversation of common folk everywhere? You will find a person who doesn't even know the pillars of the prayer, the rulings of worship, or the things that invalidate ritual ablution, yet he raises his voice without fear or worry, speaking about the most serious issue in Islam: the attributes of Allah. The only reason this occurs is because the ambiguous texts that the scholars forbade us from narrating—as was quoted from Imām Mālik—are being repeated over and over again to the common folk. Commenting on Imām Mālik's prohibition, Imām Ibn Rushd said: "The only reason Mālik forbade it was..., out of fear lest it is spoken about, and then discussed more and more and spread among the people, until it is heard by the ignorant who do not know its interpretation, and resemblance [between Allah and the creation] occurs in their minds."

DISAGREEMENTS IN THE FUNDAMENTALS OF AHL AL-SUNNA

We have explained the disagreements in the fundamental religious beliefs and the ruling on someone who goes against any of that. What remains is to explain the disagreements in the fundamentals of Ahl al-Sunna wal-Jamā'a. Now, in these fundamentals, the opponent is not charged with disbelief, however, disagreements in these things are no light matter; nay, they are very dangerous.

Examples of these fundamentals include: the belief in the torment or delight in the grave, the Traverse [*ṣirāṭ*], the Scale, abstaining from speaking ill of the Companions of the Messenger of Allah ﷺ, invoking Allah's pleasure upon them, belief in the Divine decree, not charging the disobedient believers with disbelief, and other matters and issues that are agreed upon among Ahl al-Sunna wal-Jamā'a from the time of the Companions, the followers, and their followers.

The judgement on the person who goes against these fundamentals is that he is charged with corruption, misguidance, and has left the fold of Ahl al-Sunna wal-Jamā'a and that which the Prophet ﷺ and his Companions were upon. May Allah protect us from tribulations.

As for the subsidiary issues of doctrine that are not found in the two aforementioned categories, they are minor details related to doctrine. An example of that is found in the disagreement among the Companions—may Allah be pleased with all of them—regarding the Prophet's ﷺ vision of his Lord on the night he was taken to the heavens. Some affirmed it, such as Ibn 'Abbās ؓ, while others negated it, such as the Mother of the believers, lady 'Ā'isha ؓ. Another example of a minor detail that was differed over is the punishment allotted to the deceased on account of his family's wailing over him. This was affirmed by some and negated by others, and there are other smaller details of creed and the unseen realm that they differed over.

The disagreement between the pious predecessors over specific figurative interpretation and non-specific interpretation is included in these minor disagreements. The scholars have reported that the majority of the *Salaf* took the position of non-specific interpretation, and that some groups among them took the position of specific figurative interpretation. Among those who took the latter position was our liege lord Ibn ʿAbbās ﷺ and others among the Companions and major followers and those after them.

It is certain that disagreements in these minor issues do not entail anything negative, for it is not narrated from the Companions or the *Salaf* in general that they charged each other with misguidance because of this issue—especially in light of the fact that their disagreement in this matter was well-known and widespread.

Also included in these minor disagreements are the differences that occurred between the factions of Ahl al-Sunna, such as the differences between the Ashʿarīs and the Māturīdīs—none of that implies charges of misguidance or innovation.

Al-Ḥāfiẓ Ibn ʿAsākir—may Allah have mercy upon him—said: "Our colleagues [*al-aṣḥāb*], despite their disagreements in some issues, are nevertheless united in their abandonment of mutual accusations of disbelief—contrary to others among the various groups and the rest of the sects. When the other groups differed on account of abominable desires and ways, they charged each other with disbelief and saw it a duty to declare their innocence of those who differed with them."[140]

Imām Tāj al-Dīn al-Subkī—may Allah have mercy upon him—said:

> I perused the books of the Ḥanafīs [Māturīdīs] and I found that the issues in which there is disagreement between us and them amount to thirteen issues: six issues among them are differences in meaning, and the remaining issues

[140] *Tabyīn Kadhib al-Muftarī*, p. 409.

> are differences in semantics. And those six issues do not necessitate—on either our part or theirs—accusations of disbelief or blameworthy innovation. This was explicitly stated by Ustādh Abū al-Manṣūr al-Baghdādī and others among our Imāms and theirs. It is in fact too obvious to warrant explicit declarations.[141]

The erudite scholar, Imām Mullā ʿAlī al-Qārī—may Allah have mercy upon him—said: "In reality, the disagreements that occurred between the Ashʿarīs and Māturīdīs in certain issues go back to subsidiary matters, for they are speculative [*ẓanniyāt*] in nature and consequently, and not from the matters of belief that are based on certainties. Nay, some of the verifying scholars [*muḥaqqiqūn*] said that the disagreements between them are merely semantic."[142]

This illustrates the mistake of those who hasten to charge their opponents with misguidance and innovation, issuing general rulings and neglecting to look at the category in which disagreements fall—especially in those issues where there is a reported difference of opinion among the pious predecessors and in which they did not censure each other.

This also illustrates the recklessness of those who ignorantly level charges of misguidance against the Ashʿarīs and Māturīdīs; feigning ignorance of the fact that all of the religious texts have reached us through them, and feigning ignorance of the fact that the issue of non-specific and specific figurative interpretation are both reported from the Companions and pious predecessors, and that both are in the category of differences that do not necessitate rulings of misguidance or innovation.

---

141 *Ṭabaqāt al-Shāfiʿiyya al-Kubrā*, 3:378.
142 *Mirqāt al-Mafātīḥ*, 1:206.

CHAPTER SEVEN

NON-SPECIFIC INTERPRETATION [*TAFWĪḌ*] AND SPECIFIC FIGURATIVE INTERPRETATION [*TA'WĪL*]

TAFWĪḌ – NON-SPECIFIC INTERPRETATION

Tafwīḍ is taken from the statement: *fawwaḍ ilayhi al-amr* ("He entrusted the matter to him.") In other words, he referred it back to him. The legal meaning is no different than the semantic meaning. Legally, *tafwīḍ* is to refer the knowledge of the ambiguous texts to Allah, the Exalted, and to abstain from delving into their meanings—after declaring Allah transcendent above their outward meanings that are not intended in the Sacred Law.

TA'WĪL – SPECIFIC FIGURATIVE INTERPRETATION

Ta'wīl is taken from the word *al-awl* which means to return. Legally, it is to disregard the outward meaning of a word or phrase in favour of an alternative meaning supported by a context or element [*qarīna*] that would support it.

As we have mentioned, these two positions are well-considered and reported from Ahl al-Sunna wal-Jamā'a with respect to the ambiguous texts. No consideration should be given to those who incline to either extreme denial [*ta'ṭīl*] or resemblance [*tashbīh*] from the adherents of the other sects that have been rejected by the Umma.

The ambiguous texts regarding the Divine attributes are either affirmed or negated. To negate them is clear denial, because it is a denial of that which was affirmed by Allah and His Messenger ﷺ. For instance, when Allah says: ﴿*The All-Merciful rose above the Throne*﴾ the denier says: "No, He did not." When Allah says: ﴿*...to the one I created with My two hands*﴾ the denier says: "No, He doesn't have *yadān* (two hands)." This is manifest falsehood, because he denies that which Allah affirmed. Allah's refuge is sought.

As for affirmation, it either includes understanding the words in their literal and outward sense, as known to humans, or the outward and literal meanings are disregarded. The first possibility clearly leads to resemblance, because the literal and outward meanings of these phrases and words are corporeal bodies and created modalities that the creation uses to express what it sees in the created world, and Allah is transcendent above that.

It should not be said: "We understand them according to their outward meaning and leave the knowledge of their modalities (the 'how') to Allah." This is a clear contradiction, because the only outward and literal meaning to them is corporeality, and in no way can Allah be described with that. Furthermore, this so-called modality, the knowledge of which is supposedly left to Allah, is the exact meaning that they claim to affirm, because the meanings [they give] to these words and phrases are modalities. So, if the meaning is affirmed then the modality is affirmed as well, and if the modality is left [to Allah] then the meaning is left [to Him] as well. This is why we say this is a contradiction.

The alternative to this is to disregard the outward and literal meaning and after that either refrain from giving it a meaning and entrusting knowledge of it to Allah—and this is *tafwīḍ* that the majority of the *Salaf* followed—or give it a meaning that befits Allah and is according to the speech of the Arabs and what is in conformity with their language—and this is *ta'wīl* that the latter-day scholars of the Umma and some groups of the *Salaf* followed.

These two positions are the only correct positions that can be taken in this issue. This is why the scholars say, whenever they are faced with any of the ambiguous texts, that their meanings are entrusted to Allah, or that they are interpreted, for besides these two positions, there remains no other alternative besides denial [*ta'ṭīl*] or resemblance [*tashbīh*]. Imām al-Ubbī—may Allah have mercy upon him—said in his commentary on the Ḥadīth: "Verily Allah grasps the heavens on a *iṣba'* [finger]": "This Ḥadīth is among the Ḥadīth reports pertaining to the Divine attributes, so the outward meaning of the word that is [rationally] impossible and which seemingly alludes to a body part is disregarded. There are two positions taken regarding this: either refraining from figurative interpretation and having faith in it in a manner that befits [Allah], relegating knowledge of it to Allah, or employing figurative interpretation."[143]

---

[143] *Sharḥ Ṣaḥīḥ Muslim*, 7:190.

The Imām and erudite Badr al-Dīn b. Jamā'a said: "The *Salaf* and the people of *ta'wīl* both agreed that things that do not befit the Majesty of the Lord, Exalted is He, ...are not intended, ...they differed regarding the specification of what possible meaning befits His Majesty. The *Salaf* remained silent without specifying what was meant, and the people of *ta'wīl* interpreted it."[144]

Imām al-Nawawī—may Allah have mercy upon him—said in his commentary on the Ḥadīth of the servant girl: "This Ḥadīth is among the Ḥadīth reports pertaining to the Divine attributes. There are two positions concerning it. The first position is to have faith in it without delving into its meaning, while at the same time believing that there is nothing like unto Allah, the Exalted, and declaring Him Divinely transcendent above the traits of the creation."[145]

In his commentary on the Ḥadīth about the heavens being grasped on one finger and the earths being grasped on another, he said: "This is from the Ḥadīth reports pertaining to the Divine attributes, and the two positions regarding them have already been mentioned: *ta'wīl*, and abstaining from that with faith in it accompanied with the belief that its outward meaning is not intended."[146]

Al-Ḥāfiẓ Ibn Ḥajar quoted the words of Ibn Daqīq al-'Īd regarding the Ḥadīth: "No one is more jealously protective than Allah": "Those who believe in Allah's transcendence are either silent, refraining from *ta'wīl*, or they employ *ta'wīl*."[147]

In conclusion, the statements of the scholars in which they confine the truth to these two positions are innumerable. What we have cited here from their works should prove convincing.

THE POSITION OF THE MAJORITY OF THE *SALAF* WAS *TAFWĪḌ*

Imām al-Tirmidhī—may Allah have mercy upon him—affirmed that the doctrine of the pious predecessors was *tafwīḍ*. He said:

---

[144] *Īḍāḥ al-Dalīl fī Qaṭi' Ḥujaj Ahl al-Ta'ṭīl*, p. 103.
[145] *Sharḥ Ṣaḥīḥ Muslim*, 5:24.
[146] Ibid., 17:129.
[147] *Fatḥ al-Bārī*, 13:411.

> The [correct] position on this according to the people of knowledge from the Imāms, such as Sufyān al-Thawrī, Mālik b. Anas, Ibn al-Mubārak, Ibn 'Uyayna, Wakī', and others is that they would narrate these things [reports] and then say: "These Ḥadīth are to be narrated, and we believe in them; it is not to be said: 'how?'"
>
> This is [the position] chosen by the traditionists [*ahl al-Ḥadīth*]; these things [reports] should be narrated as they appeared and they should be believed in; they should not be explained, be subject to conjectures, and it should not be asked: "how?" This is the command of the people of knowledge that they chose and adopted.[148]

His phrase "they should be believed in" is an affirmation of them, and by this, they [the traditionists] were distinguished from the people of denial. His statement: "...they should not be explained, be subject to conjectures, and it should not be asked: 'how?'" relegates their meaning to Allah, the Exalted. His statement: "...and it should not be asked: 'how?'" means that no one should seek out their meanings or specify what is intended by them; and by this they [the traditionists] were distinguished from the people of resemblance.

Al-Khallāl narrated with a rigorously authentic chain from Imām Aḥmad ﵀ who said regarding these texts: "We believe and have conviction in them, and there is no modality or meaning."

Imām al-Bayhaqī narrated with his chain from Imām al-Awzāʿī—may Allah have mercy upon him—who said: "The explanation of everything Allah described Himself with in His Book is their recital and silence concerning them."[149]

There are many texts from the *Salaf* to this effect, all of which indicate that they had faith in them [the attributes], passed them along, and refrained from delving into the explanation of their meanings. Al-Ḥāfiẓ Ibn Ḥajar quoted Imām Ibn al-Jawzī who explained the meaning of their phrase: "Pass them along as they have come."

---

[148] *Sunan al-Tirmidhī*, 4:493.
[149] *Al-'Itiqād*, p. 93.

Ibn al-Jawzī said: "Most of the *Salaf* refrained from giving figurative interpretations to the likes of this,[150] and they would pass it along as it came. In the context of passing it along, it is a must that one believes that the attributes of Allah do not resemble the attributes of creation. The meaning of 'passing it along' is to not know the intended meaning of it[151] while at the same time maintaining belief in Divine transcendence."[152]

Imām ʿAdī b. Musāfir[153]—may Allah have mercy upon him—said: "The way of the *Salaf* [regarding the Divine attributes] is to affirm them as they came without drawing likeness [between Allah and the creation], giving modality, making resemblance, or understanding them according to their outward meanings [*ḥamluha ʿalā al-ẓāhir*]."[154]

Al-Ḥāfiẓ Ibn Ḥajar quoted the words of Imām Ibn al-Munīr who said:

> Regarding these attributes, such as *ʿayn* (eye), *wajh* (face), and *yad* (hand), the theologians have three views... The third view is that they should be passed on as they came while entrusting their meanings to Allah, the Exalted.

---

[150] Referring to the Ḥadīth in which it states that Allah laughs at two men. [t]

[151] In the coming chapters we shall explain in more detail what it means to not know the intended meaning. It does not mean that they understood no meaning from the words whatsoever. If that were true, then the speech would be akin to the disjoined letters in the beginning of the Qurʾānic chapters, which would entail that the words of Allah and His Messenger ﷺ have no useful meaning, which is of course impossible with respect to Allah and His Prophets—upon them all be peace.

[152] *Fatḥ al-Bārī*, 6:48.

[153] He is Abū Muḥammad ʿAdī b. Musāfir al-Shāmī al-Hakkārī, the Shaykh, righteous Imām, exemplar, and ascetic of his era. He travelled the earth for years on end and kept the company of the Shaykhs and engaged in various forms of spiritual struggles. He later settled in some of the mountains around Mosul, in an area uninhabited by anyone and bereft of intimate companions. After that Allah made him the intimate companion of that place and he filled it with his blessings. He died in the year 557 AH (*Siyar ʿAlām al-Nubalāʾ*, 20:342 and *Wafiyāt al-Aʿyān*, 3:254.)

[154] *ʿItiqād Ahl al-Sunna wal-Jamāʿa*, p. 26.

> Shaykh al-Suhrawardī said in his book of creed: "Allah informed [us] in His Book and the Messenger affirmed [for us]: *istiwā'* (rising), *nuzūl* (descent), *nafs* (being), *yad* (hand), and *'ayn* (eye); they should not be handled with either resemblance [*tashbīh*] or denial [*ta'ṭīl*], for were it not that Allah and His Messenger informed us, the intellect would not dare venture around this topic. Al-Ṭībī said: "This is the relied upon doctrine and it is the view of the pious predecessors."[155]

Imām al-Nawawī—may Allah have mercy upon him—said:

> They disagreed regarding the verses pertaining to the Divine attributes and reports: should they be given figurative interpretation or not?
>
> Some said that they should be given figurative interpretation according to what is fitting—and this is the more famous of the two positions held by the theologians.
>
> Others said that they should not be given figurative interpretation, rather, there should be no discussion regarding their meanings and the knowledge of that should be entrusted to Allah, the Exalted, and it should be believed that Allah is Divinely transcendent and that the qualities of contingent beings are negated from Him.
>
> For instance, it is said regarding the verse: ﴾*The All-Merciful rose above the Throne*﴿: We do not know its real meaning or intent, however, we believe that there is nothing like unto Allah, the Exalted, and that He is transcendent above indwelling and possessing the traits of contingent beings—and this is the way of the *Salaf* or their majority, and it is the safest way.[156]

Imām Jalāl al-Dīn al-Suyūṭī—may Allah have mercy upon him—said: "The verses pertaining to the Divine attributes are from the ambiguous [texts]... The majority of Ahl al-Sunna, from them the *Salaf* and traditionists, believe in having faith in them while [at

[155] *Fatḥ al-Bārī*, 13:190.
[156] *Al-Majmū'*, 1:25.

the same time] entrusting their intended meanings to Allah, the Exalted; we do not explain them, while at the same time we declare Him transcendent above their literal meanings."[157]

These citations are clear in affirming the position of *tafwīḍ* held by the pious predecessors. There is no way to deny it or give it an alternative meaning that goes against their lofty rank and their belief in the Creator's transcendence—as is done by those who say that they [the *Salaf*] affirmed the literal meanings that are known to humans and entrusted knowledge of their modalities to Allah, the Exalted. Those who make this claim say that they affirm the literal meaning and entrust the knowledge of the modality [to Allah]. The one who says this does not know what he is talking about, for the literal realities of these expressions *are* their modalities, so how can someone claim to affirm their meanings while taking a position of *tafwīḍ* regarding their modalities?

What led to this understanding was the expression "without modality" that was oft-repeated in the statements of the pious predecessors when they would speak about the ambiguous texts. So, those who hold the aforementioned view understood that they [the *Salaf*] affirmed the literal meaning and entrusted the modality [to Allah]. This is a false understanding. Nay, this expression "without modality" is to prevent the questioner from research and inquiry. It is not an affirmation of a literal meaning and [at the same time] a position of *tafwīḍ* regarding the modality!

Whenever there is an expression that has a literal meaning indicating something corporeal and with a modality, and the intended meaning is unknown, when one wants to ask about it, he uses the word "how" [*kayf*]. This is proven in the Ḥadīth that speaks about the virtue of visiting the sick, narrated by Muslim. In the Ḥadīth it states that Allah says to His servant: "...I was sick and you did not visit Me... I was hungry and you did not feed Me... And I was thirsty and you did not give Me drink..." Responding to each of those statements, the servant said: "O my Lord! How can I visit You when You are the Lord of the worlds? O my Lord! How can I feed You when You are the Lord of the worlds? O my Lord!

---

[157] *Al-Itqān fī 'Ulūm al-Qur'ān*, 2:10.

How can I give You drink when You are the Lord of the worlds? After realizing that the literal meaning of those words was impossible, the servant did not understand what was meant by them, so he asked "how," inquiring about the intended meaning. He did not affirm the literal meaning of sickness, seeking food, and seeking drink to Allah without knowledge of their modalities!

When someone is answered with the phrase "without modality/how" it is understood to mean "without a meaning," because the expression of "how" is an interrogative in which one is asking about the meaning. By negating it the meaning that is asked about is negated as well. This is akin to negating what implies something by negating that thing which it implies. So "how" is implied in the outward meaning, and by negating it one negates the outward meaning. This is similar to when someone says to you: "This number is not an even number," which implies that it is not two, four, six, and so on, because these [even] numbers and the concept of even numbers are inseparable from each other.

This clarifies the meaning of the statement repeated by the *Salaf*: "Without modality/how." From this we also learn that those who claim the *Salaf* affirmed the literal meanings of the texts pertaining to the attributes and entrusted their "how" [to Allah] are in fact, and unbeknownst to them, accusing the *Salaf* of anthropomorphism [*tajsīm*].

Important Notice

Did the *Salaf* understand any meaning from the ambiguous texts or were those texts like the disjoined letters in the beginning of the chapters? If they did understand meanings from them, how can that be reconciled with the explanation of the phrase "pass them on," which we said means not knowing the intended meanings of them?

At first glance, it would seem that there is a mutual contradiction between understanding meanings from these [ambiguous] texts and "passing them on" which means not knowing their intended meanings. In reality, however, there is no contradiction between these two things. What is meant by the phrase "not knowing the intended meanings" (which is itself an explanation of the phrase "pass them on") is not knowing what is intended by those texts in detail and with incontrovertible evidence and specification. This does not necessarily mean that they did not know the general intended meanings.

An example of this is in the statement of the Exalted: ﴾*Nay, His two hands are outstretched.*﴿ The general meaning understood from this verse is complete generosity, magnanimity, and unending bestowal of gifts that befits the attribute of the Lord, Exalted is He. As for the expression "two hands" that is ascribed to Allah in this verse, we say, after negating the outward and linguistic meaning that was coined to indicate the physical limbs of creation, that this expression carries many metaphorical meanings that are possible. The majority of the *Salaf* stopped short of specifying one of these meanings—and this is what is meant by not knowing what is intended. It is not because they didn't understand any meaning from these texts whatsoever. Far exalted is Allah from addressing the people with something they would not understand!

This position taken by the *Salaf* is commensurate with their station in knowledge, for it is inconceivable that they would hear the words of Allah: ﴾*Allah's hand is above their hands*﴿, ﴾*Nay, His two hands are outstretched: He spends how He wills*﴿, ﴾*The All-Merciful rose above the Throne*﴿, ﴾*Then He rose above the Throne*﴿ and ﴾*on the day a sāq (shin) is unveiled*﴿ or the words of the Messenger ﷺ: "Our Lord laughs...," "Our Lord descends..." or "Our Lord is amazed..." and not understand any meaning from those texts whatsoever, like the disjoined letters in the beginning of [some] Qur'ānic chapters.

Of course, these expressions have metaphorical meanings in the Arabic language that are well-known and famous, and there is no doubt that the *Salaf* understood them in that general sense; however, due to their immense fear of Allah and awe for that holy station, and because they had no need to specify a particular meaning—because their era was free of innovators who sought to explain the words of Allah and His Messenger ﷺ in a corrupt manner that is not supported by the language and that violates the principle of transcendence—they withheld from doing so and they sufficed themselves with a general understanding of those texts. The reason the latter-day scholars after them spoke about those texts with detail was because of the mitigating factors and challenges they were faced with.

Shaykh Salāma al-ʿAzzāmī al-Quḍāʿī said:

> The Exalted said: ﴾*Allah is the Light of the heavens and the earth.*﴿ Did any of the *Salaf* understand that He is the light that shines on the walls and interiors and that is spread about outside? The station of the scholars who are knowledgeable regarding Allah and His Book is too sacrosanct for them to understand it in this general and literal meaning!
>
> The learned-man [*ḥabr*] of this Umma, Ibn ʿAbbās, said in a narration mentioned by al-Ṭabarī with a rigorously authentic chain: "Allah, the Glorified, is the Guide of the people of the heavens and earth."
>
> A similar report was narrated from Anas b. Mālik. It was narrated from Mujāhid that it [al-Nūr: the Light] means the Disposer of Affairs. The Imām [al-Ṭabarī] preferred the first view and refuted the other views...
>
> Allah is transcendent above the qualities of corporeal bodies and the traits of contingent beings. If you were to read with detail the statements of the *Salaf* found in their appropriate places, you would see a good portion of it clarifying the specific meanings that befit Allah. Whoever claims that the *Salaf* did not specify [any meaning] whatsoever has not researched or read in detail.[158]

He also said:

> *Important notice*: If you hear in some of the expressions of the *Salaf*, statements like: "We believe that He has a *wajh* (face) unlike faces and a *yad* (hand) unlike hands," do not think that they meant that His lofty Essence is divided into parts and portions; a hand here and a face there, without resembling the hands and faces of the creation!
>
> Allah forbid that they believe such a thing. That is nothing but unmitigated resemblance. What they meant was only that the expressions *wajh* and *yad* have been used to convey a particular meaning and are attributes that befit the lofty Essence, such as tremendousness and

[158] *Furqān al-Qurʾān*, p. 104.

omnipotence; however, due to their scrupulousness and fear of treading on that sacred station, they did not specify those attributes.

Shaykh Muḥammad Abū Zahra—may Allah have mercy upon him—said:

> Is it conceivable that those who pledged their fealty to the Prophet ﷺ under the tree, understand when they recite the words of the Exalted: ﴿*Indeed, those who pledge their fealty to you only pledge their fealty to Allah. Allah's hand is above their hands. So, whoever breaks his word only breaks it to the detriment of his own self. And whoever fulfils that which he promised Allah—He will give him a great reward*﴾ that the word "hand" here is a hand unlike that of the creation—in other words, that it is a literal hand as the literalists say, however, it is not like the hands of creation? Is it conceivable that they do not understand that its intended meaning is the authority and power of Allah, as proven by the threat it contains towards those who break their oaths, that it will only be to their detriment?
>
> For this reason, we prefer the method of the Māturīdīs and the method of Ibn al-Jawzī and al-Ghazālī. We believe that the Companions used to explain the metaphorical expressions if applying the literal meanings proved impossible, just as they would explain the literal expressions themselves.[159]

This is strengthened by the quotes taken from groups among them in which they clearly explained these metaphorical meanings, such as our liege lord Ibn ʿAbbās, Ibn Masʿūd, ʿAlī ﷺ and al-Ḥasan al-Baṣrī, Mālik, al-Awzāʿī, Qatāda, al-Thawrī, Mujāhid, and ʿIkrima—may Allah have mercy upon them—as well as many others whose statements fill the books of Qurʾānic exegesis, Ḥadīth, and more.

[159] *Tārīkh al-Madhāhib al-Islāmiyya*, 1:237.

FIGURATIVE INTERPRETATION IS A CORRECT METHOD TAKEN FROM THE *SALAF* AND THE ARABIC LANGUAGE

Due to the proverbial dust-storm that blinds the eyes and intellects of many, some think that figurative interpretation is an innovated and blameworthy method, especially when considering the false interpretations of the innovators, such as the Bāṭinī sects, and the extreme negation of the Jahmīs and others who took extreme and far-fetched interpretation as a vehicle or bridge to demolish the religion or destroy the edifice of the Sacred Law.

The undeniable truth that any fair-minded and intelligent person would agree with is that figurative interpretation, provided that it is used with its proper conditions and guidelines, is a sound and necessary epistemological tool for understanding the Book and the Sunna, and it is reported from groups of the *Salaf*.

Imām al-Zarkashī—may Allah have mercy upon him—said:

> The people differ regarding what is cited from them [the ambiguous texts] in the verses and Ḥadīth reports, and they are three groups:
>
> 1- [Those who believe that] there is no room for figurative interpretation of them, rather [they posit], they should be relayed according to their outward meanings and nothing of them should be interpreted. They are the anthropomorphists.
>
> 2- [Those who believe that] the [ambiguous texts] do have an interpretation, however, we are to refrain from that, while at the same time not believing in any resemblance or outright denial. [According to this view] we are to say: ﴾*None know its interpretation except Allah.*﴿ This is the view of the *Salaf*.
>
> 3- [Those who believe that] they are interpreted. They interpreted them according to what befits Him. The first position is false, and the other two positions are recorded from the Companions, ...and those who have been reported using figurative interpretation include ʿAlī, Ibn Masʿūd, Ibn ʿAbbās, and others.[160]

[160] *Al-Burhān fī ʿUlūm al-Qurʾān*, 2:207.

Imām al-Nawawī—may Allah have mercy upon him—said in his commentary on one of the Ḥadīth mentioning the Divine attributes:

> This Ḥadīth is from the Ḥadīth reports pertaining to the Divine attributes, and there are two well-known positions the scholars take concerning it... The first position is the position of the majority of the *Salaf*... The second position, which is the position of most of the theologians, some groups among the *Salaf*, and it is related from Mālik and al-Awzā'ī, is that these reports are to be given figurative interpretation according to what is appropriate for them and according to their context.[161]

We have already mentioned Imām Mālik's figurative interpretation of the Lord's descent and Ibn 'Abd al-Barr's comments regarding that.

Imām Abū Muḥammad al-Juwaynī,[162] the father of Imām al-Ḥaramayn—may Allah have mercy on both of them—said:

---

[161] *Sharḥ Ṣaḥīḥ Muslim*, 6:36.

[162] He is 'Abdullāh b. Yūsuf, the father of Imām al-Ḥaramayn. He was the unrivalled scholar in his time in knowledge, piety, and asceticism. Shaykh al-Islām Abū 'Uthmān al-Ṣābūnī said concerning him: "Had Abū Muḥammad been among the Children of Israel, his descriptive traits would have been narrated to us and they would have taken pride in him." He died in the year 438 AH. His written works include *Al-Furūq*, *Al-Silsila*, *Al-Tadhkira*, *Al-Tabṣira*, and others.

With regards to the so-called essay on *istiwā'* that some attempt to pass off and ascribe to him, it is falsely attributed to him; the last book he wrote was called *The Creed of the Companions of Imām al-Maṭlibī al-Shāfi'ī and the Remainder of Ahl al-Sunna wal-Jamā'a*. In his final book he lauded Imām Abū al-Ḥasan al-Ash'arī with goodly praise. See *Tabyīn Kadhib al-Muftarī* (p. 115 and before it on p. 113), where he added his signature in pleasure and support to the signatures of a large group of Imāms, such as Shaykh al-Islām Abū 'Uthmān al-Ṣābūnī and his son Abū Naṣr and others, attesting to the written statement of Imām Abū al-Qāsim al-Qushayrī.

In it, it reads: "The traditionists agreed that Abū al-Ḥasan 'Alī b. Ismā'īl al-Ash'arī was an Imām among the Imāms of the traditionists and that his doctrine was the doctrine of the traditionists. He spoke about theological matters according to the way of Ahl al-Sunna... Whoever

> As for what appears in the outward [*ẓāhir*] texts of the Book and the Sunna, the apparent meanings of which seem to allude to resemblance, the *Salaf* have two methods regarding them: refraining from delving into them and entrusting knowledge of them to Allah, the Exalted, ...and that was the position of many of the *Salaf*...
>
> The second method is: speaking about them and their interpretation by tracing them back from attributes of the Essence to attributes of action; so "descent" is interpreted as the proximity of mercy, "hand" is interpreted as bounty, and "rising" [*istiwāʾ*] is interpreted as overpowering and omnipotence. He [the Prophet] ﷺ said: "Both of His hands are right." Whoever contemplates this expression will have the doubt of resemblance removed from his heart.
>
> The Exalted said: ﴾*The All-Merciful rose above the Throne*﴿ and ﴾*There is no secret conversation of three except that He is the fourth, and there is no secret conversation of five except that He is the sixth.*﴿ How can He be on the Throne at the same time He is the sixth among them, unless that it is given the meaning of encompassment and knowledge, not the meaning of place, settlement, direction, and limits?[163]

The erudite scholar, Imām al-Shawkānī—may Allah have mercy upon him—said:

---

maligns, attacks, curses, or insults him has spoken ill of Ahl al-Sunna entirely." That was in the year 436 AH and was presented by al-Ḥāfiẓ Ibn ʿAsākir. This is also found in *Al-Ṭabaqāt al-Kubrā* of al-Tāj al-Subkī (3:374).

Al-Ḥāfiẓ Ibn ʿAsākir included him in the third tier of those who followed Imām al-Ashʿarī (*Tabyīn*: p. 257), as did al-Subkī in *Al-Ṭabaqāt al-Kubrā* (3:370). Furthermore, none of the many scholars who wrote about his life mentioned this so-called essay. Assuming that he actually did write it, the scholars of his time and after him would have refuted him. Certainly they refuted him for much less than that. For instance, Imām al-Bayhaqī refuted him in a letter he sent to him as the latter was writing his book *Al-Muḥīṭ*. The text of that letter is found in al-Subkī's *al-Ṭabaqāt al-Kubrā* (5:77).

[163] *Itḥāf al-Sāda al-Muttaqīn*, 2:110 (Taken from *Kifāya al-Muʿtaqad*).

Section two: Regarding that to which interpretation applies. It is two categories. One: most of the branch subsidiary matters [*furū'*]—and there is no disagreement regarding that. Two: the fundamentals, such as doctrine and theological matters and the attributes of the Creator ﷻ. They [the scholars] have differed regarding this and have taken three separate positions:

1- That there is no room for figurative interpretation of them, rather [it is posited], they should be relayed according to their outward meanings and nothing of them should be interpreted. This is the view of the anthropomorphists.

2- That they do have an interpretation, however, we are to refrain from that, while at the same time not believing in any resemblance or outright denial. [According to this view] we are to say: ﴾*None know its interpretation except Allah.*﴿ Ibn Burhān said: "This is the view of the *Salaf*."

3- That they are interpreted. Ibn Burhān said: "The first position of these three is false, and the other two positions are recorded from the Companions. This third position was recorded from 'Alī, Ibn Mas'ūd, Ibn 'Abbās, and Umm Salama."[164]

These quotes from the scholars clearly affirm the positon of figurative interpretation for the pious predecessors.

Let us assume for argument's sake that there is not a single person among the *Salaf* who is reported to have used figurative interpretation. Still, what harm shall be met by the one who takes the way of the Arabs in understanding Arabic speech, and interprets these texts in a manner that is consistent with what their language allows?

It is very common in the Arabic language for something to be given the name of that which is close to it or cause for it, such as calling rain [*maṭr*] "gale" [*nawa'*], and hand [*yad*] "power" [*quwwa*]. Similarly, it is very common in the Arabic language for an action to be ascribed to other than its real doer, if that action was done with the approval or command of that person. For instance, it is said: "The Emir did such-and-such," and "The Emir

[164] *Irshād al-Fuḥūl*: p. 176.

struck so-and-so." The doer and striker are the real actors, however, the actions are ascribed to the Emir because he ordered or approved of them.

In general, this and its likes are wide-spread and common in their language and there is no room to censure or deny it, and the Qur'ān and the Ḥadīth reports of the Messenger ﷺ have come in the Arabic tongue and in their language.

In his commentary on the Ḥadīth: "Indeed, you shall see your Lord, ...and nothing remains between the people looking upon their Lord except the cloak of Highness [*kibriyā'*] upon His *wajh* (face)" Imām Ibn Ḥajar quoted Imām al-Māzirī who said: "The Prophet ﷺ used to speak to the Arabs in a way they would understand, and he would extract spiritual meanings from physical things in order to bring it closer to their understanding. So, he spoke of the removal of the preventative barrier and being raised from the visions in that manner."[165]

Ibn Ḥajar said:

> 'Iyāḍ said: "The Arabs would frequently use metaphorical expressions, and it is the loftiest device of its succinctness and eloquence. An example of it is in the words of the Exalted: ﴾*The wing of humility.*﴿ The Prophet ﷺ addressing them with: '...the cloak of Highness [*kibriyā'*] upon His *wajh* (face)' and what resembles it and what is ambiguous and that from which it is known that Allah is Divinely transcendent above, either the transmitter is rejected or it is interpreted, such as saying: [this phrase] 'the cloak of highness' is a metaphorical expression denoting the tremendous authority of Allah, His Highness, His greatness, His awe, and His might that prevents the visions of man—with their weakness—from encompassing Him. So when He wishes to strengthen their visions and hearts, He unveils from them the veil of His awe, the barriers of His tremendousness."[166]

Imām al-'Izz b. 'Abd al-Salām—may Allah have mercy upon him—preferred the position of figurative interpretation. He said:

---

[165] *Fatḥ al-Bārī*, 13:144.
[166] Ibid.

"The method of figurative interpretation with its prerequisite conditions is the closest of them to the truth." Imām al-Zabīdī commented on his statement, saying: "He means, with its condition of being consistent with the Arabic language."[167]

The Imām and erudite scholar, al-Ālūsī—may Allah have mercy upon him—encouraged interpreting the ambiguous texts as figures of speech: "To interpret according to the figurative use that is wide-spread in the Arabic language, [as well as] a metaphor that is so well-known that it is near equal to the literal [meaning], is more obvious than interpreting it according to an unknown meaning."[168]

He also said: "As far as I see it, there is no problem with the figurative interpretation that is approximate and close to the mind and that has similar well-known examples in the Arabic language—considering that there are some verses that are interpreted by the agreement of the *Salaf* and latter-day scholars."[169]

Shaykh [Muḥammad Sa'īd] Ramaḍān al-Būṭī—may Allah have mercy upon him—said:

> The way of the *Salaf* is to refrain from delving into any figurative interpretation or specific explanation of these texts, and to suffice with affirming that which Allah affirmed for Himself, while at the same time, declaring Him Divinely transcendent above every imperfection and resemblance to contingent beings. This path is a non-specific interpretation of these texts and passing the detailed knowledge of what is intended by them to the knowledge of Allah ﷻ.
>
> As for leaving these texts upon their outward meaning without either figurative interpretation—specific or non-specific—that is impermissible, and it was not done by either the *Salaf* or latter-day scholars...
>
> However, when you declare Allah—through all of these verses—to be transcendent above resembling His creation by being restricted to a place, possessing dimensions,

---

[167] *Itḥāf al-Sāda al-Muttaqīn*, 2:109.
[168] *Rūḥ al-Ma'ānī*, 3:89.
[169] Ibid: 3:116.

parts, form, and shape, and conversely, you affirm for Allah what He affirmed for Himself in a manner that befits His perfection, and by entrusting the details of what is intended in these texts to Allah ﷻ you are safe from contradictions in understanding and you have sanctified the Qurʾān from any illusions of contradiction within it.

This is the path of the *Salaf*—may Allah have mercy upon them all. Do you not see how they said regarding them [the attributes]: "Pass them along without any modality." Were it not that they gave these texts a non-specific interpretation, according to the meaning we have just explained, it would not be correct for them to say that.

The way of the latter-day scholars who came after them is to give these texts a figurative interpretation, in a way that places all of them on one path, consistent with the clear-cut texts that unequivocally declare Allah transcendent above direction, place, or bodily limbs.

You should know that the way of the *Salaf* in their own era was superior, safer, and more consistent with the innate faith that is within both the rational faculty and the heart.

The way of the latter-day scholars in their own era became the inescapable destiny due to the ideologies that came into being during their time and the resultant debates that took place...

What's important is for you to know that both positions are two ways to the same goal: to establish that Allah ﷻ does not resemble His creation, and that He is transcendent above all qualities of imperfection. The disagreement we see between them is merely semantical.

Shaykh ʿAlī al-Ṭanṭāwī—may Allah have mercy upon him—said:

The Qurʾān was revealed in the Arabic language, and it addressed the Arabs; consequently, everything that a genuine Arab understands from it and that is consistent with the principles of Arabic and the nomenclature of its people—be it literal when looked at literally, or figurative when it is understood as such—is a correct understanding.

> However, since all languages have been developed for expressing earthly and material meanings, they are not able to encompass all human feelings, much less the Divine attributes.[170]

This is a reality that no one possessed of intelligence can deny. Speech should be taken literally and upon its apparent meaning when possible; however, figurative speech is also an alternative. Since the literal meanings of these expressions are limited to the physical and sensory, it is an egregious error to apply that [the literal] to the [attributes]. Nay, they must be given an alternative, figurative meaning.

That being the case, there is no harm or blame upon the scholars of the Umma when they explain the words of Allah and His Messenger ﷺ—which are in Arabic—according to the way of the Arabs, their rhetorical devices, and their manners of speech, as it befits the exaltedness of Allah and averts the specious doubts of the anthropomorphists. When the scholars do this, are they not following the guidance of the majority of the *Salaf* who understood from Allah and His Messenger ﷺ, though as we mentioned, did not openly state it or announce it due the absence of need for that in their era and time?

That is how it was in their era and in the era of those who came after them, until a time came in which the heads of blameworthy innovation manifested and the people of heresy raised their banner and confronted people with things that were previously unheard of, and they gained ascendency over the minds of the common folk with their corrupt doctrines, and interpolated meanings into the words of Allah and His Messenger ﷺ that were impermissible. When that occurred, the scholars of Ahl al-Sunna were duty-bound to defend the creed of the Muslims. The most they did—may Allah be pleased with all of them—was to openly state that which the majority of the pious predecessors and Companions and followers did not state because of their lack of need.

Imām al-ʿIzz b. ʿAbd al-Salām said:

170 *Taʿrīf ʿĀm bi-Dīn al-Islām*, p. 81.

> Engaging in this [figurative interpretation] is not an odious innovation; engaging in it is rather a good innovation that is obligatory when specious doubts are made manifest. The reason the *Salaf* were silent and did not speak about it was because there was no one in their era who understood the words of Allah and His Messenger in an impermissible way. Had doubt spread in their era they would have most certainly denied and censured them [its proponents] to the utmost. Indeed, the Companions and the *Salaf* refuted the Qadariyya when they manifested their innovation, whereas they did not speak about that [predestination] before their appearance.[171]

The Shaykh, Imām, and lordly exemplar, ʿAdī b. Musāfir al-Shāmī—may Allah have mercy upon him—said:

> And we believe in that which is cited in the Book and the Sunna and we do not seek recourse in figurative interpretation after we know that Allah ﷻ does not resemble anything from the creation, and that nothing of the creation resembles Him. Certainly He is the Apportioner and Creator of everything that is given likeness in the imagination, and this [belief] was held by the *Salaf* before the appearance of vain desires and before the spread of base opinions. When blameworthy innovation manifested and resemblance [*tashbīh*] and extreme denial [*taʿṭīl*] spread among the masses, the people of truth sought recourse in figurative interpretation.[172]

The opinion stated by Imām ʿAdī b. Musāfir is the same opinion and belief held by the Ashʿarīs. Were it not for the spread of tribulations and the doctrines of the heretics, and their specious doubts against the beliefs of the common folk, the Ashʿarīs would not have openly spoke about that which the *Salaf* passed on and believed in general.

---

[171] *Fatāwā al-ʿIzz b. ʿAbd al-Salām*, p. 22.

[172] *ʿItiqād Ahl al-Sunna wal-Jamāʿa*, p. 26.

The erudite Mullā ʿAlī al-Qārī—may Allah have mercy upon him—said in his apologetic defence of the scholars who employed figurative interpretation:

> By that they did not intend opposition to the pious predecessors—Allah forbid that such things are thought regarding them—rather, the exigencies of their time obligated that due to the large number of anthropomorphists, Jahmīs, and other misguided sects, and due to their hold on the minds of the common folk. So by that [figurative interpretation] they tried to repel them and invalidate their false beliefs. Moreover, many of them excused themselves, saying: "If we were in the same situation as the *Salaf*, with the purity of creed and absence of deniers, we would not have delved into figurative interpretation one bit."[173]

Imām al-Zarkashī—may Allah have mercy upon him—said: "I say: They were only motivated to use figurative interpretation because of the obligation of interpreting the words in a manner contrary to their literal understanding, due to the evidence establishing that resemblance and corporeality are impossible for the Creator, Exalted is He."[174]

Mullā ʿAlī al-Qārī quoted Imām Ibn Ḥajar al-Haytamī as saying:

> Due to the fact that the people of innovation were not manifest in their time, most of the *Salaf* would entrust the knowledge of them [the verses pertaining to the Divine attributes] to Allah, the Exalted, while at the same time declaring Him transcendent above their outward meanings that do not befit the Majesty of His Essence. On the other hand, most of the latter-day scholars—forced due to the large number of heretics and innovators in their times—would give them figurative interpretation by explaining them in a manner that befits His Holy Majesty and complete perfection.[175]

---

[173] *Mirqāt al-Mafātīḥ*, 2:136.
[174] *Al-Burhān fī ʿUlūm al-Qurʾān*, 2:209.
[175] *Mirqāt al-Mafātīḥ*, 1:134.

Imām al-Ḥaramayn al-Juwaynī—may Allah have mercy upon him—said: "If the people had remained on that which they [the *Salaf*] were upon, we would not have been ordered to engage in theological rhetoric [*'ilm al-kalām*]. As for now, innovations have increased and become rife and there is no way [we] can let the waves of tribulation crash."[176]

Imām al-Nawawī—may Allah have mercy upon him—said: "When there was a need for figurative interpretation in order to refute an innovator, they would employ it; and this is how the reports from the scholars concerning this are understood."[177]

Mullā 'Alī al-Qārī said:

> Both the *Salaf* and the latter-day scholars agreed in declaring Allah transcendent above the outward meanings of the ambiguous texts and meanings that are impossible for Allah, the Exalted...
>
> Most of the latter-day scholars engaged in figurative interpretation, although they were not absolutely certain that [those interpreted meanings] were the definitive intent of Allah, the Exalted, behind those texts. By it they only intended to prevent the common folk from believing in the outward meaning of the ambiguous texts, and to refute the innovators who held firmly to most of those outward meanings.[178]

The erudite scholar, Maḥmūd b. Khaṭṭāb al-Subkī—may Allah have mercy upon him—said:

> As with regards to the ambiguous verses and Ḥadīth reports, both the *Salaf* and the latter-day scholars—may Allah be pleased with them—concurred that their outward meanings are disregarded, due to the words of the Exalted: ﴿*Say: "He is Allah, the One. Allah, the Eternal Refuge. He neither begets, nor is He begotten. And there is not any equivalent to Him.*﴾ And: ﴿*There is nothing like unto Him, and He is All-Hearing and All-Seeing.*﴾

---

[176] Ibid.

[177] *Al-Majmū'*, 1:25.

[178] *Mirqāt al-Mafātīḥ*, 1:189.

They did, however, disagree regarding the level of explanation to be given to these verses and Ḥadīth reports. The *Salaf* would entrust the knowledge of their meanings unto Him, the Exalted, and say: "The 'rising' [*istiwā'*] mentioned in the verse ﴾*The All-Merciful rose above the Throne*﴿ is known to none but Allah ﷻ."

At the same time, they were clear in their belief that it is impossible for Him ﷻ to be settled upon the Throne or be attached to it, or to be sitting upon it, because He, the Exalted, is the Pre-eternal Deity Who is described with being risen above the Throne before the creation of the Throne, because the Qur'ān—in which this verse is found—was existent before the creation of the Throne, so how is it conceivable that He, the Exalted, could be settled upon a Throne that was non-existent? When He created the creation He did not need a place in which to subsist, nay, He is free of needing that. He, the Exalted, is pre-eternally described with His attributes.

The latter-day scholar say concerning it: "The meaning of 'rising' is ability and free-disposal, etc." The way of the *Salaf* is safer. The validity of the way of the latter-day scholars is [proven by the fact] that they interpreted the verse according to what the Arabic expression indicates—and of course the Qur'ān is in Arabic.

The reason they upheld the aforementioned interpretation and did not take a position of *tafwīḍ* as the *Salaf* did, was because of the presence of anthropomorphists in their time who claimed that the outward meanings of these verses prove that He, the Exalted, is a corporeal body. They did not understand that corporeality and indwelling in places are impossible for Him ﷻ.

Hence, it was obligatory upon them [the latter-day scholars] to explain to the common folk the meanings of these ambiguous verses and Ḥadīth reports according to the [attributes] that were proven in the Qur'ān and Prophetic Ḥadīth reports, that Allah, the Exalted, is qualified with—in order to make the truth known so they may act upon it, and in order to leave falsehood and its people. May Allah reward them with the best reward.

> The erudite scholar, [Aḥmad] Zarrūq quoted Abū Ḥāmid [al-Ghazālī] as saying: "There is no disagreement that figurative interpretation is obligatory when a specific doubt [is brought] which cannot be eliminated without it."
>
> The upshot of this is that the latter-day scholars did not disagree with the *Salaf* in doctrine, rather they disagreed with them in the interpretation of the ambiguous texts due to the mitigating circumstances of their time that were not found in the time of the *Salaf*—as you know. Nay, their doctrine was one, namely that the outward meanings of the ambiguous verses and Ḥadīth reports that would seem to allude to Him, the Exalted, resembling anything from the qualities of contingent beings are disregarded. He is absolutely dissimilar to contingent beings; He is not a corporeal body [*jism*], an indivisible element [*jawhar*], an accident [*'araḍ*], and He is not settled upon the Throne or in the heavens; He is not subject to the vicissitudes of time; He is not in a direction, and He is not qualified by any other trait of the creation.[179]

In conclusion, figurative interpretation is the truth, whether it is authentically cited from the *Salaf* or not (although it is, as we shall soon see). It is a deep-rooted style of Arabic for understanding Arabic speech, and that includes the speech of Allah and His Messenger ﷺ. The one who employs figurative interpretation has not brought a novel and innovated thing; rather, he has followed the way of the Arabs in understanding speech.

EXAMPLES OF FIGURATIVE INTERPRETATION GIVEN BY THE SCHOLARS

Imām al-Khaṭṭābī—may Allah have mercy upon him—said in his commentary on the Ḥadīth: "Indeed, a squeak is heard like the squeaking of a new leather saddle...":

> If these words are taken upon their outward meaning there will be a type of modality inferred, and modality is negated from Allah and His attributes. So it is understood

[179] *Al-Dīn al-Khāliṣ*, 1:27.

> that its intended meaning is not the affirmation of this attribute or the specification of this form [*hay'a*]; rather, it is an approximation expressing the tremendousness of Allah ﷻ. The intent behind it is to make the questioner comprehend in a way he could understand, for he was a Bedouin ruffian who was not acquainted with the meanings of precise speech and the subtleties of understanding. In this speech [the Ḥadīth] there is both ellipsis and omission. Thus the meaning of his statement: "Do you know what is Allah?" is "Do you know what is Allah's tremendousness?" And his statement: "Indeed, a squeak is heard..." means that it is so utterly incapable that it squeaks due to His tremendousness and Majesty—for it is known that a new leather saddle squeaks due the force of what is above it and due to its inability to bear it.
>
> So, through this type of similitude, it establishes Allah's tremendousness and Majesty and the elevation of His Throne, that it be known that the One Who is described with the Exalted Status, Mighty Rank, and Grand Mention is not to be made an equal to one who is less than Him in rank and lower than Him in level. Far exalted is Allah from resembling anything or being given modality through a created form or being encompassed with a limit: ﴾*There is nothing like unto Him, and He is All-Hearing and All-Seeing.*﴿[180]

He also said regarding the Ḥadīth on "descent" and other ambiguous reports:

> This Ḥadīth and its likes are only denied by the one who compares them to what he sees of "descent," which is moving from an upward position to a downward position, and displacement from above to below—and this is the attribute of corporeal bodies and forms. As for the descent of the One Who does not possess the qualities of corporeal bodies, then these aforementioned meanings are not imagined with respect to Him; it is only a report [alluding] to His omnipotence, His pity towards His servants, His kindness towards them, His response to their supplications, and His forgiveness of them. He does what

[180] *Maʿālim al-Sunan*, 4:328.

> He wills. His attributes are not subject to modality and His actions are not subject to quantification. Glorified is He: ﴿*There is nothing like unto Him, and He is All-Hearing and All-Seeing.*﴾[181]

The reviver of the Sunna, Imām al-Baghawī—may Allah have mercy upon him—gave a figurative interpretation for Allah's love [*ḥubb*] of the believers, saying that it is His lauding them, granting them reward, and pardoning them.[182] His exegesis is filled with that which brings delight to the eyes of the people of transcendence.

Al-Ḥāfiẓ Abū Bakr al-Bayhaqī said in his commentary on the Ḥadīth: "Whoever comes close to Me a hand-span...":

> The servant draws near by excellence [*iḥsān*] and the Real [Allah] draws near by the bestowing favour... The servant draws near to Him by repentance and penitence, and the Creator draws near to Him with mercy and forgiveness... The servant draws near to Him with petitioning, and He draws near [to the servant] with conferring... The same is said regarding "running": it only denotes quick acceptance and the reality of responsiveness and the level of arriving [at the Divine]. The [outward] description that refers to Allah ﷻ is disregarded by the tongue of Divine Oneness and the exposition of Oneness, and [instead] explained [in light of] His lofty attributes and beautiful names.[183]

Imām Abū Naṣr al-Qushayrī—may Allah have mercy upon him—said:

> How can it be permitted for someone to say regarding the Book of Allah, the Exalted, that it contains what no one among creation has recourse to knowing, and whose interpretation is unknown to all but Allah? Is that not the greatest insult to Prophethood [*nubuwwāt*]—that the

---

[181] *Al-Asmā' wal-Ṣifāt*, p. 453.
[182] See: *Tafsīr al-Baghawī*, 1:293.
[183] *Al-Asmā' wal-Ṣifāt*, p. 453.

Prophet ﷺ did not know the interpretation of what was mentioned of Allah's attributes, and that he called the creation to have knowledge of what is unknown? Did not Allah say: ﴾*In a clear Arabic tongue...*﴿

Therefore, according to their claim it is necessary to say that He lied when He said: ﴾*In a clear Arabic tongue...*﴿; for it was unknown to them—otherwise, where is the clear exposition? If it is indeed in the Arabic language, how can it be claimed that it contains what the Arabs do not know? If that were the case, it would not be Arabic...; to claim that the Prophet ﷺ invited to a Lord that is described with attributes that cannot be understood is a heavy matter than no Muslim could ever imagine. Indeed, ignorance of the attributes leads to ignorance of the One described with them.

So to the point, it is clear to anyone with a modicum of intellect that the statement of the one who says: "His rising [*istiwā'*] is an attribute of self [*ṣifa dhātiyya*] whose meaning is unknown, and *yad* (hand) is an attribute of self whose meaning is unknown, and *qadam* (*foot*) is an attribute of self whose meaning is unknown"—is a distortion of the facts and implies modality, resemblance, and is a call to ignorance. The truth is clear to anyone who possesses two eyes.

Would that I knew: does the one who censures figurative interpretation apply this same censure to everything and to every verse, or is he satisfied to merely refrain from interpreting the attributes of Allah, the Exalted? If he refrains from interpretation entirely he has invalidated the Sacred Law and the sciences, for there is not a single verse or report except that it needs an interpretation and explanation of its words. Furthermore, there are things that must be given interpretation—and in that there is no disagreement between the people of intellect, except the outright atheists whose intent is to invalidate the Sacred Laws. Believing in this leads to the invalidation of that which he holds firm to in the Sacred Law.

If he retorts: "Figurative interpretation is permissible in general, except in those things that pertain to Allah and His attributes, for there is to be no figurative interpretation of them," we respond by saying: this implies that the things that do not pertain to Allah must be known, whereas that which pertains to the Maker must be distanced. No Muslim would be pleased with this.

The secret behind this issue is that those who forbid figurative interpretation actually believe in resemblance [between Allah and His creation]; however, they are deceptive and say: "He has a hand unlike hands, a foot unlike feet, and a rising with His Essence—not as we understand it among ourselves."

Let the person of inquiry say: Clarity must be sought from these words. Your statement that we "pass them along according to their outward meaning while their meaning is unknown" is a contradiction. If you pass them along according to their outward meaning, then the outward meaning of "shin" [*sāq*] in the words of the Exalted: ﴾*On the day a sāq is unveiled...*﴿ is a physical limb that is composed of skin, flesh, bone, veins, and sinew. If you adopt this outward meaning and attest to it [being a] limb, that is disbelief. If you are unable to adopt that, then how are you holding fast to the outward meaning? Have you not disregarded the outward meaning and known that the Lord, Exalted is He, is transcendent above what the outward meaning alludes to? How can you be holding fast to the outward meaning? If the opponent retorts: "These outward expressions have no meanings whatsoever," then he has ruled that they are cancelled out and consequently, there is no benefit in them being relayed to us. This, of course, is useless and is impossible.

In the Arabic language there are many rhetorical devices and expressions. The Arabs knew the meanings of speech and the intent behind words. The one who shuns figurative interpretation does so only due to his own weak understanding of Arabic. Conversely, the one who is well-acquainted with the Arabic language will easily comprehend the realities. It was said: ﴾*...yet none know its explanation save Allah, and those who are of sound knowledge...*﴿ so it was as if He said that those who are of sound knowledge also know it, and they say "we believe in it." Certainly, faith in something is only conceivable after

> someone has knowledge of it. What faith is there in something that is unknown? This is why Ibn ʿAbbās said: "I am from those of sound knowledge."[184]

Al-Ḥāfiẓ Ibn Ḥajar quoted the words of Ibn Daqīq al-ʿĪd regarding the Ḥadīth: "No one is more jealously protective than Allah":

> Those who believe in Allah's transcendence are either silent, refraining from figurative interpretation, or they employ figurative interpretation. The second one [i.e., the one who employs figurative interpretation] says that what is meant by jealously protective is protection and defence of something—and both of these are implications of jealously protective. So, it was used as a figurative statement [*majāz*], such as close attachment and other common meanings found in the Arabic language.[185]

Imām al-Nawawī—may Allah have mercy upon him—said in his commentary on the Ḥadīth that mentions the heavens being grasped on one finger [*iṣbaʿ*] and the earths being grasped on another:

> This is from the Ḥadīth reports pertaining to the Divine attributes, and the two methods, both figurative interpretation and *tafwīḍ* have been explained... As for using the expression "two hands" for Allah, it is interpreted as power. "Two hands" is used as a metonym for power because our actions are performed with two hands, so we have been addressed with that which we understand in order that it may be clearer and more emphasised in the souls. There is no resemblance in the transmitted [*samʿiyya*] attribute[186] that is called *yad* (hand)—that is not a physical limb, and Allah, the Exalted, knows best the intent of His Prophet ﷺ concerning the recondite statements reported in these Ḥadīth. We believe

---

184 *Itḥāf al-Sāda al-Muttaqīn*, 1:211.

185 *Fatḥ al-Bārī*, 13:411.

186 That is, an attribute that can only be known via revelation and which the intellect cannot independently know. [t]

> in Allah, the Exalted, and His attributes and we do not believe that He resembles anything nor do we believe that anything resembles Him.[187]

The Imām, linguist, and grammarian, Ibn al-Sayyid al-Baṭlayūsī—may Allah have mercy upon him—said after mentioning the Ḥadīth of "descent" in the context of affirming figurative speech [*majāz*]:

> The anthropomorphists believe that it is a literal descent—and exalted is Allah above what the wrongdoers say! Those who know Allah ﷻ concurred that He does not displace Himself, because displacement is from the qualities of contingent beings. This particular Ḥadīth has two sound interpretations, neither of which implies any resemblance whatsoever. The first interpretation was indicated by Mālik—may Allah have mercy upon him—when he was asked about this Ḥadīth. He said: "His command descends each night. As for Him ﷻ, He is Permanent and does not pass or displace Himself—there is no god but He." Al-Awzāʿī was asked and he replied: "He does what He wills."[188] This is an intimation in need of an open statement, and an allusion in need of a clear expression...

Ibn al-Sayyid went on to explain the meanings of what both Mālik and al-Awzāʿī said according to the figurative speech of the Arabs and their rhetorical styles. He mentioned that the Arabs ascribe an action to the one who ordered it just as they ascribe it to the one who performed it directly. He mentioned that the meaning of "descent" in the Ḥadīth is that Allah, the Exalted, commands an Angel to descend to the heavens of this world and call out with His command. He then said: "As you see, this is a sound interpretation according to the eloquent language of the Arabs and is used in their speech and is well-known in their

---

[187] *Sharḥ Muslim*, 5:24.

[188] Imām Abū ʿAmr al-Dānī mentioned this statement of al-Awzāʿī and then said: "In other words, He manifests of His actions what He wills." (*Al-Risāla al-Wāfiya*: p. 137).

rhetorical styles and address. This is an explanation of what Mālik and al-Awzāʿī intended—may Allah have mercy upon both of them."[189]

Imām Abū Bakr b. al-ʿArabī—may Allah have mercy upon him—said:

> As for al-Awzāʿī—and he was a great Imām—he partook of figurative interpretation when, after being asked about the statement of the Prophet ﷺ: "Our Lord descends," he said: "He does as He wills." So he opened a great door of knowledge and paved a straight path for figurative interpretation... Indeed, Allah, the Exalted, is transcendent above movement and displacement because He is not bound by place, just as He is not subject to time. He does not occupy a space just as He does not come close to something by way of distance. He is not absent from anything with His knowledge; His Divine Essence is free of all faults and exalted above change and transformations; He is worshipped in the earth and He is worshipped in the heavens. This is the firm creed entrenched in the hearts and affirmed with clear proof.[190]

He also said in his commentary on the *Sunan* of al-Tirmidhī:

> The people differed regarding this Ḥadīth and its likes and they held three positions. Some of them rejected it because it is a singular narration [*khabar wāḥid*] reporting something that, in its outward meaning, is impermissible [to be ascribed] to Allah: these people are innovators. Some accepted it and passed it along as it came and neither interpreted it nor spoke about it, while at the same time believing that there is nothing like unto Allah. Some of them interpreted and explained it—and this is the view I hold, because it is an approximate meaning in eloquent Arabic.
>
> With that said, a folk who are not from the people of knowledge have transgressed the limits by interpreting it, leading them to believe in multiplicity. They said: "In this

---

[189] *Al-Inṣāf*, p. 82.
[190] *Sharḥ al-Muwaṭṭā'*, 1:288–289.

Ḥadīth there is proof that Allah is above the heavens, on the Throne, and above the seven heavens." We retort: this is major ignorance. He ﷺ only said: "Our Lord descends" and he did not say from where He descends or how He descends. They say—and their proof here is the outward meaning—"Allah, the Exalted said: ﴾*The All-Merciful rose above the Throne.*﴿" We retort: what is the [meaning] of throne in Arabic? What is the meaning of *istiwā'*?...

What must be believed regarding this, is that Allah was, and there was nothing along with Him, then He created the creation entire, and He did not undergo change through that nor did He [obtain] a direction from it [the creation] nor did He have a place within it. He does not indwell or cease; He is the Divinely transcendent; He does not undergo change or transformation. In the Arabic language, the word *istiwā'* has fifteen meanings, some of which are literal and some of which are figurative. Some of them are permissible [to be ascribed] to Allah—and thus can be the meaning of the verse—and some are in no way permissible [to be ascribed] to Allah, such as if *istiwā'* is taken to mean fixation, settlement, connection, or attachment. None of these meanings are permissible [to be ascribed] to Allah, the Exalted. Similitudes from the creation are not to be struck for Him. Either [this verse] is not interpreted—as Mālik and others said: "Rising is known...," meaning its mention in the language is known, and the meaning that Allah intended and which is permissible [to be ascribed] to Him of the meanings of "rising" is unknown, for who is able to specify, and asking about it is an innovation, because delving into it is clearly seeking the meanings of that which is ambiguous and an attempt to stir up tribulation. The upshot of the statement of the Imām of the Muslims, Mālik, is that "rising" is known and that which is permissible [to be ascribed] to Allah is not specified, and that He is transcendent above that which is impossible for Him. So, to specify the intent [behind "rising"] with that which is impermissible [to be ascribed] to Him is of no benefit to you, for you have already obtained faith and belief in Divine Oneness by negating resemblance and impossibilities for Allah ﷻ—so nothing else besides that is binding upon you...

As for his statement about Him [Allah] descending, coming, arriving, and similar expressions whose meanings are impermissible [to be ascribed] to Allah in His Essence, then all of these expressions refer to Allah's actions. Herein lies an important point: your actions, O servant, are in your self, and the actions of Allah are not in His Self and they do not go back to Him, rather they are within His creation. So, if you hear: "Allah says such-and-such," its meaning is within the creation and not in [His] Essence. This was clarified by al-Awzāʿī when he was asked about the Ḥadīth [of "descent"]. He said: "Allah does as He wills." Or[191] you should know and believe that Allah cannot be imagined to have the attributes of contingent beings, and that He does not resemble anything from the creation —and you do not enter a single door of figurative interpretation.

The literalists say: "We say that He descends and we don't ask how." We retort: we seek Allah's refuge from saying such a thing! We only say as the Messenger of Allah ﷺ instructed us and how the Arabic in which the Qur'ān was revealed has taught us. The Prophet ﷺ said: "Allah says: 'I fell ill and you did not visit Me... I was hungry and you did not feed Me... And I was thirsty and you did not give Me drink....'" None of these things are permissible [to be ascribed] to Him, yet He honoured them by addressing them in this way. Similarly, his ﷺ statement: "Our Lord descends..."—in this, he ﷺ is speaking about His servant and Angel that descends with His command and with His name, giving of His mercy... "Descent" can be metaphorical and it can be in the literal-physical sense. If you interpret the "descent" that Allah informed us about in the physical sense, then it refers to His Angel, Messenger, and servant. If you interpret it saying that He did none of that, then He did in the last third of the night: responding, forgiving, and bestowing, and He called that "descent" from one level to another and from one attribute [of action] to another, then that is pure Arabic addressed to those who are more aware than you, O

---

[191] This is the second part of the clause mentioned on the previous page: "Either [this verse] is not interpreted..." [t]

> literalists, and who are more intelligent and possessing more [firmness] in Divine Oneness and having less confusion than you—nay, having no confusion at all.
>
> They say out of their ignorance: "If He meant by that the descent of His mercy, He would not have specified the last third of the night because His mercy descends day and night." We retort: However, at night and on the day of Arafat and in the last hour of Friday its descent is even more and its giving even more expansive, and Allah informed us of this in His statement: ﴿*And those who seek forgiveness in the early morning hours.*﴾[192]

We took the liberty to mention this long quote because of its value and precision. By Allah we do not know how the likes of this lofty and splendid speech can be considered misguidance.

In *Al-Bayān wal-Taḥṣīl*, Ibn Rushd al-Jadd—may Allah have mercy upon him—said:

> He said [i.e. Mālik's companion Ibn al-Qāsim]: "I asked Mālik about the Ḥadīth in the reports of Sa'd b. Mu'ādh regarding the Throne. He replied: 'Do not speak of them...'" [He also said the same regarding] the Ḥadīth: "Indeed, Allah created Ādam with his image," and the Ḥadīth regarding the *sāq* (shin). Regarding all of these, Ibn al-Qāsim said: "It is not fitting for one who is conscientious and fearful of Allah to speak about these."[193]

After mentioning the Ḥadīth alluded to by Ibn al-Qāsim, Imām Ibn Rushd said:

> The only reason Mālik forbade speaking about these two Ḥadīth reports and the Ḥadīth that mentions Allah creating Ādam with his image—and other Ḥadīth reports that imply resemblance when taken in their outward meaning—is out of fear lest they are spoken about and then discussed more and more and spread among the people, until they are heard by the ignorant who do not

---

[192] *Tuḥfa al-Aḥwadhī*, 2:234.

[193] *Al-Bayān wal-Taḥṣīl*, 18:504. See also: *Siyar 'Alām al-Nubalā'*, 8:104, *Al-Nawādir wal-Ziyādāt*, 14:553.

> know their interpretation, and resemblance [between Allah and the creation] occurs to their minds. The [proper] method regarding them—if they are authentic—is to give them a sound interpretation by which any resemblance between Allah ﷻ and His creation can be negated—as is done with the many things in the Qur'ān that have outer meanings implying resemblance, such as the "coming" [*ityān*] mentioned in His words: ﴿*Do they await but that Allah should come to them...*﴾ and the "rising" [*istiwā'*] mentioned in His words: ﴿*The All-Merciful rose above the Throne*﴾ and as is done with similar things reported in the mass-transmitted *Sunan* collections, such as "laughter," "descent," and other things that are transmitted without reprehensibleness due to mass-transmissions to that effect. This is because these narrations, in their outward meanings, all imply resemblance and carry the possibility of being interpreted in such a way as to negate Allah's resemblance to His creation, Exalted is He.[194]

Al-Ḥāfiẓ Abū al-Ḥasan 'Alī b. al-Qaṭṭān—may Allah have mercy upon him—cited a consensus regarding non-specific interpretation and specific interpretation. He said:

> And they concurred that He, the Exalted, comes on the Day of Judgment, along with the Angels in rows upon rows, in order to present the nations and to take them to account and punish and reward them. He shall forgive whom He wills from the believers and punish from them he whom He wills, as the Exalted said. His coming is not through movement or displacement. They also concurred that He, the Exalted, is pleased with those who are obedient to Him, and that His pleasure with them is His will to bestow upon them His bounty. They also concurred that He loves the penitent and is displeased and angry with the disbelievers, and that His anger is His will to punish them, and that nothing stands in the way of His anger...[195]

---

[194] Ibid.
[195] *Al-Iqnā' fī Masā'il al-Ijmā'*, 1:32–43.

Imām al-Shāṭibī—may Allah have mercy upon him—said:

> Those who are firmly grounded [*al-rāsikhūn*] possess a path they traverse in following the truth, and the deviants are on another path besides theirs. So, we are in need of explaining the path travelled by the latter in order to avoid it, just as we need to explain the path travelled by those who are firmly grounded so as to travel it...
>
> From it [i.e., from the path of the deviants]: their reliance upon weak and flimsy Ḥadīth... From it is also the opposite of that, namely their rejection of Ḥadīth reports that do not agree with their desires and doctrines...
>
> From it: their surmises about the speech in the Arabic Qur'ān and Arabic Sunna, along with their non-existent knowledge of Arabic by which Allah and His Messenger ﷺ are understood...
>
> From it: their deviation away from the clear fundamentals and their following of the ambiguous texts in which the intellects stumble...[196]

He provided an example of this group from the Christians, then he said: "And the example of this in the Umma of Islam is the doctrine of the literalists in their affirmation of physical limbs for the Lord—who is transcendent above imperfections—such as a physical eye, hand, leg, and face, and other things that are affirmed for contingent beings."[197]

The meanings of his words are obvious. What is forbidden is to understand them as physical objects—which is the implication of understanding them literally with their outward meaning. Now, the truth is to affirm them while at the same time upholding belief in Allah's transcendence above the outward meanings and literal and well-known linguistic meanings. That is the way of the majority of the pious predecessors of this Umma—may Allah be pleased with all of them.

He also said, interpreting Allah's love and anger:

---

[196] *Al-I'tiṣām*, 1:298.
[197] Ibid.

> The love and anger from Allah, the Exalted, either mean the actual bestowal of bounty or vengeance, in which case they both go back to the attributes of action according to those who held that view. Or, they mean the will to bestow bounty or take vengeance, in which case they refer back to the attributes of the Essence, because the literal meanings of love and anger, as understood in the Arabic language, are impossible for Allah, the Exalted.[198]

Imām Ibn al-Athīr—may Allah have mercy upon him—said:

> "The Black Stone is Allah's right [hand] on Earth," ...these words are a similitude and imagery. Its basis lies in the fact that when a king shakes a man's hand, that man kisses his hand. So it is as if the Black Stone—with Allah—is in the position of the right hand of the king, insofar as it is kissed and rubbed.
>
> Similarly, in another Ḥadīth: "And both of His hands are right." This means that His two hands, Blessed and Exalted is He, are attributes of perfection with no imperfection in them, because the left [hand] is less in stature than the right. Every mention of hand, hands, or right hand or any other name for a physical limb in the Qurʾān and Ḥadīth reports ascribed to Allah, the Exalted, are taken as figures of speech; Allah is transcendent above resemblance [*tashbīh*] and anthropomorphism [*tajsīm*].[199]

He also said regarding the Ḥadīth of "descent":

> Descent and rising [*ṣuʿūd*] and movement and stillness are all qualities of corporeal bodies, and Allah is exalted and transcendent above that. What is meant by "descent" is mercy and Divine benevolence and its proximity to the servants. It is been specially marked for the night time, and in particular the last third of it, because that is the time of the night vigil prayer [*tahajjud*] in which people are unaware of those who present themselves for

---

[198] Ibid.

[199] *Al-Nihāya fī Gharīb al-Ḥadīth*, 5:300.

> receiving the outpourings of Allah's mercy. During that time, the intention is pure and the longing desire for Allah is plentiful and it is a time apt for Divine acceptance and response.[200]

Imām al-Qurṭubī—may Allah have mercy upon him—said in his commentary upon the Ḥadīth: "The hearts of children of Ādam are between the two fingers [*iṣba'ayn*] from the fingers of the All-Merciful.": "The outward meaning of finger is clearly impossible for Allah, the Exalted... Some of our Imāms interpreted this Ḥadīth and said: 'This is a figure of speech that is likened to their statement: "So-and-so is in my hand and in my grasp," meaning that he is able to control him or has free disposal over him as he wills.'"[201]

Al-Ḥāfiẓ Ibn Ḥajar—may Allah have mercy upon him—interpreted the expression "shyness" [*ḥayā'*] ascribed to Allah, the Exalted, in the Ḥadīth. He said: "His ﷺ statement: 'Allah is shy of him...' means that He was merciful towards him and did not punish him. His statement: 'So Allah turned away from him...' means that He was displeased with him..."[202]

He also interpreted the expression "hand" saying: "What is meant by hand here is power."[203] And before that he said:

> The mention of "hand" appears in the Qur'ān and Ḥadīth reports and is ascribed to Allah, the Exalted. Ahl al-Sunna wal-Jamā'a are in agreement that the meaning of "hand" is not the physical limb that is from the qualities of contingent beings. They [Ahl al-Sunna] affirmed that which mentions it [the revelation] and they believed in it. Some of them stopped there and did not engage in figurative interpretation, whereas some of them interpreted each wording with a meaning that seemed obvious to them—and this is how they dealt with everything that has appeared similar to it.[204]

---

[200] Ibid., 5:42.
[201] *Al-Mufhim*, 6:672.
[202] *Fatḥ al-Bārī*: 1:189.
[203] Ibid: 1:419.
[204] *Hadī al-Sārī*, p. 219.

You see that this matter is minor and does not call for all of the fearmongering around it. There is no serious danger in interpreting words in a figurative manner as long as that is readily understood from the Arabic language. Here we see that al-Ḥāfiẓ Ibn Ḥajar said that after declaring Allah's transcendence above the outward meanings, Ahl al-Sunna either employ figurative interpretation or take a position of *tafwīḍ*—and there is no rebuke from one against the other.

Imām al-Ubbī—may Allah have mercy upon him—mentioned words that deserve to be considered a golden principle in this issue. He said:

> The principle that must be given consideration is: that which is impossible to ascribe to the Divine Essence or the attributes, is impossible for to be found in a mass-transmitted decisive text that does not carry the possibility of interpretation. The most that can occur is for a mass-transmitted text to indicate something impossible via its outward indication [*dilāla ẓāhira*], and that which is outwardly apparent can accept interpretation. So, if such [a text] is cited, its outward and impossible meaning must be disregarded.
>
> After that, there was a difference of opinion. Most of the *Salaf* refrained from figurative interpretation and said: "We believe in it as it is with Allah in reality, and we entrust the knowledge of that to Allah, the Glorified." Some folk, nay even among the first group [the *Salaf*], took the position of figurative interpretation... And if a singular report contains a decisive text with something that is impossible, its narrator is unequivocally judged as a liar, and if it carries the possibility of figurative interpretation it is given an alternative meaning as we mentioned previously.[205]

These words are clear-cut and precise and presented in a comprehensive yet succinct manner. His statement: "...And if a singular report contains a decisive text with something that is impossible, its narrator is unequivocally judged as a liar..." means

205 *Sharḥ Muslim*, 7:54.

that the narrator is rejected because it is something speculative that opposes what is clear-cut and certain, and it has been established via unequivocal legal and rational proof that there is nothing like unto Him, the Exalted. So it can be clearly stated that a narrator is lying if he brings any report that goes against that, because the proofs in the Sacred Law mutually support each other and they do not contradict each other.

Whoever peruses the books of our Islamic heritage written by the Imāms of Islam will find innumerable quotes like the ones we have presented here—which are only a small sample—and he will attain absolute certainty that this is the correct methodology that the Umma has concurred upon.

Shaykh al-Zurqānī—may Allah have mercy upon him—said:

> Our scholars—may Allah bestow them with a generous reward—agreed upon three things concerning these ambiguous texts, and beyond that they disagreed. The first thing they agreed upon was to disregard their outward meanings that are impossible, while believing that these outward meanings are false, as proven by unequivocal proofs and what is known in the Sacred Law by its own clear-cut texts. The second thing they agreed upon was that if the defence of Islam is conditioned upon the interpretation of these ambiguous texts, then it is obligatory to interpret them in a manner that will refute the obfuscations of the anthropomorphists and avert the attacks of the opponents. The third thing they agreed upon was that if an ambiguous text has one interpretation that is understood closely [i.e., without detailed explanation], then by consensus it is obligatory to hold to it. An example of this is found in the words of the Exalted: ﴾*And He is with you wherever you may be.*﴿ It is clearly impossible for the Divine Essence to be with the creation [physically], so after that there remains but one interpretation, namely that He is with them by encompassing knowledge, sight, power, and will.
>
> As for the disagreements of the scholars beyond that, they have three schools of thought...[206]

---

[206] *Manāhil al-'Irfān*: 2:286.

Al-Zurqānī went on to mention the method of figurative interpretation and *tafwīḍ*, and then mentioned the view of Imām Ibn Daqīq al-ʿĪd, which was a third and middle view between figurative interpretation and *tafwīḍ*. Ibn Daqīq al-ʿĪd said: "Regarding the recondite attributes, we say that they are real and the truth according to the meaning intended by Allah. Whoever interprets them, we look: if his interpretation is proximate based on the Arabic language we do no censure him, and if it is far-fetched we hold back from it and return to conviction coupled with belief in Divine transcendence."[207]

In reality, his view is included in the way of figurative interpretation because there is no one from Ahl al-Sunna except that he agrees with Ibn Daqīq's view of rejecting far-fetched interpretations that are not based on the Arabic language.

The Shaikh and erudite scholar, Muḥammad al-Ḥāmid—may Allah have mercy upon him—said:

> The clear-cut revealed texts, in other words, those texts that are explicit in their meaning, are the basis upon which the ambiguous texts are to be interpreted —ambiguous, meaning that which gives a meaning of resemblance to the mind. ﴿*It is He Who has revealed unto you the Book, wherein are plain verses, which are the foundation of the Book; others are ambiguous. As for those in whose hearts is deviation: they seek out that which is unclear of it, seeking mischief, and seeking its explanation—yet none know its explanation save Allah, and those who are of sound knowledge say: "We believe in it. All of it is from our Lord." And none take the reminder except those of understanding.*﴾
>
> In other words, "we believe in all of it: its clear-cut and its ambiguous;" however, their belief in its ambiguous parts does not contradict their belief in its clear-cut p arts that form the basis. Hence, they do not believe that Allah resembles His creation; rather, they entrust the knowledge of the meaning of the ambiguous verses to Allah ﷻ, believing that they have noble meanings that befit Him, the Glorified. So they are in no way deniers of the texts, nor are they anthropomorphists. Their way is a

[207] *Fatḥ al-Bārī*: 13:395.

> moderate middle-way between the two groups that have swerved from the path of the people of truth: the extreme deniers and the anthropomorphists.
>
> This was the way followed by the early generations of this Umma, from the Companions, their followers, and their followers. Were I to quote their words it would be long-winded. However, when blameworthy innovations appeared and the heads of deviancy raised their heads and began to confuse the Muslims regarding their creed, the scholars of the Muslims became fearful over the beliefs, lest they be tarnished by corruption, and consequently they relied upon figurative interpretation of the ambiguous texts within the framework of the Arabic language and within the confines of the Sacred Law.[208]

His statement: "...however, their belief in its ambiguous parts does not contradict their belief in its clear-cut parts that form the basis" is a clear refutation against those who understand the ambiguous texts in a physical sense. Instead of understanding the ambiguous texts in light of the clear-cut texts, they did the exact opposite; by this action of theirs they negated their faith in the clear-cut texts, such as Allah's words: ﴾*There is nothing like unto Him, yet He is All-Hearing, All-Seeing.*﴿ The esteemed caller, Sayyid Quṭb—may Allah have mercy upon him—said:

> Likewise the Throne: We believe in it as He mentioned it; we do not know its reality. As for "rising" above the Throne, we are able to say that it is a figure of speech denoting complete control over the creation. We say this based on what we know from the Qur'ān with certainty, that Allah, the Glorified, is not subject to change, so He is not in a state of not being risen above the Throne, and then followed by a state in which He is risen above it. The statement that we believe in, *istiwāʾ*, while not comprehending its modality, does not explain the statement of the Exalted: ﴾*Then He performed the act of istiwāʾ.*﴿ It is more fitting that we say: it is a figure of speech denoting complete control—as we mentioned. This

---

[208] *Rudūd ʿalā Abāṭīl.*

> interpretation does not depart from the method we mentioned just now, because it does not spring from our conceptions and ideas.[209]

He also said in his explanation of Allah's words: ﴾*The All-Merciful rose above the Throne*﴿: "Rising above the Throne is a figure of speech indicating the utmost domination and exaltation."[210] The methodology of Sayyid Quṭb in the *Ẓilāl* is between figurative interpretation—which he first held to before revising the *Ẓilāl*—and *tafwīḍ* that he inclined to later on. Both methods are the truth. Nay, the way of *tafwīḍ* which is the way of the majority of the pious predecessors is more fitting to be followed as long as there is no need for figurative interpretation.

The final view that Sayyid Quṭb settled upon is much like what is ascribed to some of the Imāms, such as Imām al-Juwaynī, al-Rāzī, al-Ghazālī, and others. Some people understood from it that they abandoned the way of al-Ash'arī. We have already refuted that notion and explained its falsehood, just as we explained that the methodology of al-Ash'arī was both figurative interpretation and *tafwīḍ*, and that they left figurative interpretation and returned to *tafwīḍ*, which is what the majority of the *Salaf* were upon. We mentioned that there is no contradiction between the two methods; both state that Allah is transcendent above the traits of imperfection and contingency; both engage in interpretation: the *Salaf's* interpretation was non-specific, and the latter-day scholars' interpretation was specific.

Shaykh 'Umar al-Tilmisānī—may Allah have mercy upon him—said regarding Allah's words: ﴾*And the heavens are enveloped with His right hand*﴿: "This right [hand] that is indicated in the noble verse is the power to fold the heavens and the earth, i.e., the ability that does what it wills, as it wills, and when it wills."[211]

Sayyid Quṭb—may Allah have mercy upon him—said: "All of the images and scenes that appear in the Qur'ān and Ḥadīth are only approximations of realities that man is not capable of comprehending without them being expressed in a way they can

---

[209] *Fī Ẓilāl al-Qur'ān, Sūra al-Ḥadīd.*

[210] Ibid., 4:2328.

[211] *Ba'ḍ mā 'Allamanī al-Ikhwān*, p. 17.

understand and in an image they can conceptualize. That includes this image that expresses the reality of universal power that is not restricted by a shape, bound by a direction, or limited by a limit."[212] The Imām and caller, Ḥasan al-Bannā—may Allah have mercy upon him—said:

> Regarding this issue, the people are divided into four groups. The first group took the outward meanings as they are and ascribed to Allah a face like the faces of the creation, a hand like their hands, laughter like their laughter... These are the Mujassima (anthropomorphists) and Mushabbiha (corporealists). They have nothing to do with Islam and their belief has not one iota of validity.
>
> The second group denied the meanings of these [attributes] from all angles. Their intention was to negate all of what they indicate [*madlūlātiha*] from Allah, the Blessed and Exalted. According to them, Allah, the Blessed and Exalted, does not speak, hear, or listen... These are the extreme deniers, and some of the scholars in the history of the Islamic beliefs called them the Jahmiyya... These two viewpoints are false and have no basis whatsoever. Remaining in front of us are two opinions that have been the subject of scholarly investigation regarding doctrine; they are the opinion of the *Salaf* and the opinion of the latter-day scholars.
>
> The way of the *Salaf* is that we believe in these verses and Ḥadīth reports as they have appeared and we entrust the explanation of their intended meaning to Allah, the Blessed and Exalted. So, they affirmed a *yad* (hand), *ʿayn* (eye), *aʿyun* (eyes), *istiwāʾ* (rising), *ḍaḥak* (laughter), *taʿajjub* (amazement)..., and so on—All of that with meanings we do not comprehend, and which we entrust to Allah, the Blessed and Exalted, the encompassment thereof. As for the latter-day scholars: they said: "We declare with certainty that the outward meanings of the expressions in these verses and Ḥadīth reports are not intended, consequently they are figurative expressions and there is nothing preventing their interpretation...[213]

---

[212] *Fī Ẓilāl al-Qurʾān*, 5:3062.
[213] *Majmūʿa Rasāʾil al-Imām*, p. 411.

Then he said:

> Between the *Salaf* and the latter-day scholars: You have come to know that the way of the *Salaf* regarding the verses and Ḥadīth reports concerning the attributes of Allah, the Blessed and Exalted, was that they passed them on as they came and remained silent, refraining from explanation or interpretation, and the way of the latter-day scholars was to interpret them in a manner consistent with Allah's transcendence, Blessed and Exalted is He, above resembling the creation.[214]

Afterwards, the Imām explained that both ways are the truth and that their disagreement does not warrant accusations of disbelief or corruption. That is the truth, for there is no disagreement between the *Salaf* and the latter-day scholars regarding this matter. It is only a permissible and allowable difference that occurred due to the different circumstances faced in their respective times. The time of the *Salaf* was free from the innovated belief of anthropomorphism and literalism, so its absence necessitated that they stop short and not interpret these texts. On the other hand, the time of the latter-day scholars was one in which the doctrines of the many innovators spread, thus there was a need for figurative interpretation.

The real difference is between the *Salaf* and the latter-day scholars on one hand, and those who understand these texts according to their outward meaning and physical sense on the other. The pious predecessors and the latter-day scholars were both in agreement that the outward meanings [of these texts] that are impossible for Allah are to be disregarded. Nay, the Umma as a whole concurs upon that. How can that not be the case when these outward meanings are negated from Allah, the Exalted, by unequivocal textual and rational proofs?

Regarding those who insist on affirming the outward meanings that necessitate false meanings and impossible conclusions, they do not differ with us that these false implications such as corporeality, limits, and the like are negated from Allah, the Exalted, however, they are ignorant of the fact that affirmation of

---

[214] Ibid.

these literal linguistic meanings that are well-known, and affirmation of these apparent meanings of the ambiguous texts, imply the affirmation of what they negate and what the Umma has negated from Allah, such as limits, boundaries, corporeality, and the like.

It is surprising that they do not admit to these implications, because affirmation of the outward meanings coupled with the negation of their implications—namely corporeality—is inconceivable because they are inseparable from each other.

If it is said to them: "These expressions have only been coined to indicate [things within] the creation, and that is the only thing that is understood if they are held with their outward meaning" they retort: "What is said regarding the attributes is also said regarding the Divine Essence; so just as you affirm an Essence unlike essences—described with life, knowledge, hearing, seeing, and other things you call qualitative attributes [*ṣifāt al-maʿānī*] and that you do not interpret—they affirm for Him, the Exalted, rising, a face, a hand, laughter, boredom, a finger, and so on—literally and without figurative interpretation!"

This is fallacious reasoning, although it might seem true at first glance to those who do not contemplate it deeply. However, with a bit of thought its false meanings become clear. The premise here is that the qualitative attributes and the expressions and ascriptions mentioned in the ambiguous texts are equal. This premise is flawed as we shall demonstrate.

The distinction between the expressions that indicate corporeal bodies and those that indicate qualitative meanings is vast. The first thing that comes to mind when the former is heard is a limb and body—for which the terms were coined. When those expressions are ascribed to Allah, the Exalted, the one who knows Allah clearly and incontrovertibly knows that the outward and primary meanings are impossible and are negated from Allah, the Exalted, and that the context of the words indicates a metaphor or figurative speech. This is like the expressions hand, finger, foot, shin, face, laughter, rising, descent, and other expressions that, in their literal sense that first appears to the mind, refer to sensory objects.

As for the latter [the qualitative attributes], they refer to a meaning, such as power, will, hearing, seeing, and so on. There is no implication of resemblance for the one who understands them in their outward and literal sense, because they are meanings and expansive realities. When ascribed to the Creator, they have realities that befit Allah, the Exalted, and when they are ascribed to the creation, they have realities fitting for them. For this reason, the scholars of the Umma were not obliged to disregard their outward meanings.

Strengthening this view is the fact that it is not reported from any of the pious predecessors ﷺ that they said regarding the qualitative attributes "Pass it along without 'how'" or "Pass it along without explanation," and so on. This was due to their awareness of the distinction between the two types of expressions. This matter is clear to all who are well-read in the sciences of Arabic.

Consider the statement of Imām Aḥmad ﷺ as found in his creed that was recorded in *Ṭabaqāt al-Ḥanābila* (2:291):

> Indeed, Allah, the Exalted, possesses "two hands" and both are an attribute of His in His Essence. They are not physical limbs; they are not composite; they are not corporeal or from the genus of corporeal bodies; they are not from the genus of that which is limited and composite or [the genus] of parts and limbs. Analogy is not to be made with them; He does not possess a wrist or forearm; nor that which is implied when they [people] apply their statement "hand" except what is articulated in the Holy Qur'ān or authentically reported from the Messenger of Allah ﷺ in the Sunna regarding it.

Here we see that Imām Aḥmad ﷺ negated everything that was linked to the false outward meanings, such as physical limb, parts, compositeness, and so on. He clarified that further with his statement: "...nor that which is implied when they [people] apply their statement 'hand.'" What this means is that all of the aforementioned meanings that apply to the word "hand," such as it being a physical limb and body, are negated from our Lord ﷻ. Consider his statement "that which is implied" and you will realize that when expressed unrestrictedly, these false meanings are implicit. The word used here, *al-iqtiḍā'*, is to search, so it is as if these expressions seek out the sensory and corporeal meanings and call them to the mind when used.

He also said ﷺ regarding the attribute of "rising" [*istiwā'*]: "And it is impermissible to say that He rose with touching or spatial contact; far exalted is Allah above that!" This is a decisive quote in which he negates the common outward meaning of the expression, and this is what the Ash'arīs say. They affirm for Allah hands, a face, eye, and that He rose above the Throne as He, the Glorified, informed us regarding Himself. They affirm everything that Allah affirmed for Himself and that His Messenger ﷺ affirmed for Him. They declare Him transcendent above the outward and conventional meanings of these expressions that occur to the creation within themselves and what they understand from their languages that were developed for the purpose of communicating their needs to one another. Allah is exalted above all that.

Perhaps someone will retort: "But when you negate these outward meanings you are cancelling out what Allah affirmed for Himself or what His Messenger ﷺ affirmed for Him!" To that we respond: We only negate the outward meanings and declare Allah transcendent above them. Clearly the outward meanings are not Allah's intended meanings or that of His Messenger ﷺ. Rather, these outward meanings are negated—rationally and textually—by the consensus of the *Salaf* and the latter-day scholars. Extreme denial [*ta'ṭīl*] is to outright negate the Creator or His attributes.

When we negate these outward meanings we do not negate the attribute that Allah affirmed for Himself. No one among Ahl al-Sunna said that Allah does not possess *yadān* (two hands), or that He does not possess an *'ayn* (eye), or that He is not risen above the Throne. Nay, they said that Allah, the Exalted, possesses two hands; however, His hand is not a physical limb. This is the belief of the *Salaf* as seen in the quote from Imām Aḥmad. They believe that Allah possesses a face that is not a body part, image, or substance. This is the belief of the *Salaf*, as stated in Imām Aḥmad's creed: "Indeed, Allah possesses a face that is not like the fashioned images or shaped concrete entities [*al-'ayān al-mukhaṭṭaṭa*]..."

Allah possesses an "eye" that is not a body part, and Allah is risen above His Throne in manner that befits Him, without touching or spatial contact. This is the view of Imām Aḥmad as we just demonstrated. They affirm for Allah what is affirmed in the Book and the authentic Sunna and they declare Allah transcendent above the outward meanings of the words as they are understood among creation. When the outward and literal meaning that occurs to the minds is disregarded, nothing else remains but figurative speech.

Due to the fact that an expression carries many possible meanings, you see that the majority of the *Salaf* stopped short of specifying one of them, sufficing themselves with a general understanding of the text according to its overall context. From Allah's statement: ﴾*Nay, His hands are outstretched...*﴿ they understood that Allah, the Exalted, is Generous and Magnimous; His treasures do not fade into oblivion and His giving does not cease. From Allah's statement: ﴾*Allah's hand is above their hands*﴿ they understood that it was victory and reward, and so on. Having said that, the majority of them did not speak about these meanings due to their clarity and their lack of need to declare them explicitly—because their era was free of what would necessitate it. Nevertheless, this did not prevent some of them —may Allah be pleased with them—from openly speaking on some of these meanings, as we shall demonstrate in the coming chapter on the figurative interpretations of the *Salaf*.

In addition to all this we say: Allah, the Exalted, is the One Who taught us how to declare His Divine transcendence and how to negate from Him the outward meanings that do not befit His Exalted Essence—as we see in the Ḥadīth *qudsī* narrated by Imām Muslim regarding the virtue of visiting the sick, in which the Lord, Exalted is He, says to His servant on the Day of Resurrection: "O My servant! I fell ill and you did not visit Me... O My servant! I sought food from you and you did not feed Me... O My servant! I sought drink from you and you did not give Me drink!..." In response to those questions, the servant says: "O my Lord! How can I visit You when You are the Lord of the worlds? O my Lord! How can I give You food when You are the Lord of the worlds? O my Lord! How can I give You drink when You are the Lord of the worlds?"

Since that servant believed that his Lord and Master is transcendent above the qualities of the creation and the traits of corporeal bodies and the incidental qualities of imperfection and flaws, he realised that it is impossible for his Lord to fall ill and for him to literally visit Him, and for Him to become hungry and thirsty. This is why the servant asked: "O my Lord! How can I...., when You are the Lord of the worlds?" In other words, since the literal meanings of these words do not befit Him, the Exalted, and are negated from Him, they were not understood, so the servant asked: "How can I..." This applies to every similar expression whose literal meanings are impossible; the intended meaning is asked about with "how?"

This is exactly what occurred to some common people in the early generations. They asked: "How did He rise?" "How does He descend?" "How does He laugh?" For this reason, the scholars of the *Salaf* forbade inquiry into their meanings, saying: "without 'how'" and they ordered them to declare Allah's transcendence above the outward meanings and to then remain silent after believing that there is nothing like unto Allah, the Exalted.

Imām al-ʿIzz b. ʿAbd al-Salām—may Allah have mercy upon him—said:

> As for his ﷺ statement reporting from his Lord: "O My servant! I fell ill and you did not visit Me... O My servant! I sought food from you and you did not feed Me... O My servant! I sought drink from you and you did not give Me drink!..."—it is interpreted as having an omitted ascription, and it is estimated as "My servant fell ill and you did not visit him; My servant sought food from you yet you did not feed him; and My servant sought drink from you yet you did not give him drink."
>
> This is proven by the fact that the one blamed, when it was said to him: "...I sought food from you and you did not feed Me...," was shocked and amazed—since he didn't realize that the ascription was omitted and didn't know what his Lord meant—and he said: "How can I feed You when You are the Lord of the worlds?"—understanding the words according to their apparent meaning. So the Lord ﷻ made clear His intent by interpreting His words:

> "My servant fell ill and you did not visit him; My servant sought food from you yet you did not feed him; and My servant sought drink from you yet you did not give him drink."[215]

His statement: "understanding the words according to their apparent meaning" means that the servant said that out of amazement, not realizing the other meanings that befit Allah, the Exalted.

The erudite Ibn Khaldūn—may Allah have mercy upon him—said:

> Until Shaykh Abū al-Ḥasan al-Ash'arī appeared and debated some of their Shaykhs on the issue of best interests [*al-ṣalāḥ wal-aṣlaḥ*][216] and rejected their path. He held the views of 'Abdullāh b. Sa'īd b. Kullāb, Abū al-'Abbās al-Qalānisī, and al-Ḥārith al-Muḥāsibī among the followers of the *Salaf* and the path of the Sunna." He aided their doctrines—i.e., the doctrines of the *Salaf*—with rational proofs and affirmed the attributes that subsist with the Essence of Allah, the Exalted, such as knowledge, power, will...
>
> Their doctrine also included the affirmation of speech, hearing, and seeing, because they [these attributes], even if their outward meanings allude to imperfection, and physical sound and letter, have another meaning found in the language of the Arabs that does not include letters and sound, and it is what exists eternally in reality, contrary to the former [meaning]...
>
> As for hearing and seeing, [it is because] even if they seemingly allude to comprehension via a body part, the language indicates that it means the perception of that which is heard and that which is seen, thus dispelling any imagined imperfection because it is the literal linguistic meaning of it.[217]

---

[215] *Al-Ishāra ilā al-Ījāz*, p. 7.
[216] That is, the belief of the Mu'tazila who stated that it is necessary for Allah to observe benefit and what is in the best interest of creation. [t]
[217] *Al-Muqaddima*, 3:1088.

That is with respect to the qualitative attributes. As for the other attributes that they [the literalists] wish to equate with the qualitative attributes, saying that it is obligatory to affirm their literal and outward meanings just as we affirm the qualitative attributes, Imām Ibn Khaldūn said regarding that:

> As for the expressions: rising, coming, descent, face, two hands, two eyes,[218] and so on, they [Ahl al-Sunna] disregard their literal linguistic meanings due to the allusion of imperfection and resemblance, in favour of their figurative meanings according to the way of the Arabs—when the literal meanings of expressions are impossible. They refer them back to the figurative meaning, such as the words of the Exalted [regarding the wall]: ﴾*It wants to fall...*﴿ and its likes. This is a well-known method of theirs and it is neither censured nor innovated.[219]

Clarifying why the latter-day scholars took the position of figurative interpretation, he said:

> What motivated them to employ figurative interpretation —even though it was against the way of the *Salaf*, which was *tafwīḍ*—was that a group endeavoured to interpret these verses, explaining them as affirmed attributes of Allah, the Exalted, Whose modalities are unknown. Regarding [the verse] ﴾*The All-Merciful rose above the Throne*﴿ they say: "We affirm for him rising as the [literal] wording indicates, so as to flee from denial, and we do not state a [particular] modality, so as to flee from resemblance that is negated in the negating verses [*āyāt al-sulūb*], such as His statement: ﴾*There is nothing like unto Him...*﴿, ﴾*Exalted is Allah above what they describe*﴿, ﴾*Exalted is Allah above what they associate* [*with Him*]﴿ and ﴾*He neither begets, nor is He begotten*﴿" They don't know that they

---

[218] The wording "two eyes" is found neither in the Qur'ān nor the Sunna. Perhaps this is an error on the part of the copyist. The correct position is the singular form, as the Exalted said: ﴾*In order that it be made under My eye.*﴿

[219] Ibid.

entered the door of resemblance by their affirmation of [a literal] rising, and the meaning of rising according to the scholars of the language is settlement and fixation, both of which are corporeal.

As with regards to the denial whose implications they so odiously hold others to, it is the denial of the expression—its outward meaning—so there is no harm in that. The only harm is in denial of the Deity...[220] Then they claim that this is the way of the *Salaf*. Allah forbid! The way of the *Salaf* is what we have established, namely, entrusting the intended meaning to Allah and remaining silent regarding its understanding... Then they [the literalists] applied their position that they innovated to the outward expressions of: face, two eyes, two hands, descent, speech with letter and sound—giving them indications that are more general[221] than corporeality and declaring Him transcendent above the corporeal indications: and this is unknown in the language. This was

---

[220] In other words, negation of His attributes, such as saying He did not rise [above the Throne] or that He does not possess two hands or a face, or that He does not become angry, or that He does not love, and other examples that some of the extreme groups of denial fell into. This is what is forbidden. As for negating the outward meaning that is impossible and affirming the attributes that Allah affirmed for Himself or what His Messenger affirmed for Him, that is not forbidden, and this is what Ahl al-Sunna, the Ashʿarīs, do.

[221] What Ibn Khaldūn mentions here is exactly what we meant when we said that the qualitative attributes have meanings that are more expansive than corporeal meanings, and for that reason the scholars were not obliged to disregard their outward indications. They have a unique indication when ascribed to Allah, the Exalted, and another indication when ascribed to the creation. As for the expressions of the ambiguous texts, their outward indications are narrow and only corporeal things are understood from them. This is why the scholars were obliged to disregard their outward meanings by either taking a position of *tafwīḍ* or employing figurative interpretation. This is exactly what Ibn Khaldūn means here in this expression, for it is inconceivable, for example, for them to say: "We do not affirm a physical limb for Allah," and then to understand the word in its outward meaning, because there is no outward meaning here besides that of a physical limb and corporeality.

> followed by the first and last of them, and the Ash'arī and Ḥanafī theologians from Ahl al-Sunna contended with them and rejected their beliefs regarding this.[222]

If it is said: "But the statements of the *Salaf* 'without 'how' and 'pass them along as they came...,' and other expressions quoted from them indicates a position of *tafwīḍ* regarding the *modality*, after having affirmed the outward meanings," we retort: The negation of these outward meanings is agreed upon by everyone who knows Allah, the Exalted. We mentioned earlier that these sensory modalities are the things from which Allah is transcendent and that it impermissible to describe Him with them because they are implications that are inseparable from the outward meanings of these expressions. Allah forbid that the pious predecessors could affirm for Allah that which is impossible for Him, while they were the most knowledgeable of the creation—after the Messenger of Allah ﷺ—regarding Allah!

STATEMENTS FROM THE SCHOLARS IN WHICH THEY NEGATE SENSORY MODALITIES

Imām al-Bayhaqī narrated with his chain from Imām al-Awzā'ī—may Allah have mercy upon him—who said: "The explanation of everything Allah described Himself with in His Book is their very recital and silence concerning them."[223] Imām al-Bayhaqī commented: "He only meant—and Allah knows best—that which, when explained, would lead to establishing a modality, and establishing a modality leads to Him being made to resemble His creation in qualities of contingency."

We say: since all of the ambiguous texts that mention the attributes are in this category (because their outward and literal meanings lead to establishing a modality, which inevitably leads to resemblance), there is no distinction between affirming the literal meaning of these expressions and establishing an impossible modality for Allah, the Exalted. This is exactly what Imām Mālik pointed to in his famous words regarding *istiwā'*: "*Istiwā'* is not unknown, and the modality is inconceivable..." In

---

[222] Ibid.
[223] *Al-'Itiqād*, p. 93.

other words, it is impermissible [to be ascribed] to Allah, the Exalted, because establishing a modality is to limit Him, which is impossible.

Shaykh al-Islām Abū 'Uthmān al-Ṣābūnī—may Allah have mercy upon him—said in his legacy: "Hence, modality is negated from the attributes of our Lord."[224]

Imām al-Nawawī—may Allah have mercy upon him—quoted Qāḍī 'Iyāḍ who said:

> There is no disagreement between the Muslims: their jurists, Ḥadīth scholars, theologians, investigators, and conformists [*muqallidīhim*] that the outward meanings that mention Allah, the Exalted, being in the heavens, ...are not understood according to their outward meaning; nay they are interpreted according to all of them...
>
> Is there a distinction between establishing a modality and affirming directions? To the contrary, to say what the Sacred Law states, namely, that He is the Irresistible, above His servants, and that He rose above the Throne, while holding fast to the comprehensive verse that establishes the universal transcendence, besides which nothing else is rationally sound, the statement of the Exalted: ﴾*There is nothing like unto Him*﴿ is the Divine protection for the one to whom Allah grants success.[225]

Echoing the amazing statement of Qāḍī 'Iyāḍ quoted by Imām al-Nawawī, we ask: Is there a distinction between establishing a modality and affirming the outward meanings of these texts? There is an inseparable link between establishing a modality and affirming the outward meanings. Imām Aḥmad's statement: "We believe in them and have conviction in them without modality and without meaning" is explicit in affirming that they ﷺ used to entrust the meaning to Allah. This statement cannot be interpreted in any other way.

Imām al-Khaṭṭābī—may Allah have mercy upon him—said in his commentary on the Ḥadīth: "Indeed, a squeak is heard like the squeaking of a new leather saddle...": "If these words are

---

[224] *Ṭabaqāt al-Shāfi'iyya al-Kubrā*, 4:287.
[225] *Sharḥ Muslim*, 5:24.

taken upon their outward meaning there will be a type of modality inferred, and modality is negated from Allah and His attributes..."

Al-Ḥāfiẓ Ibn ʿAbd al-Barr—may Allah have mercy upon him—said in response to those who claimed that Allah descends with His Essence: "This is rejected [*laysa bi-shay'in*] according to the people of understanding among Ahl al-Sunna because it is a modality [*kayfiyya*], and they flee from that because it is only suitable for something that is directly encompassed, and Allah, the Exalted, is transcendent above that."[226]

Al-Ḥāfiẓ Ibn Kathīr took a position of *tafwīḍ* and criticized those who understood the ambiguous texts according to their outward meanings. In his exegesis of *Sūra al-ʿArāf*, commenting on the verse ﴾*Then He rose above the Throne*﴿ he said:

> Regarding this issue, the people have many positions, and this is not the proper place to mention them at length. In this matter we traverse the path of the pious predecessors: Mālik, al-Awzāʿī, al-Thawrī, al-Layth b. Saʿd, al-Shāfiʿī, Aḥmad, Isḥāq b. Rāhawayh, and others from the Imāms of the Muslims both early and contemporary, namely to pass it along as it came without establishing a modality and without resemblance and nullification. And the outward meaning that appears to the minds of the anthropomorphists is negated from Allah, for nothing of His creation resembles Allah.[227]

Shaykh Salāma al-ʿAzzāmī al-Quḍāʿī—may Allah have mercy upon him—said:

> The general statement in this matter is that the qualities of contingent beings are two categories: The first category is that which indicates contingency, possibility, want, and need intrinsically, from its essence, and by implication, such as being in a direction and place, and largeness and smallness of size and receptivity to division. These things that are unique to [contingent] beings cannot in any way

[226] *Al-Tamhīd*, 7:143.
[227] *Tafsīr Ibn Kathīr*, 2:220.

be used to describe the Creator. Moreover, some of these things are considered disbelief by consensus if applied to Allah, such as saying that He, the Exalted, begets or is begotten, or that He has a wife or a partner, and other things in which imperfection is evident. Some of these things are differed over, there being different opinions concerning them, although this is not the appropriate place to go into that. The most correct view is that it [those things that are differed over] is misguidance, blameworthy innovation, and odious corruption much more egregious than the bodily acts of corruption.

The common person might be excused due to ignorance in some of that, but as for the one whose rank is elevated above that of lay person, he is not excused, nay he is to be punished. And if he is a caller to his belief then his sin is greater and the matter is even more dangerous—Allah's refuge is sought!

The second category is that which does not indicate the aforementioned things intrinsically and does not indicate imperfection for His exalted perfection, such as existence, life, knowledge, will, power, and their likes of every attribute that is perfection in itself. This category is attributed to the Real in its most perfect levels and in a way that is most distant from imperfection and farthest removed from contingency and its implications. These attributes are necessary just as the One described with them is necessary, the Blessed and Exalted. He is Pre-eternal with His pre-eternality and Everlasting with His everlastingness.

As for the portion of the creation thereof, for them it is an incidental quality that is emergent within them due to the Real bringing them into being. It is contingently possible and not necessary; in a lower level that befits the state of that which is possible. There is no relation between what the Real, Exalted is He, is described with, and what the creation is described with. How can a contingent and possible existent that is subject to diminishment and that does not even possess its own qualities compare to the necessary existent that is Pre-eternal and Everlasting: One Who is Exalted above having a beginning or an end, and Who will never perish?

This explains to you the meaning of Allah's statement regarding the attribute of His Exalted Essence and perfection: ﴾*There is nothing like unto Him, and He is All-Hearing, All-Seeing*﴿, ﴾*He is the Living*﴿, ﴾*He is the Kind, the Well-Aware*﴿, ﴾*He is the All-Knowing, the All-Powerful*﴿ and ﴾*None in the heavens and the earth known the unseen but Allah*﴿—and other noble verses, all of which prove that these attributes are limited to Him only.

Due to the vast distinction between the realities of these attributes as they apply to the creation and their realities as they apply to Allah, the Exalted, some of the virtuous people have said: "Describing the contingently possible [the creation] with existence, life, knowledge, and so on is nothing but figurative."

After clarifying these two categories, I hope that the fallacies used by those who attempt to debate Ahl al-Sunna are disclosed to you, namely their statement: "Face, eye, two hands, two feet, and shin are all attributes just as life, knowledge, will, and power are attributes. Since you [Ahl al-Sunna] believe in the latter with regard to Allah's Essence, why don't you say the same thing regarding the face and the other things mentioned with it? Just as you say He possesses knowledge unlike 'knowledges' and power unlike 'powers,' you should also say that He possesses a literal face unlike faces, and a literal hand unlike hands, and a literal leg unlike legs, and a literal shin unlike shins."

They go into detail regarding that until virtuous people are fooled by them due to their stratagems and are deceived by them due to their beautified speech. What adds even further beauty to their deceitful speech is that some of the major believers in Allah's Divine transcendence above parts and corporeality are reported to have said: "He possesses a face unlike faces..." But this is a fallacy on the part of the literalists, because face, eye, hand, foot, and shin are all parts, organs, and limbs, since they are concrete things and not qualitative meanings that subsist in the one described with them. How can these compare to life, knowledge, will, and power? Is this not similar to a knower resembling knowledge and the colour white resembling whiteness?

> If they retort: "By 'face' and the others, we do not intend parts and limbs, rather we intend real attributes like tremendousness [*'aẓama*], dominion, sight, and power, however, we do not specify what is intended," we say in response: Welcome to those who return to the truth; there is no dispute between us![228]

Shaykh al-Zurqānī—may Allah have mercy upon him—said:

> Some people in this time have gone to extremes, delving into the ambiguous attributes without right. In their discussions and comments regarding them, they have mentioned things that Allah has not permitted. In this topic they have obscure words that carry the possibility of [both] resemblance and transcendence..., so much that these words have themselves become ambiguous. Unfortunately, they present these things to the common folk and their like. It is saddening that they ascribe their views to the pious predecessors... That is like their statements "Indeed, Allah can be pointed to in a physical-sensory way, and among the six directions, to Him belongs the direction of above." They say that He, the Exalted, rose upon the Throne with a literal rising, i.e., that He settled upon it literally, although they backtrack and say: "Not like our settlement and not as we know."
>
> They take verses like this, and as far as we know they have nothing more than clinging to the outward meanings. We have already made clear to you the way of the *Salaf* and the latter-day scholars, so we will not bother to repeat it... If only these people were to put themselves in their proper places they would have remained silent regarding the ambiguous verses and reports and they would have sufficed themselves with declaring Allah's Divine transcendence above what the outward meanings would suggest of contingency and its implications, then they would have entrusted the matter to Allah alone.[229]

---

[228] *Al-Furqān*, p. 78

[229] *Manāhil al-'Irfān*, 2:291.

The erudite Maḥmūd b. Khaṭṭāb al-Subkī—may Allah have mercy upon him—said: "As for the *Salaf* and the latter-day scholars, they are in agreement about affirming the attributes of Allah that are mentioned in the Mighty Book and the Muḥammadan ﷺ Sunna. Their only disagreement is with regards to the position of *tafwīḍ* towards the ambiguous [reports]—which is the way of the *Salaf*—and clarifying their meanings—which the way of the latter-day scholars."[230]

Imām Ibn al-Qushayrī—may Allah have mercy upon him—said:

> They—the literalists—say: "We hold fast to the outward meanings and adhere to a literal understanding of the verses that seemingly allude to resemblance and the reports that imply limit and parts. It is impermissible for us to give figurative interpretation to any of that." They try to support their view with the words of the Exalted: ﴾*And none know its interpretation but Allah*﴿ ...and they inspire their allies with these innovations and allow in their hearts for the Deity, Glorified is He, to be described with parts, limbs, compositeness, descent, leaning, sitting, rising with [His] Essence, and going from place to place. Whoever gives ear to these outward meanings will immediately imagine sensory things, and thus he will believe in egregious things, being swept away by a torrential flood whilst he is unaware.[231]

Shaykh al-Zurqānī—may Allah have mercy upon him—said:

> According to us, the reliance in matters of doctrine is found in the clear-cut, unequivocal proofs that amply demonstrate that He, the Exalted, is not a corporeal body, that He is not limited, that He is not divided into parts, that He is not composite, and that He is not in need of anyone or any place or time or anything of the like. The Qurʾān mentions this in its clear-cut verses. He said: ﴾*There is nothing like unto Him*﴿, ﴾*Say: "He is Allah, the One. Allah, the Eternal Refuge. He neither begets, nor is He begotten.*

[230] *Al-Dīn al-Khāliṣ*, 1:28.
[231] *Itḥāf al-Sāda al-Muttaqīn*, 2:109.

And there is not any equivalent to Him"⟫, ⟪*If you disbelieve, then indeed, Allah is free of needing you. And He is not pleased with disbelief for His servants. And if you are thankful, it will please Him*⟫ and ⟪*O people! You are all poor unto Allah. And Allah is free of all needs, worthy of praise*⟫ and there are many other examples of this in the Book and the Sunna.

So everything that appears in its outward meaning to oppose these clear-cut and unequivocal texts is from the ambiguous texts that are impermissible to follow—as has become clear to you from what has preceded.

Moreover, they—the literalists—contradict themselves; they affirm these ambiguous texts literally. Now, there is no doubt that their literal meanings imply contingency and the incidental qualities of contingency [*'arāḍ al-ḥudūth*] such as corporeality, division into parts, movement, and displacement; however, after they affirmed those ambiguous texts literally they negated these implications, despite the fact that affirmation of what implies something while negating what is implied is a contradiction that no intelligent person would be pleased with for himself—much less a student or scholar.

So their view regarding the issue of *istiwā'* mentioned above, that *istiwā'* remains upon its literal meaning, means that it is the well-known sitting [*julūs*] that implies corporeality and spatial contact. Their disclaimer after it, that it is not like the *istiwā'* that we know, indicates that it is not the well-known sitting that implies corporeality and spatial contact. So it is as if they are saying: "Indeed, He is risen in a way that is not rising, and He is settled upon the Throne in a way that is not settlement." Or it is like saying that He is both limited and unlimited; that He is both a corporeal body and not a corporeal body; or that being risen above the Throne is not being risen above the Throne, and being settled above it is not being settled above it...

So if by their statement [that they believe] He is literally risen above the Throne, they mean that is taken as a reality that Allah knows and that we do not know, then we are in agreement. However, this expression of theirs is ambiguous and it is impermissible for a believer to utter it, especially in a classroom setting, when guidance is given, and in a situation in which there is debate and proofs. This is because one does not look at a statement—be it literal or figurative—as it is with the knowledge of Allah, rather what is looked at is the meaning for which it was coined in the conventional sense of the language. In the Arabic language, *istiwā'* literally indicates that which is impossible for Allah, hence the outward meaning of it must be disregarded. When the outward coined meaning of word is disregarded and in its place another meaning for which it was not coined is used, it has gone from being literal to being figurative—without fail—as long as there is a contextual element that prevents the original meaning from being intended.

Furthermore, their [the literalists'] words deceive the common folk and cause tribulation for them, so how can they be faced with it and ordered with it? That will lead the Umma to misguidance and will rupture their unity, which is forbidden in the Qur'ān—and this is something that caused 'Umar to do what he did to Ṣabīgh, and it is what caused Mālik—may Allah have mercy upon him—to say what he said and do what he did with the man who asked him about *istiwā'*. If only these people were to put themselves in their proper places they would have remained silent regarding the ambiguous verses and reports and they would have sufficed themselves with declaring Allah's Divine transcendence above what the outward meanings would suggest of contingency and its implications, then they would have entrusted the matter to Allah alone.[232]

With these statements from the Imāms of Islam and the notables of the Umma, the truth of this issue becomes clear, and it is established with certainty that the people of truth have only two view-points regarding this issue: *tafwīḍ*, which was the way of the majority of the *Salaf*; and figurative interpretation, which was the way of the majority of the latter-day scholars and some groups among the *Salaf*. Nothing remains after these two view-points other than extreme denial [*ta'ṭīl*] and anthropomorphism [*tajsīm*].

---

[232] *Manāhil al-'Irfān*, 2:292.

Chapter Eight

Figurative Interpretation and Extreme Denial

Both figurative interpretation and extreme denial are ascribed to the Ashʿarīs as a type of insult and defamation. As for figurative interpretation, it has already been demonstrated that it has been a distinguishing mark of the people of truth in contradistinction to the people of innovation from the anthropomorphists and corporealists. So figurative interpretation deserves to be counted as a compliment and not an insult.

As for extreme denial [*taʿṭīl*], they are innocent of it. How can the Ashʿarīs be accused of extreme denial when they affirm the attributes and declare Allah transcendent above all faults and traits of imperfection found in the creation? They are ascribed to the Imām of Ahl al-Sunna and the thorn of the people of truth in the throats of the innovators.

The only reason some people accuse the Ashʿarīs of extreme denial is because they did not comprehend the very real distinction between figurative interpretation and extreme denial; or they did not comprehend the distinction between negating an attribute and negating the sensory and outward and literal meaning that does not befit Allah, the Exalted. Nevertheless, in this section we shall endeavour to explain this distinction. Before that, however, we must explain the meaning of denial.

The Reality of Extreme Denial

Lexically, denial [*taʿṭīl*] means to empty and negate. It is said: "This woman is *ʿāṭil*" if she is free of jewellery and adornment. The Muʿaṭṭila (extreme deniers) are those who negate the Maker of the universe. Here, they are referred to as the negators of the Creator's ﷻ attributes such as the Jahmiyya who negated and denied Allah's attributes.

Do the Ashʿarīs Negate Allah's Attributes?

In this research we have demonstrated the beliefs of the Ashʿarīs and their figurative interpretation of some of the expressions whose outward and literal meanings that mankind know in themselves and around them are impossible for Allah. This figurative interpretation of theirs is exactly what the pious predecessors knew and believed in, although the majority of them ﷺ refrained from openly stating that or specifying the meaning of an expression that had more than one meaning. They would abstain from that out of scrupulousness and awe of the Divine. In addition, they had no need for that because their era was relatively pure from the blameworthy innovations that emerged after them.

This is attested to by the many citations we provided here in which they said the same things the Ashʿarīs say. If it were allowable to accuse the Ashʿarīs of extreme denial because of their use of figurative interpretation, that same ruling would just as equally apply to the generation of the Companions, the followers, and their followers.

The scholars have textually stated that the way of figurative interpretation was cited from pious predecessors. That the majority of them held fast to *tafwīḍ*—that the scholars call non-specific interpretation—does not negate the fact that groups among them used figurative interpretation.

Imām al-Nawawī—may Allah have mercy upon him—said:

> This Ḥadīth is from the Ḥadīth reports pertaining to the Divine attributes, and there are two well-known positions the scholars take concerning it... In summary, the first position, ...is the position of the majority of the *Salaf* and some of the theologians The second position, which is the position of most of the theologians, some groups among the *Salaf*, and it is related from Mālik and al-Awzāʿī, is that these reports are to be given figurative interpretation according to what is appropriate for them according to their context.[233]

Imām al-Zarkashī—may Allah have mercy upon him—said:

> The people differ regarding what is cited from them [the ambiguous texts] in the verses and Ḥadīth reports, and they are three groups:

[233] *Sharḥ Ṣaḥīḥ Muslim*, 6:36.

> 1 [Those who believe that] there is no room for figurative interpretation of them, rather [they posit], they should be relayed according to their outward meanings and nothing of them should be interpreted. They are the anthropomorphists.
>
> 2 [Those who believe that] the [ambiguous texts] do have an interpretation, however, we are to refrain from that, while at the same time not believing in any resemblance or outright denial. [According to this view] we are to say: ﴾*None know its interpretation except Allah.*﴿ This is the view of the *Salaf.*
>
> 3 [Those who believe that] they are interpreted. They interpreted them according to what befits Him. The first position is false, and the other two positions are recorded from the Companions, ...and those who have been reported using figurative interpretation include ʿAlī, Ibn Masʿūd, Ibn ʿAbbās, and others.[234]

The erudite scholar, al-Shawkānī—may Allah have mercy upon him—said:

> Section two: Regarding that to which interpretation applies. It is two categories. One: most of the branch subsidiary matters [*furūʿ*]—and there is no disagreement regarding that. Two: the fundamentals, such as doctrine and theological matters and the attributes of the Creator ﷻ. They [the scholars] have differed regarding this and have taken three separate positions:
>
> 1 That there is no room for figurative interpretation of them, rather [it is posited], they should be relayed according to their outward meanings and nothing of them should be interpreted. This is the view of the anthropomorphists.
>
> 2 That they do have an interpretation, however, we are to refrain from that, while at the same time not believing in any resemblance or outright denial. [According to this view] we are to say: ﴾*None know its interpretation except Allah.*﴿ Ibn Burhān said: "This is the view of the *Salaf.*"

[234] *Al-Burhān fī ʿUlūm al-Qurʾān*, 2:207.

3 That they are interpreted. Ibn Burhān said: "The first position of these three is false, and the other two positions are recorded from the Companions. This third position was recorded from 'Alī, Ibn Mas'ūd, Ibn 'Abbās, and Umm Salama."[235]

This is also supported by the quotes taken from some of the Imāms of the *Salaf* in which they gave figurative interpretations for some of the ambiguous texts. Here, we shall cite a small sample of them:

Ibn 'Abbās ﷺ interpreted the word *sāq* (shin) as a severe matter [*shidda al-amr*], as did Mujāhid, 'Ikrima, al-Ḍaḥḥāk, Qatāda, Sa'īd b. Jubayr, and others.[236] They also interpreted the word *wajh* in Allah's statement: ﴾*So wherever you turn there is the wajh (face) of Allah.*﴿ Mujāhid said: "It is Allah's *qibla*."[237] Regarding Allah's words: ﴾*Everything shall perish except His wajh (face)*﴿ Mujāhid, Abū 'Ubayda and al-Ḍaḥḥāk said: "Except for Him."[238] Abū 'Āliya and Sufyān said: "Except that which was intended for His sake." Al-Ṣādiq said: "His religion." Abū 'Ubayda also said: "Except His rank."[239]

Ibn Jarīr al-Ṭabarī interpreted *istiwā'* as loftiness and authority[240] and a similar interpretation is reported from al-Ḥasan [al-Baṣrī] and Sufyān al-Thawrī.[241]

Aḥmad interpreted Allah's words: ﴾*...and your Lord comes...*﴿ He said: "His reward comes." This was mentioned by Ibn Kathīr from the narration of al-Bayhaqī. After mentioning this, Ibn Kathīr quoted al-Bayhaqī, who said: "There is nothing wrong with this chain [*lā ghubār 'alayhi*]."[242] It is also narrated from our master Ibn 'Abbās ﷺ.[243]

---

[235] *Irshād al-Fuḥūl*, p. 176.
[236] *Tafsīr al-Ṭabarī*, 29:38; *Tafsīr al-Qurṭubī*, 18:249.
[237] *Tafsīr al-Ṭabarī*, 1:402.
[238] *Tafsīr al-Qurṭubī*, 13:322.
[239] Ibid.
[240] *Tafsīr al-Ṭabarī*, 1:192.
[241] *Mirqāt al-Mafātīḥ*, 2:137; *Tafsīr al-'Izz b. 'Abd al-Salām*, 1:485–486.
[242] *Al-Bidāya wal-Nihāya*, 10:327.
[243] *Tafsīr al-Nasafī*, 4:378 in the margins of *Tafsīr al-Khāzin* [*Al-Musammā li-Bāb al-Ta'wīl fī Ma'ānī al-Tanzīl*].

Al-Bukhārī interpreted "laughter" [ḍaḥak] as mercy.[244] He also interpreted Allah's words: ﴾*Everything shall perish except His wajh (face).*﴿ He said: "Except His dominion."[245]

There are many other examples of figurative interpretation we will mention in the chapter on the figurative interpretation of the pious predecessors. There are many examples that fill the books of Qur'ānic exegesis and Ḥadīth. It is an established and undeniable fact that no stubborn person can deny.

As is clear from its definition, extreme denial is to negate the attributes of the Creator, Glorified is He; but the Ash'arīs have not negated a single attribute that has been established in a sound manner. Their written works attest to this fact. The most they did was take the texts that have outward and literal meanings that indicate resemblance between Allah and His creation and understand them in a manner known to the Arabs and that do not contradict Allah's transcendence. There is a vast difference between negating what Allah has affirmed, as the Jahmīs did, and affirming them and then giving them—after declaring that the outward meanings are impossible—a meaning that befits Allah, the Exalted, and is well known in the Arabic language.

Let us mention an example of this for added clarity. The Exalted said: ﴾*The All-Merciful rose above the Throne.*﴿ In the Arabic language, *istiwā'* has many different meanings, some of which are figurative and some of which are literal. Of all of the meanings that indicate a corporeal reality, none of them befit Allah, the Exalted, so anything like that in its literal and outward sense clearly does not befit Allah, the Exalted. For this reason, it is inevitable that we seek recourse in the figurative meanings—and this is what the scholars did.

When they—may Allah have mercy upon them—established that it is impossible for the literal and sensory meaning of *istiwā'* to apply to Allah, they affirmed what Allah affirmed for Himself and what His Messenger ﷺ affirmed for Him, then they declared Allah's transcendence above the outward meaning of the text and negated the literal meaning as it is known to the creation. They said: "Our Lord performed the act of *istiwā'* as He informed: an

---

[244] Al-Bayhaqī, *Al-Asmā wal-Ṣifāt*: p. 470.
[245] *Fatḥ al-Bārī*, 8:464.

istiwā' that is not like the *istiwā'* of man—the first meaning of the word that comes to the mind. It is an *istiwā'* that is exalted above contact, indwelling, settlement, and other false meanings."

Imām al-Ghazālī—may Allah have mercy upon him—said: "And He, the Exalted, is risen above the Throne in the sense that He said and with the meaning that He intended; a rising that is exalted above contact, settlement, fixation, indwelling, and displacement. The Throne does not carry Him; rather, both the Throne and its carriers are carried by His subtle power and they are overpowered in His grasp."[246] He also said: "The eighth fundamental: Knowing that He, the Exalted, is risen above His Throne with the meaning that Allah, the Exalted, intended by *istiwā'*; it does not negate exaltedness, and the traits of contingency and extinction do not approach it."[247]

By Allah! Where is the denial here? Has anything here been negated besides that which must be negated from Allah, the Exalted, and that which is forbidden to affirm for Him?

The Ash'arīs did not negate the attribute of *istiwā'* and they did not say: "He did not perform the act of *istiwā'*" or that He is not risen. Rather, they declared Allah transcendent above the sensory meanings that are impossible for Him, namely sitting and settlement, both of which are the literal meaning of the word. Undoubtedly, those who affirm sitting have fallen into resemblance [*tashbīh*] and are inclining towards it. The scholars have textually stated that to understand it in its literal sense is resemblance.

Al-Ḥāfiẓ Ibn Ḥajar—may Allah have mercy upon him—said in his commentary on the Ḥadīth on "descent": "There are different opinions regarding the meaning of 'descent': some understood it in its literal and outward sense, and they are the Mushabbiha (corporealists)—exalted is Allah from what they say..."[248]

Imām al-Qurṭubī—may Allah have mercy upon him—said in his explanation of Allah's words: ﴾*Do you feel safe from He Who is in the heavens...*﴿:

---

[246] *Iḥyā' 'Ulūm al-Dīn*, 1:90.
[247] Ibid.
[248] *Fatḥ al-Bārī*, 3:36.

> The verifying scholars [*al-muḥaqqiqūn*] said that it means: "Do you feel safe from He Who is above the heavens," like Allah's words: ﴾*So travel in the earth.*﴿ In other words, [travel] above it; [this verse means] without contact and limits, rather with overpowering and managing...
>
> The reports in this section are many, authentic, and widely disseminated; they indicate loftiness, and no one but a heretic or ignorant obstinate person can deny that. What is meant by it is His exaltation and transcendence above [the qualities of] beneath and below. His is described with loftiness and tremendousness; not by places or directions or limits because those things are from the qualities of corporeal bodies.
>
> The only reason the hands are raised upwards to the heavens in supplication is because the heavens are where the revelation descended..., and because He created all places and He is not in need of them. He was in pre-eternity before the creation of place and time; there was no place or time, and He is now as He always was.[249]

Imām al-Ṭabarī—may Allah have mercy upon him—said in his exegesis regarding the statement of the Exalted: ﴾*And He is the Irresistible, above His servants*﴿: "He is above them with His overpowering of them and they are beneath [*dūn*] Him."[250] His last phrase means that they are beneath Him in this sense, i.e., that they are overpowered by Him, not that they are beneath Him by way of sense perception and place. We see here that he interpreted aboveness [*fawqiyya*] as the aboveness of overpowering.

In his explanation of "rising" [*istiwā'*] he said: "He rose above it in the sense of dominion and authority; not a loftiness of displacement and movement."[251]

Imām al-Qurṭubī said in his exegesis regarding the words of the Exalted: ﴾*And He is the Irresistible, above His servants*﴿: "The meaning of 'above His servants' is the aboveness of domination

---

[249] *Tafsīr al-Qurṭubī*, 18:216.
[250] *Tafsīr al-Ṭabarī*, 7:103.
[251] Ibid., 1:192.

by overpowering and overmastery over them. In other words, they are under His control; it is not the aboveness of place."[252]

Al-Ḥāfiẓ Ibn Ḥajar said: "That the directions of above and below are impossible for Allah does not preclude Him from being described with loftiness; because His description of loftiness is in meaning, whereas the impossible [loftiness] is that of sense perception."[253]

Ibn Ḥajar al-ʿAsqalānī also said in his commentary on the Ḥadīth: "When one of you stands up to pray, he is in intimate conversation with his Lord..., [or alternatively,] his Lord is between him and the *qibla*...": "This contains a refutation against the one who claims that He [Allah] is above the Throne with His Essence."[254] Imām Badr al-Dīn al-Jamāʿa—may Allah have mercy upon him—said:

> [The wording:] ﴾*Then He rose above the Throne*﴿ appears in five verses and in the sixth verse in [*Sūra*] *Ṭāhā*: ﴾*The All-Merciful rose above the Throne.*﴿ The Qurʾān was revealed in the Arabic language and with the meanings of their words and that which they understood from their speech...
>
> The *Salaf* and the people of figurative interpretation agreed that the things that do not befit the Majesty of the Lord, such as sitting and being upright [in a sitting position] are not intended. They disagreed regarding the specification of the possible meanings that befit His Majesty, such as "intended" and "conquered;" the *Salaf* remained silent whereas the people of figurative interpretation interpreted it as conquering and overpowering, due to the exaltedness of the Lord ﷻ above the traits of corporeal bodies, such as needing a boundary and a place. In addition, He is not to be described with movement or stillness or gathering or separation, because all of those things are from the traits of contingent beings and incidental accidents. The Lord, Exalted is He, is transcendent above them. Hence, His statement: ﴾*Then He rose...*﴿ must take the meaning of conquering and

---

[252] *Tafsīr al-Qurṭubī*, 6:399.

[253] *Fatḥ al-Bārī*, 6:158.

[254] Ibid., 1:598.

overpowering and not sitting and settlement, for were His existence bound by time or place, it would imply that time and place are eternal or that they precede Him, the Exalted, and both propositions are false...

If it is retorted: "Negating a direction for an existent being implies the negation of that existent being as well, for it is impossible for a being to exist without a direction," we respond: That which exists is of two categories: [1] an existence that cannot be engaged with the imagination, intuition, or sense-perception; an existence that cannot receive connection or separation, and [2] an existence that can be engaged with and receive all of the above. The impossibility of the first one is itself impossible. In other words, its existence without a direction is not deemed [rationally] impossible. The Lord, Exalted is He, is not subject to that [a direction], for He is not a corporeal body [*jism*], accident [*'araḍ*], or indivisible element [*jawhar*]. Hence it is rationally valid for Him to exist without a direction or spatial boundary. Just as the rational evidence proves His existence with the negation of corporeality and the [indwelling] of accidents—even though the sensory understanding deems this difficult to conceive—similarly it proves the negation of direction and spatial boundary...

If it is retorted: "Allah, the Exalted, said: ﴾*Unto Him the good words ascend*﴿ and this clearly indicates a direction, and the Exalted also said: ﴾*The Angels and the Spirit rise unto Him*﴿ and ﴾*Then it rises unto Him,*﴿" we respond: "unto" here does not mean on of direction, rather it means that all matters are with Him, as He said elsewhere: ﴾*Certainly to Allah do all matters return*﴿ and ﴾*And unto Him all matters return*﴿ and the statement of the intimate friend [Ibrāhīm ﷺ]: ﴾*Indeed, I am going to my Lord. He shall guide me.*﴿

So it means that with Him are all the rewards, ranks, and honour that He has prepared for His servants and Angels. If it is retorted: "'Conquering' is only said with respect to that which was previously dominant or for that which contends and is dominated over, or for that which was incapable and then capable," we respond: what is meant by conquering here is the complete and perfect power that is from any contender...

> If it is retorted: "Well in that case, 'conquering' with that meaning is true for all of His creation, so what is the benefit in Him mentioning it specifically in reference to the Throne?" we respond: it was given special mention because it is the most tremendous creation—by consensus—just as He said: ﴾*...the Lord of the Throne*﴿ even though He is the Lord of everything. So, if He overpowers the Throne which encompasses everything, then clearly He overpowers everything as well.
>
> If this is established, then we say that whoever explains *istiwā'* in a manner that is understood from the qualities of contingent beings, and says: "He rose with His essence," or: "He rose literally," he has innovated this additional wording that is affirmed by neither the Sunna nor any of the Imāms who are to be emulated.[255]

Apply this same ruling to all of the attributes affirmed in the texts. They affirm all of that without resemblance or likeness, and if the outward meaning is impossible they interpret it without denial. They affirm what Allah affirmed for Himself in His Book or what He affirmed upon the tongue of His Prophet ﷺ—after having declared His transcendence above everything that does not befit Him in the outward expression.

The outward meaning of the expression is negated according to them because it is impossible for Allah to be described with it and it must be negated from Him. There is no doubt that the one who affirms the outward meaning has fallen into resemblance [*tashbīh*] and anthropomorphism [*tajsīm*], or has inclined to it.

Moreover, there is no escape from figurative interpretation. All those who flee from it are forced to use it, otherwise what can they possibly say regarding Allah's words: ﴾*They forgot Allah so He forgot them*﴿ and ﴾*Today We forget them just as you forgot the meeting of this day of yours.*﴿ They are forced by implication to affirm literal forgetfulness for Him because He affirmed it for Himself—however, with the caveat that it is unlike the forgetfulness of man, which the Lord has negated from Himself when He said: ﴾*And your Lord is not forgetful!*﴿

[255] *Īḍāḥ al-Dalīl*, pp. 101–107.

What can they possibly say regarding Allah's words: ﴾*And He is with your wherever you may be*﴿, ﴾*There is no secret conversation of three except that He is the fourth, and there is no secret conversation of five except that He is the sixth, and no less than that or greater than that except that He is with you wherever you are*﴿, ﴾*Allah mocks them*﴿, ﴾*Allah is the best of plotters*﴿ and ﴾*They seek to deceive Allah but Allah deceives them.*﴿

What can they possibly say regarding the statements of the Prophet ﷺ: "Allah does not become bored until you become bored," and [in the Ḥadīth *qudsī*] "...and whoever comes to me walking I come to him running..." and "My servant was sick yet you did not visit Me..."

What can they possibly say regarding His statements: "Allah's razor is sharper than your razor and Allah's forearm is stronger than your forearm," "Indeed, Allah is Shy and Generous; He is shy before His slave when he raises his hands in supplication to return them emptyhanded...," "Indeed, Allah laughs...," "Indeed, Allah is jealously protective..." and his statement: "Indeed, Allah is amazed..."

Can you imagine anyone affirming the outward and literal meanings of these things as they are conventionally known to man, saying: "We affirm for Allah a literal forgetfulness, a literal plotting, a literal deception, a literal mocking, a literal sickness, a literal running, a literal strong forearm, a literal sharp razor, a literal boredom, a literal amazement, jealousy, shyness, hesitation, laughter, and a literal 'withness' [*maʿiyya*] and closeness with His Essence and with distance—all literally and as conventionally known to man in their languages." Allah's refuge is sought!

We don't think anyone can be as stubborn and bold as to deny that these outward meanings are impossible and are negated from Allah, the Exalted. So, just as these outward meanings are impossible, so are "rising," "descent," "coming," and other expressions whose literal meanings must be negated and prevented because of their unifying factor, namely the impossibility of their outward and literal meanings.

Al-Ḥāfiẓ Ibn ʿAsākir—may Allah have mercy upon him—said:

All praise is due to Allah. They [the Ashʿarīs] are neither Muʿtazila nor Muʿaṭṭila (deniers) who negate Allah's attributes; they affirm for Him ﷻ the attributes He affirmed for Himself and they describe Him with what He described Himself with in the clear-cut verses and with what His Prophet ﷺ described Him with in the rigorously authentic narrations. They declare Him exaltedly transcendent above imperfections and faults. If they find anyone who believes in corporeality or modality among the anthropomorphists or corporealists, or if they meet anyone who describes Him with the qualities of contingent beings—among those who believe in limits and directions—then they tread the path of figurative interpretation and affirm His transcendence with the clearest of proofs. They go to great lengths in affirming His sanctity and transcendence for fear that those who do not know might fall into the darkness of resemblance.

When they are safe from that, they believe that silence is safer and that refraining from figurative interpretation—except when there is a need—is more judicious. In this they may be likened to an experienced doctor who treats every illness with the generally agreed upon medicine; however, when it is ascertained that a patient is overcome with coldness, he prescribes him with hot medicines, and treats him with cold medicine when he is sure that the patient is suffering from a hot illness. This similitude is akin to the report narrated from Sufyān who said: "When in the Levant, speak about the excellent virtues of ʿAlī ؓ, and when in Kufa, speak about the excellent virtues of ʿUthmān ؓ."

The one who engages in figurative interpretation with a clear proof may be likened to a swimmer. He is not in need of swimming skills so long as he is on land. If, however, he finds himself at some point sailing the ocean and faces its terrifying tempests and witnesses its crashing waves and is struck by powerful winds until the ship is torn apart and faces certain destruction if he does not swim, he should then swim with his utmost effort in order to seek safety. In that scenario he will not be remiss due to his love of life. Similar is the case with the believer in Divine Oneness. As long as he treads the clear path of

> transcendence and is safe in his creed from sailing on the waves of corporeality, then he has not need of delving into figurative interpretation—as his beliefs are safe from resemblance and falsehood. If, however, his purity is soiled by the grime of seeking modality or likeness, he must then purify his heart from that by the cleansing interpretation and he must clean his mind with clear proofs, so as to save his creed from resemblance [*tashbīh*] and denial [*taʿṭīl*].[256]

Imām Abū Naṣr al-Qushayrī—may Allah have mercy upon him—said:

> If it is retorted: "Did not Allah say: ﴾*The All-Merciful rose above the Throne*﴿ and it must be believed literally?" we respond: Allah also said: ﴾*And He is with you wherever you may be*﴿ and ﴾*Certainly, He is All-Encompassing over everything.*﴿ So these two verses must also be taken literally, which would mean that He, the Exalted, is upon the Throne, with us, and encompassing the universe with His Essence all at the same time. It is impossible for one to be everywhere with his essence. They say: "Allah's statement: ﴾*And He is with you*﴿ means with His knowledge, and His statement: ﴾*He is All-Encompassing over everything*﴿ means an encompassing of knowledge." We say: Similarly, Allah's words: ﴾*The All-Merciful rose above the Throne*﴿ means overpowering and overseeing.[257]

The Imām and *Ḥujja al-Islam*, al-Ghazālī—may Allah have mercy upon him—said:

> The eighth fundamental: Knowing that He, the Exalted, is risen above His Throne with the meaning that Allah, the Exalted, intended by *istiwā'*; it does not negate exaltedness, and the traits of contingency and extinction do not approach it. This is what is intended by "rising unto the heavens," where He said in the Qur'ān: ﴾*Then He rose* [*istawā'*] *to the heavens while they were smoke.*﴿ That is only via overpowering and dominion...

---

[256] *Tabyīn Kadhib al-Muftarī*, p. 388.
[257] *Itḥāf al-Sāda al-Muttaqīn*, 2:108.

> The people of truth were obliged to give this interpretation just as the people of falsehood were obliged to interpret Allah's words: ﴾*And He is with your wherever you may be.*﴿ Hence, by agreement, that is understood to refer to encompassment and knowledge. And his ﷺ statement: "The heart of the believer is between the two fingers of the fingers of the All-Merciful" is understood to mean power and dominion. And his ﷺ statement: "The Black Stone is Allah's right hand on earth" is understood to mean nobility and honouring, for if it remained on its outward meaning, that which is impossible would be implied.
>
> Similarly with *istiwā'*: if it were left [with it outward meaning of] settlement and fixation, it would imply that the being that is fixed upon it is a corporeal body that is touching the Throne and is either larger than it or smaller, and that is impossible. Whatever leads to an impossible [conclusion] is itself impossible.[258]

The scholars have cited a consensus that these outward meanings are not intended in the Sacred Law. This consensus was mentioned by al-Ḥāfiẓ Abū al-Ḥasan ʿAlī b. al-Qaṭṭān—may Allah have mercy upon him:

> And they concurred that He, the Exalted, comes on the Day of Judgment, along with the Angels, in rows upon rows, in order to present the nations and to take them to account and punish and reward them. He shall forgive whom He wills from the believers and punish from them he whom He wills, as the Exalted said. His coming is not through movement or displacement. They also concurred that He, the Exalted, is pleased with those who are obedient to Him, and that His pleasure with them is His will to bestow upon them His bounty. They also concurred that He loves the penitent and is displeased and angry with the disbelievers, and that His anger is His will to punish them, and that nothing stands in the way of His anger...[259]

---

[258] *Iḥyā' ʿUlūm al-Dīn*, 1:90.
[259] *Al-Iqnāʿ fī Masā'il al-Ijmāʿ*, 1:32–43.

Do you think that they would concur upon falsehood by agreeing that the outward meanings of "coming," "pleasure," and "anger" are negated and impossible? Does the Umma of Muḥammad ﷺ unite upon misguidance or blameworthy innovation? Do you think they would concur upon denying the attributes of the Creator ﷻ?

We have already quoted the words of Qāḍī 'Iyāḍ—may Allah have mercy upon him:

> There is no disagreement among the Muslims whatsoever —not between their jurists, Ḥadīth scholars, theologians, investigators, and common folk—that the outward meaning of the texts that mention Allah, the Exalted, being in the heavens, such as His statement: ﴿*Do you feel safe from He Who is in the heavens that he would not cause the earth to swallow you*﴾ and its likes are not to be taken upon their outward meaning, nay, they are interpreted according to all.[260]

The Imām, ascetic, and exemplar, Abū 'Amr al-Dānī—may Allah have mercy upon him—said:

> Indeed, Allah, the Exalted, has not ceased being a "willer" [willing], determiner, "lover" [loving], hating, being pleased, being displeased, being an ally, being an enemy, merciful, and compassionate—and all of these attributes refer back to His will for His servants and His determination for His creation; not to an anger that changes Him, a pleasure that calms His "nature," a displeasure and rage that comes over Him, or a hatred that He finds. He, the Exalted, is pleased in pre-eternity with the one whose actions He knows He will seal with faith and who will be rewarded in full for it, and He is angry [in pre-eternity] with the one whose actions He knows He will seal with disbelief and who will be requited for it.[261]

---

[260] *Rawḍa al-Ṭālibīn*, 10:85.

[261] *Al-Risāla al-Wāfiya li-Madhhab Ahl al-Sunna fī al-'Itiqādāt*, p. 124.

He also said regarding the Lord's descent: "And His ﷻ descent is How He wills; without limits and without establishing a modality and without the description of displacement or movement."[262]

Regarding *istiwā'* he said: "His *istiwā'*, Exalted is His Majesty, is His loftiness without modality or limits or contact or touching."[263]

Were these Imāms extreme deniers when they disregarded the outward meanings of these expressions and interpreted them in light of figurative speech and rhetorical devices? With this you know—may Allah guide you and us—that the extreme denial that the Ash'arīs and Māturīdīs—the majority of the Umma—are accused of is in fact Divine transcendence and sanctity.

Anyone who rejects their view in this and insists on affirming what they negated will inevitably fall into anthropomorphism and resemblance. It is forbidden to affirm as attributes of Allah the portions of the expressions that the Ash'arīs negated and declared Allah transcendently above, for that will necessitate impossible and false conclusions.

In general, the statements of the *Salaf* of this Umma and its latter-day scholars all declare Allah's transcendence above the outward meanings that are impossible. What we have presented here should convince the fair-minded person.

In conclusion, figurative interpretation with its guidelines and pre-requisites is a Sunni way and a genuine legal method. There is no harm in utilising it to understand the Book of Allah, the Exalted, and the Sunna of His Prophet ﷺ. It is not a way of innovation and misguidance or extreme denial. Rather, the one who understands the ambiguous texts pertaining to the attributes according to their outward meanings as they are conventionally used with the creation is in fact the one who falls into extreme denial, for he denies the meaning that is understood from the text and disregards its intended meaning.

[262] Ibid.
[263] Ibid.

CHAPTER NINE

THE *SALAF'S* FIGURATIVE INTERPRETATIONS OF THE TEXTS PERTAINING TO THE ATTRIBUTES

WHEN THE LATTER-DAY SCHOLARS OF THE UMMA upheld the way of figurative interpretation, they did not invent a novel matter from their own selves. Rather, this way was adopted by many groups from the pious predecessors. They employed figurative interpretation and spoke with it, proving definitively that this is a genuinely legal and Sunni method. The scholars have quoted a number of interpretations reported from the *Salaf*. They include the following:

Ibn 'Abbās' ﷺ interpretation of footstool [*kursī*]

In *Tafsīr al-Ṭabarī*, explaining the verse of the footstool [*āya al-kursī*], it says:

> The people of Qur'ānic interpretation disagreed regarding the meaning of the footstool that Allah, the Exalted, informed about. In this verse He mentioned that it extends over the heavens and the earth. Some of them said: "It is the knowledge of Allah, exalted is His mention."
>
> ...As for what is proven by the apparent meaning of the Qur'ān, it is the statement of Ibn 'Abbās narrated by Ja'far b. Abī al-Mughīra from Sa'īd b. Jubayr, that he said: "It is His knowledge."[264]

Ibn 'Abbās' ﷺ interpretation of the coming of the Lord ﷻ

In *Tafsīr al-Nasafī*[265] it is mentioned in the commentary on the verse: ﴾*And your Lord and the Angels shall come: row upon row*﴿:

> This is a similitude for the manifestation of the signs of His omnipotence and an explanation of the signs of His magnificent power and authority. When one of the kings

---

[264] *Tafsīr al-Ṭabarī*, 3:7.

[265] *Tafsīr al-Nasafī*, 4:378.

> is present, his presence manifests the effects of awe that are not manifested when only his soldiers or close associates are present. It is reported from Ibn ʿAbbās: "His command and decree.[266]

Imām al-Qurṭubī narrated a similar interpretation from al-Ḥasan al-Baṣrī and quoted the words of some scholars who said:

> He made the "coming" mentioned in the verses particular to Him as a way of magnifying the effect of those verses. An example of this is found in the words of Allah in the Ḥadīth [*qudsī*]: "O son of Ādam! I fell ill yet you did not visit me... I sought drink from you yet you did not give Me drink... And I sought food from you yet you did not give Me food!"
>
> Allah ﷻ is not described with moving from one place to another—and how could He possibly [be described with] movement and displacement when He has no place or time? He is not subject to the vicissitudes of time because the passing of time over something means that time is lost and whoever loses something is incapable.[267]

Ibn 'Abbās' ﵄ interpretation of the word "eye" [ʿ*ayn*]

Allah, the Exalted, said: ﴾*And construct the ship under Our eyes.*﴿ Ibn ʿAbbās ﵄ said: "You are in our vision."[268] Allah, the Exalted also said: ﴾*And be patient for the ruling of your Lord for indeed you are by Our eyes.*﴿ Ibn ʿAbbās ﵄ said: "We see what is done to you."[269]

Ibn 'Abbās' ﵄ interpretation of the word "hand" [*yad*]

Allah, the Exalted, said: ﴾*And the heavens We built with aydin (hands).*﴿ He ﵄ said: "With power and ability."[270]

---

[266] In other words, what comes is Allah's command and decree. [t]
[267] *Tafsīr al-Qurṭubī*, 20:55.
[268] *Tafsīr al-Baghawī*, 2:322.
[269] *Tafsīr al-Khāzin*, 4:190.
[270] *Tafsīr al-Qurṭubī*, 18:52.

Ibn ʿAbbās' رضي الله عنه interpretation of "light" [*nūr*]

Allah, the Exalted, said: ﴾*Allah is the light of the heavens and the earth.*﴿ In *Tafsīr al-Ṭabarī* it says: "It is related from Ibn ʿAbbās regarding His statement: ﴾*Allah is the light of the heavens and the earth*﴿: 'Allah is the Guide of the people of the heavens and the earth.'"[271]

Ibn ʿAbbās' رضي الله عنه interpretation of the texts that mention "face" [*wajh*]

Allah, the Exalted, said: ﴾*And the face of your Lord, the Possessor of might and grandeur, shall remain.*﴿ He رضي الله عنه said: "Face is an expression that means Him." Al-Qurṭubī said in his exegesis:

> In other words, Allah shall remain. The [word] "face" denotes His existence and His Essence, Exalted is He... This is the view that the verifying scholars hold. From our scholars [who held this view are] Ibn Fūrak, Abū al-Maʿālī, and others... Abū al-Maʿālī said: "As for the intended meaning of face according to most of our Imāms, it is the existence of the Creator, Exalted is He."[272]

Ibn ʿAbbās' رضي الله عنه interpretation of "shin" [*sāq*]

Allah, the Exalted, said: ﴾*On the day a shin* [*sāq*] *shall be unveiled.*﴿ Ibn ʿAbbās رضي الله عنه said: "A severe affliction."[273]

Ibn ʿAbbās' رضي الله عنه interpretation of "side" [*janb*]

Allah, the Exalted, said: ﴾*That a soul says: "O what severe regret for my negligence in the side* [*janb*] *of Allah!"*﴿ He رضي الله عنه said: "For what I abandoned of obedience to Allah and Allah's commands and rewards."[274] Imām al-Ālūsī—may Allah have mercy upon him—said: "In general, it is not possible to leave the words in their literal sense, for He ﷻ, is transcendent above possessing a literal side. I have not come across any of the *Salaf* who counted it among the transmitted attributes [*ṣifāt al-samʿiyya*]."[275]

---

[271] *Tafsīr al-Ṭabarī*, 18:135.
[272] *Tafsīr al-Qurṭubī*, 18:165.
[273] *Tafsīr al-Ṭabarī*, 29:38; *Tafsīr al-Qurṭubī*, 18:249.
[274] *Rūḥ al-Maʿānī*: *āya* 57 of *Zumar*.
[275] Ibid.

This is all from our liege lord Ibn ʿAbbās ﷺ. It goes without saying that Ibn ʿAbbās had immense knowledge in jurisprudence, the Qur'ān, and revelation. He is the one the Messenger of Allah ﷺ prayed for when he said: "O Allah! Grant him profound knowledge of the religion and teach him the interpretation." He is the *ḥabr* [scholarly ocean] of this Umma and the interpreter of the Qur'ān [*tarjumān al-Qur'ān*].

The position adopted by the Ashʿarīs and Māturīdīs with regards to these texts is the exact same position quoted from Ibn ʿAbbās ﷺ. So if it is allowable to accuse the Ashʿarīs and Māturīdīs with extreme denial and blameworthy innovation, it is also allowed to accuse our liege lord Ibn ʿAbbās with the same—and Allah's refuge is sought! Allah forbid that he says about Allah what he does not know!

Let the one who receives an admonition from His Lord fear Him and beware of high-handedness against the Imāms of this religion and the scholars of the Sacred Law. Any high-handedness against them is in reality high-handedness against the Companions of the Messenger of Allah ﷺ and those who followed them with excellence.

Mujāhid and al-Suddī's interpretation of the word "side" [*janb*]

In *Tafsīr al-Ṭabarī* there appears the following interpretation of Allah's words: ﴾*That a soul says: "O what severe regret for my negligence in the side* [*janb*] *of Allah!"*﴿: "Mujāhid said: 'In the command of Allah.' Al-Suddī said: 'For what I have abandoned of Allah's command.'"[276]

The interpretation of al-Ḍaḥḥāk, Qatāda, and Saʿīd b. Jubayr for the word "shin" [*sāq*]

It says in *Tafsīr al-Ṭabarī*, commenting on Allah's words: ﴾*On the day a shin* [*sāq*] *shall be unveiled*﴿: "Al-Ḍaḥḥāk said: 'It is a severe matter.' Qatāda said: 'A horrible matter and severe affair.' Saʿīd said: 'The severity of the matter.'"

[276] *Tafsīr al-Ṭabarī*, 24:19.

Before quoting them, Imām al-Ṭabarī said: "Groups among the Companions, followers, and people of interpretation said: 'He will disclose a severe matter.'"[277]

The interpretation of Sufyān al-Thawrī and Ibn Jarīr al-Ṭabarī for "rising" [*istiwā'*]

Imām al-Ṭabarī said in his commentary on Allah's words: ﴾*Then He rose* [*istawā'*] *to the heavens*﴿ after mentioning the lexical meanings of "rising": "He elevated above them and rose, managing them with His power... He rose above them with the loftiness of dominion and authority, not the loftiness of displacement and movement."[278]

Sufyān al-Thawrī interpreted "rising above the Throne" as "intending His command" and "rising to the heavens" as "intending them."[279]

The interpretation of Mujāhid, al-Ḍaḥḥāk, and Abū 'Ubayda for the word "face" [*wajh*]

Allah, the Exalted, said: ﴾*So wherever you turn there is the face* [*wajh*] *of Allah.*﴿ Mujāhid—may Allah have mercy upon him—said: "The *qibla* of Allah."[280]

Al-Ḍaḥḥāk and Abū 'Ubayda said regarding Allah's words: ﴾*Everything shall perish except His face* [*wajh*]﴿: "In other words, except Him."[281]

Imām al-Shāfi'ī's interpretation of the word "face" [*wajh*]

Al-Mizzī narrated from al-Shāfi'ī regarding the words of Allah: ﴾*...there is the face* [*wajh*] *of Allah*﴿: "Allah knows best, but it means there is the direction which Allah has directed you towards."[282]

---

[277] Ibid., 29:38–39.

[278] Ibid., 1:192.

[279] *Mirqāt al-Mafātīḥ*, 2:137.

[280] *Tafsīr al-Ṭabarī*, 1:402; al-Bayhaqī, *Al-Asmā' wal-Ṣifāt*, p. 309; authenticated by Ibn Taymiyya as mentioned in *Al-'Uqūd al-Durriyya*, pp. 247–248.

[281] *Dafa' Shubha al-Tashbīh*, p. 113.

[282] Al-Bayhaqī, *Al-Asmā' wal-Ṣifāt*, p. 309.

Imām al-Ṭabarī's interpretation of the word "eye" [ʿ*ayn*]

He said in his interpretation of Allah's words: ﴿*And let it be built under My eye*﴾: "In My vision and with love and will."[283]

Imām Mālik's interpretation of the Ḥadīth of "descent"

Imām Mālik ﵀ said in his figurative interpretation of "descent" [*nuzūl*] mentioned in the Ḥadīth: "His command/affair descends each night." He said: "As for Him ﷻ, He is Permanent and does not pass or displace Himself—there is no god but He."[284]

Imām Aḥmad's interpretation of Allah's coming[285]

---

[283] *Tafsīr al-Ṭabarī*, 16:123.

[284] See: *Al-Tamhīd*, 7:143; Imām al-Nawawī's *Sharḥ Ṣaḥīḥ Muslim*, 6:37; *Siyar ʿAlām al-Nubalāʾ*, 8:105; *Al-Inṣāf* of Ibn al-Sayyid al-Baṭlayūsī, p. 81.

[285] Ibn Taymiyya mentioned that the Ḥanbalīs differed regarding the affirmation of this from Aḥmad ﵀. He said: "Some of them said that [the narrator] Ḥanbal was mistaken and that Aḥmad did not say this. Others said that Ḥanbal had well-known errors and this was one of them—and this is the position of Abū Isḥāq b. Shāqilā.

Others said Aḥmad did in fact say this as an implication against the Muʿtazila during a debate... A third group of Aḥmad's companions said it at that time, and they made this a narration from him. Then there are some who adopted the way of figurative interpretation, such as Ibn ʿAqīl, Ibn al-Jawzī, and others, and they took this as their reliance...

Then he [Ibn Taymiyya] said: "And there is no doubt that what is quoted and mass-transmitted from Aḥmad contradicts this narration and clarifies that he does not say that the Lord's command come, arrives, and descends. Rather, he censures those who say that." (*Al-Fatāwā* 5:499)

He—may Allah have mercy upon him—did not bring a proof to negate and falsify this narration. The fact that the famous position recorded from Imām Aḥmad is to not engage in figurative interpretation does not contradict this narration. It is possible that the well-known position from the Imām is one thing, and the rare exception is still reported from him, especially considering that there is no contradiction between the two matters. Certainly there are reports from the *Salaf* in which they spoke about refraining from figurative interpretation and mentioned their hatred for engaging in that. At the same time, however, there are reports from them in which they interpreted certain expressions. There is no harm in either of the two methods. Their famous words against interpretation do not cancel out their other words.

In *Al-Bidāya wal-Nihāya* of the Imām and Ḥadīth master Ibn Kathīr—may Allah have mercy upon him—it reads: "Al-Bayhaqī narrated from al-Ḥākim from ʿAmr b. al-Samāk from Ḥanbal that Aḥmad b. Ḥanbal interpreted Allah's words: ﴾*And you Lord shall come...*﴿ saying that His reward shall come... And al-Bayhaqī said: 'There is no problem with its chain [*lā ghubār ʿalayhi*].'"[286]

Al-Ḥāfiẓ Ibn al-Jawzī—may Allah have mercy upon him—reported from Qāḍī Abū Yaʿlā from Imām Aḥmad regarding Allah's words: ﴾*Do they await but that Allah should come to them in covers of clouds...*﴿ that he said: "What He means is His power and command. This was clarified in the words of the Exalted: ﴾*...or the command of your Lord comes.*﴿" Another example of this in the Qur'ān is His statement: ﴾*And your Lord shall come.*﴿ He said: "This refers only to His power."[287]

Al-Ḥasan al-Baṣrī's interpretation

Regarding this verse, al-Ḥasan al-Baṣrī ﷺ said: "His command and decree come." Al-Kalbī said: "His judgement shall come."[288] He also said regarding the verse: ﴾*That a soul says: "O what severe regret for my negligence in the side* [*janb*] *of Allah!"*﴿: "In Allah's obedience."[289]

Imām al-Bukhārī's interpretation of "laughter" [*ḍaḥak*]

Imām al-Bayhaqī—may Allah have mercy upon him—said in his book *Al-Asmā' wal-Ṣifāt*:

Moreover, Ibn Taymiyya's judgment is not binding, especially considering those who oppose him from both the early and latter-day Ḥanbalīs, as well as others, such as Imām al-Bayhaqī who declared the chain of this narration from Aḥmad rigorously authentic, and those who agreed with him, such as Ibn Kathīr, who mentioned his narration without the slightest criticism or comments—and he was the verifier of reports and a student of Ibn Taymiyya. No matter the case, the other reports we have cited from the *Salaf* are sufficient, even if this report is not authentically established from Aḥmad.

[286] *Al-Bidāya wal-Nihāya*, 10:361.

[287] *Dafaʿ Shubha al-Tashbīh*, p. 141.

[288] *Tafsīr al-Baghawī*, 4:454.

[289] *Rūḥ al-Maʿānī*: *āya* 57 of *Zumar*.

> Chapter: What has been mentioned regarding "laughter"... Abū Hurayra related from the Messenger of Allah ﷺ who said: "Allah laughs at two men, one of whom kills the other and both enter Paradise..." Imām al-Bukhārī said: "The meaning of 'laughter' [here] is mercy."
>
> Abu Sulaymān [al-Khaṭṭābī] said: "The statement of Abū 'Abdillāh [al-Bukhārī] is approximate, but interpreting it as pleasure for their action [the action of the two men] is closer and more appropriate. It is known that laughter from those of discernment indicates pleasure, and that smiling and jubilance from them indicate the acceptance of the means of approach, and that they are the precursors to the fulfilment of requests. The people of nobility, when asked, are described with smiling and a cheerful countenance—hence the meaning of his statement: "Allah laughs at two men..." is that He bestows them with bountiful giving because that is what 'laughter' entails and implies."[290]

Al-Ḥāfiẓ Ibn Ḥajar supported the view of al-Khaṭṭābī and the notable knowers of Allah. He said: "Another proof that indicates that the intended meaning of 'laughter' is pleasure is that it is made transitive by the governing particle *ilā* (to/at). You say: 'So-and-so laughed at [*ilā*] so-and-so' if he smiled at him, manifesting pleasure with him."[291]

Imām al-Bukhārī's interpretation of the word "face" [*wajh*]
Imām al-Bukhārī—may Allah have mercy upon him—said in his exegesis of Allah's words: ﴾*Everything shall perish except His face* [*wajh*]﴿: "Everything except His dominion. It is also said: 'Except that which is intended for Allah's sake.'"[292]

We have previously mentioned the consensus of the Umma regarding the method of figurative interpretation. Al-Ḥāfiẓ Abū al-Ḥasan 'Alī b. al-Qaṭṭān—may Allah have mercy upon him—said:

---

[290] *Al-Asmā' wal-Sifāt*, p. 470.
[291] *Fatḥ al-Bārī*, 6:486.
[292] Ibid., 8:364.

> And they concurred that He, the Exalted, comes on the Day of Judgment, along with the Angels, in rows upon rows, in order to present the nations and to take them to account and punish and reward them. He shall forgive whom He wills from the believers and punish from them he whom He wills, as the Exalted said. His coming is not through movement or displacement.
>
> They also concurred that He, the Exalted, is pleased with those who are obedient to Him, and that His pleasure with them is His will to bestow upon them His bounty.
>
> They also concurred that He loves the penitent and is displeased and angry with the disbelievers, and that His anger is His will to punish them, and that nothing stands in the way of His anger...[293]

The Umma's consensus to disregard the outward meaning of "coming" that is impossible for Allah, the Exalted, which is movement and displacement, is a consensus to *tafwīḍ*, and their consensus to understand the expression "pleasure" as His will to bestow bounty and goodness, and the expression "anger" as His will to punish and take vengeance is a consensus to figurative interpretation. This once again emphasizes the point we have made that both the way of *tafwīḍ* and the way of figurative interpretation are two well-pleasing paths that are well-considered and relied upon by the Umma.

These quotes of figurative interpretation from the *Salaf* are only a small sample. Whoever would like more examples should refer back to the books of our heritage, such as the books of Qur'ānic exegesis, Ḥadīth, legal theory, and more.

Notice

There is a misconception that is often repeated by those who affirm the outward meanings of these ambiguous texts. They say that the affirmation of general meanings for these texts does not negate the specific affirmation of the attributes mentioned within them. So, for example, when Allah says: ﴾*Rather, His two hands are outstretched*﴿ they say: "We do not deny that this text indicates the affirmation of His generosity and magnimity,

---

[293] *Al-Iqnāʿ fī Masāʾil al-Ijmāʿ*, 1:32–43.

Exalted is He, and the negation of stinginess; this meaning of "outstretched hands" is well-known with the Arabs. With that, however, it does not negate the affirmation of the attribute of a "hand" for Allah, the Exalted. And the same may be said regarding all of the texts that pertain to the Divine attributes, such as shin in Allah's words: ﴾*On the day a shin is unveiled*﴿; the fact that it means the severity of the matter or a tribulation does not negate that Allah possesses a literal shin."

Response

If by affirming the attributes he means affirming them as they have appeared without providing an explanation or imparting a specific meaning, and that it is sufficient to recite them and remain silent—which is clearly after disregarding the outward meaning that is impossible for Allah—and that it is not said "with His Essence" or "literally," then that is the truth without doubt. That is the way of the pious predecessors and it does not contradict the way of the latter-day scholars.

This can be explained by the following example. In the text, it is mentioned that Allah, the Exalted, possesses "two hands," therefore we affirm for Him "two hands" that are not physical limbs and then we remain silent and entrust the knowledge of what is meant to Allah, the Exalted. There is no disagreement regarding the soundness of this approach and it is the way of the pious predecessors. If, by affirming it, one means that the wording is understood according to its outward and literal meaning as conventionally known in the language, then that is clearly false, and we have quoted many statements from the scholars where they negated this and refuted it, so there is no need to mention them again.

Having said that, we must add: not everything that is ascribed to Allah, the Exalted, is meant to be affirmed as an attribute. An ascription might be a type of similarity or converse statement, such as mocking, plotting, deception, and other similar expressions. These expressions cannot be used to affirm attributes for Allah, such as saying that Allah has a plot that befits Him and a mocking that befits Him—Exalted is He above that! Included with that are the attributes of imperfection, such as boredom, forgetfulness, sickness, amazement, hesitation, and so on. Allah is transcendent—both rationally and textually—from these things and their likes. He is not to be described with any of that. Also included with that are the expressions that have well-known figurative meanings, such as the expressions side, finger, and so on. There is no disagreement that these expressions and their likes are interpreted according to their well-known meaning.

Al-Ḥāfiẓ Ibn Ḥajar quoted the words of Ibn Daqīq al-ʿĪd:

> "Regarding the recondite attributes, we say that they are real and the truth according to the meaning intended by Allah. Whoever interprets them, we look; if his interpretation is proximate based on the Arabic language we do no censure him, and if it is far-fetched we hold back from it and return to conviction coupled with belief in Divine transcendence.
>
> If it has an apparent meaning that is understood in the speech of the Arabs we interpret it as such, like Allah's words: ﴾*...for my negligence in the side [janb] of Allah!"*﴿ What is meant by this, according to their widespread usage, is the right of Allah; so there should be no hesitation in interpreting it as such. Similarly his ﷺ statement: "Indeed, the heart of the son of Ādam is between the two fingers of the fingers of the All-Merciful." This means that the will of the son of Ādam is changed by the power of Allah and what He places in it. Similarly, Allah's words: ﴾*So Allah came to their structures from the foundations.*﴿ This means that Allah demolished their structures. His statement: ﴾*We only feed you for the face of Allah*﴿ means "for the sake of Allah"—and so on. This is a great amount of detail and few are those who are attentive to it.[294]

Shaykh ʿAlī al-Ṭanṭāwī—may Allah have mercy upon him—said:

> If languages are unable to encompass human emotions, then they are even more incapable of encompassing the attributes of Allah. Hence, it is impermissible for one to understand the words used in the verses of the attributes

[294] *Fatḥ al-Bārī*, 13:395.

according to their lexical meaning, and it is impermissible for us to say: "Allah possesses a hand like our hands, as proven by the words of the Exalted: ﴾*Allah's hand is above their hands*﴿ because the meaning of 'hand,' as found in the dictionary, proves that." This is the foundation for understanding the verses pertaining to the attributes, as the Exalted said: ﴾*There is nothing like unto Him*﴿ and because the Creator does not resemble the creation.

In addition, it is impermissible for us to negate every meaning and cancel out any indication [*dilāla*], for Allah did not reveal the Qur'ān in order for its meanings to be cancelled out and He did not make it a collection of empty words that indicate nothing. Therefore, how do we understand the verses pertaining to the attributes? I have found that these verses take on three forms.

[1] Verses in which Allah is informing us of something, such as His words: ﴾*The All-Merciful rose above the Throne.*﴿ We do not say that He didn't perform the act of *istiwā'*, thereby negating what Allah affirmed. Similarly, we do not say that He rose above the Throne as a seated person rises above a chair, thereby having the Creator resemble the creation. Rather, we believe that this is the speech of Allah and that Allah has an intended meaning whose reality and details we do not understand, because He did not detail it to us, and because the human intellect is incapable of reaching that on its own. We do not delve into the matter; nay, we follow the way of the *Salaf* in it. The *Salaf* did not look into the matter to begin with and they did not say: "Literally" or "Figuratively."

[2] Verses that employ a rhetorical style known by the scholars of rhetoric as similarity [*mushākala*]...There are many verses that express this style, such as the words of the Exalted: ﴾*They forgot Allah so He forgot them*﴿, ﴾*And they plotted and Allah plotted...*﴿ and ﴾*The seek to deceive Allah but Allah deceives them.*﴿

[3] Verses that have intended meanings that are indicated in other verses, such as Allah's words: ﴾*The Jews said: "Allah's hand is tied up." May their hands be tied up and may they be cursed on account of what they said. Nay, His hands are outstretched; spending how He wills.*﴿ The intended meaning of this verse is indicated in the other verse:

> ﴾*And do not tie your hands up to your neck and do not outstretch them completely.*﴿ It is understood from this that the outstretching of the hand means generosity and magnimity. That does not necessitate—nay it is impossible—that Allah possesses two literal hands like the hands of people, and in the Qur'ān He said: ﴾*Between the two hands of His mercy*﴿ and ﴾*Between the two hands of a severe torment.*﴿ Mercy, torment, and the Qur'ān do not possess two literal hands [either].[295]

It is important to mention here and warn against a strange method and path that deviates from the fundamentals of knowledge—especially in the realm of doctrine and the Divine attributes that depends on decisive and certain evidence. This path is one in which its adherents affirm attributes for Allah from Ḥadīth reports and texts that are not suitable for being evidence in the subsidiary details of jurisprudence, much less the fundamentals of the religion and what pertains to Allah's Entity and attributes.

Those who follow this strange path are contradictory in their rulings, for while they are lax in the area of affirmation, affirming attributes for Allah based on spurious Ḥadīth and weak reports,[296] they are extreme in subsidiary branches of jurisprudence, nay, even in the area of encouragement and discouragement [encouragement to good actions and discouragement from bad actions: *al-targhīb wal-tarhīb*], virtuous actions [*faḍā'il al-ʿamāl*], and merits [*manāqib*]—areas in which the scholars were not so stringent in accepting Ḥadīth related to them with their well-known prerequisites.

They censure people for acting in accordance with weak Ḥadīth in these areas, but they affirm attributes for Allah based on Ḥadīth that are at the exact same level of authenticity—nay, what is weaker still. They are extreme in areas of ease and they are lax in areas where one must be strict and certain, like

---

[295] *Taʿrīf ʿĀm bi-Dīn al-Islām*, p. 82.

[296] Nay, if the Ḥadīth was authentic and was a singular report [*āḥād*] but contained that which contradicted the unequivocal rational proofs and could not possibly be interpreted in a manner that conforms to these unequivocal proofs, it is obligatory to reject it and it cannot be used.

doctrine. What we have said here is if, for argument's sake, the contents of those Ḥadīth reports and narrations that they affirm for Allah as attributes contain that which is textually and rationally possible, what, then, if the matter is quite the opposite and the outward meanings of those reports are textually and rationally impossible? No doubt the tribulation would be greater and the danger more severe!

Earlier we mentioned the golden principle of Imām al-Ubbī. There is no harm in repeating it once more:

> The principle that must be given consideration is: that which is impossible to ascribe to the Divine Essence or the attributes, is impossible for to be found in a mass-transmitted decisive text that does not carry the possibility of interpretation. The most that can occur is for a mass-transmitted text to indicate something impossible via its outward indication [*dilāla ẓāhira*], and that which is outwardly apparent can accept interpretation. So, if such [a text] is cited, its outward and impossible meaning must be disregarded.
>
> After that, there was a difference of opinion. Most of the *Salaf* refrained from figurative interpretation and said: "We believe in it as it is with Allah in reality, and we entrust the knowledge of that to Allah, the Glorified." Some folk, nay even among the first group [the *Salaf*], took the position of figurative interpretation... And if a singular report contains a decisive text with something that is impossible, its narrator is unequivocally judged as a liar, and if it carries the possibility of figurative interpretation it is given an alternative meaning as we mentioned previously.[297]

This principle that is agreed upon by all the great minds from the notables of this Umma, the Imāms of the Muslims, and the knowers of Allah, shows the mistakes of those who are reckless in this issue.

---

297 *Sharḥ Muslim*, 7:54.

Chapter Ten

The Ashʿarīs and Māturīdīs are the Majority of the Umma

The scholars of the Umma are the stars of the heavens: by them, he who is covered in the darkness of perplexity and confused about the sign posts is guided aright. When he sees elders in front of him whose virtue the Umma has testified to and whom the common folk and elite meet with acceptance, he knows that their way is the way of guidance and the straight path.

The way of the Ashʿarīs and those who agree with them from Ahl al-Sunna is the way followed by the great bulk of the Umma and its senior people of virtue—as we have quoted from the words of the scholars. This is because the way of the Ashʿarīs is a natural extension of the way of the Companions, the followers, and their followers.

There remains not a single science wherein they are not its leaders; they left not a single door of knowledge save that the entered it; in every science of the Sacred Law and in other sciences they have exerted a major influence.

The Senior Qur'ānic Exegetes of the Umma from the Ashʿarīs and Māturīdīs

One of the sciences in which Ahl al-Sunna have dominance and distinction is the exegesis of Allah's Book and its ancillary sciences such as the canonical modes of recitation, the rare and obscure words [in the Qur'ān], etc. A quick glance at the notables of the science will unveil this reality.

- The esteemed Imām, Qur'ānic exegete, and Ḥadīth scholar, al-Qurṭubī—may Allah have mercy upon him. He is the author of *Al-Jāmiʿ li-Aḥkām al-Qur'ān*. His excellent exegesis is widely popular. In it, he narrated the views of all of the *Salaf*. Al-Dāwūdī said about it in his *Ṭabaqāt*: "It is from the noblest of commentaries and one of the greatest of them in benefit."

- The Imām, Ḥadīth master, and Qur'ānic exegete, Abū al-Fidā' Ismā'īl b. Kathīr—may Allah have mercy upon him. He is the author of *Tafsīr al-Qur'ān al-'Aẓīm*, *Al-Bidāya wal-Nihāya*, and others. It was mentioned that he explicitly said he was an Ash'arī. In addition to that, he was placed in charge of Dār al-Ḥadīth al-Ashrafiyya, and one of the preconditions placed on it by the initial endower was that only an Ash'arī can be placed in charge of it.[298] In addition to that, in his exegesis there are declarations of Divine transcendence and rebuke against those who take the outward meanings of the ambiguous texts, as we mentioned regarding his explanation of Allah's words: ﴾*Then He rose above the Throne.*﴿ There are other clear examples in his exegesis that show he was from Ahl al-Sunna: an Ash'arī.
- The Imām and esteemed Qur'ānic exegete, the exemplar of all exegetes, Ibn 'Aṭiyya al-Andalūsī—may Allah have mercy upon him. He is the author of *Tafsīr al-Muḥarrar al-Wajīz*. He wrote his exegesis in the best of ways. He was from the virtuous people of Ahl al-Sunna wal-Jamā'a and from the senior people of goodness. Abū Ḥayyān al-Andalūsī said concerning him: "He is the noblest of those who wrote in the science of Qur'ānic exegesis and the best of those who took it upon themselves to examine it and record it."[299]
- Imām Abū al-Ḥayyān al-Andalūsī—may Allah have mercy upon him. He is the author of *Al-Baḥr al-Muḥīṭ wal-Nahr al-Mād min al-Baḥr*. He is the reliable proof and linguist and is in no need of introduction.
- The foremost Imām, Fakhr al-Dīn al-Rāzī—may Allah have mercy upon him. He is the author of *Tafsīr Mafātīḥ al-Ghayb*. He was a Qur'ānic exegete, a theologian, the Imām of his age, and the inimitable one of his era. He was a thorn in the throats of the innovators and an unsheathed sword against the people of deviation and heresy.

---

[298] See: *Al-Ṭabaqāt al-Kubrā*, 10:200, 398.
[299] *Muqaddima al-Baḥr al-Muḥīṭ*.

- The Imām, Qur'ānic exegete, Ḥadīth master, and reviver of the Sunna, al-Baghawī—may Allah have mercy upon him. He is the author of the book *Sharḥ al-Sunna*. His exegesis is filled with that which proves the doctrine of Ahl al-Sunna and it is filled with the Sunni figurative interpretation of the ambiguous texts.
- The Imām and Qur'ānic exegete, Abū al-Layth al-Samarqandī—may Allah have mercy upon him. He is the author of *Baḥr al-ʿUlūm*, *Tanbīh al-Ghāfilīn*, and *Bustān al-ʿĀrifīn*. He was given the nickname of "Imām of guidance."
- The Imām and Qur'ānic exegete, al-Wāḥidī: Abū al-Ḥasan ʿAlī al-Naysabūrī. He was the chief scholar of his time in grammar and Qur'ānic exegesis. He was a Sunni Ashʿarī from Ahl al-Sunna wal-Jamāʿa. He is the author of many beneficial works and splendid allusions. He has a book on the circumstances behind revelation [*asbāb al-nuzūl*] and it is one of the most famous books on the topic.
- The Imām and Qur'ānic exegete, Abū al-Thanā' Shihāb al-Dīn al-Ālūsī al-Ḥusaynī al-Ḥasanī—may Allah have mercy upon him. He was the seal of the Qur'ānic exegetes and the cream of the Ḥadīth scholars, as described by Shaykh Bahja al-Bayṭār. He also said about him: "He ﷺ was one of the unique ones of the world; he would speak the truth and would never swerve from veracity; he used to cling firmly to the Sunna and keep away from tribulations."[300]
- The Imām and Qur'ānic exegete, al-Samīn al-Ḥalabī—may Allah have mercy upon him. He is the author of *Al-Durr al-Maṣūn*.
- The Ḥadīth master and Qur'ānic exegete, Jalāl al-Dīn al-Suyūṭī—may Allah have mercy upon him. He is the author of *Al-Durr al-Manthūr fī al-Tafsīr bil-Ma'thūr*.
- The Imām, al-Khaṭīb al-Shirbīnī—may Allah have mercy upon him. He is the author of *Al-Sirāj al-Munīr*.

There are many other Qur'ānic exegetes who were from Ahl al-Sunna: Ashʿarīs or Māturīdīs. Were we to mention all of them it would take us away from the goal of this book.

[300] *Ḥilya al-Bashar*: 3:1450.

Notice

We have only mentioned those who came after Imām al-Ash'arī and followed his way and we did not mention the Shaykh and head of the Qur'ānic exegetes, the Ḥadīth master and exegete Muḥammad b. Jarīr al-Ṭabarī—may Allah have mercy upon him. He was a contemporary of Imām al-Ash'arī and died before him, so it is not farfetched to imagine that he came across some of the many written works of Imām al-Ash'arī and benefitted from them, especially considering the fact that they lived in the same city.

Whoever looks deeply into the exegesis of Imām al-Ṭabarī will see that this is not farfetched. It is authentically reported from him that he engaged in some figurative interpretation for some of the ambiguous verses and he cited some of the interpretations of the *Salaf* among the Companions and followers and supported them. Moreover, it is not farfetched to imagine that he might have ascribed himself to al-Ash'arī in that which has not reached us of his books. The books of history mention that all of Ahl al-Sunna in the Islamic world came to the aid and defence of Imām Abū al-Ḥasan and Imām Abū al-Manṣūr. Perhaps the position taken by some bigoted Ḥanbalīs against Ibn Jarīr strengthens this assumption.

No matter the case, it is enough for us that he was in agreement with the doctrine of declaring Allah's transcendence, and that is enough for us to consider Imām al-Ṭabarī among the aforementioned Qur'ānic exegetes—nay, he is at their forefront. What matters is the creed of Ahl al-Sunna wal-Jamā'a, whether one ascribes to al-Ash'arī or not.

SOME OF THE LATTER-DAY ASH'ARĪ QUR'ĀNIC EXEGETES

- The Shaykh and caller, Sayyid Quṭb—may Allah have mercy upon him. He is the author of the tremendous book *Fī Ẓilāl al-Qur'ān*.
- The Shaykh and erudite scholar, al-Ṭāhir b. 'Āshūr. He is the author of the tremendous exegesis, *Al-Taḥrīr wal-Tanwīr*.

- The Ustādh and caller, Shaykh Saʿīd Ḥawwā—may Allah have mercy upon him. He is the author of *Al-Asās fī al-Tafsīr*.
- The Shaykh and erudite scholar, Muḥammad Mutawallī al-Shaʿrāwī—may Allah have mercy upon him—whose name has become connected with the Qur'ān, so much that when the Qur'ān is mentioned the Shaykh is mentioned, and when the Shaykh is mentioned, the Qur'ān is mentioned.
- The Shaykh and Professor, Wahba al-Zuḥaylī—may Allah have mercy upon him. He is the author of *Al-Tafsīr al-Munīr*, *Al-Fiqh al-Islāmī*, and other useful works.

THE SENIOR ḤADĪTH SCHOLARS AND MASTERS OF THE UMMA FROM THE ASHʿARĪS AND MĀTURĪDĪS

- The Imām and Ḥadīth master, Abū al-Ḥasan al-Dāraquṭnī—may Allah have mercy upon him. He was the Imām of his era and he did not narrate to anyone of his likes. His story with Imām al-Bāqillānī is enough to establish that he followed the way of al-Ashʿarī.[301]
- The Ḥadīth master, Abū Nuʿaym al-Aṣfahānī—may Allah have mercy upon him. He is the author of *Ḥilya al-Awliyā'* and was from the second rank of al-Ashʿarī's followers. He was from the rank of Imām al-Bāqillānī, Ustādh Abū Isḥāq al-Isfarāyīnī, al-Ḥākim, and Ibn Fūrak—may Allah have mercy upon them all.[302]
- The Ḥadīth master, Abū Dharr al-Harawī: ʿAbdullāh b. Aḥmad—may Allah have mercy upon him. Al-Ḥāfiẓ Ibn ʿAsākir counted him among the third rank, from

[301] See: *Tabyīn Kadhib al-Muftarī*, p. 255; *Siyar ʿAlām al-Nubalā'*, 17:558 (in the biography of the Ḥadīth master, Abū Dharr al-Harawī); and *Tadhkira al-Ḥuffāẓ*, 3:1104.

[302] See: *Tabyīn Kadhib al-Muftarī*, p. 246; *Al-Ṭabaqāt al-Kubrā*, 3:370; and the two events that happened to al-Aṣfahānī mentioned by al-Dhahabī in *Siyar ʿAlām al-Nubalā'*, 18:41, 459.

those who took from the companions of al-Ash'arī's companions.[303]

- The Ḥadīth master, Abū Ṭāhir al-Silafī—may Allah have mercy upon him.[304]
- The Ḥadīth master, al-Ḥākim al-Naysabūrī—may Allah have mercy upon him. He is the author of *Al-Mustadrak 'alā al-Ṣaḥīḥayn*. He was the Imām of the traditionists [*ahl al-Ḥadīth*] in his time and he is in no need of introduction. The scholars are in agreement that he was one of the most knowledgeable Imāms by whom Allah protected this religion. Al-Ḥāfiẓ Ibn 'Asākir mentioned him among the second rank, from the companions of those who took directly from al-Ash'arī.[305]
- The Ḥadīth master, Ibn Ḥibbān al-Bustī—may Allah have mercy upon him. He is the author of *Ṣaḥīḥ Ibn Ḥibbān, Kitāb al-Thiqāt*, and others. He is the reliable Imām and the exemplar of his time who was at the forefront. His *Ṣaḥīḥ* collection is the best testimony to that.
- The Ḥadīth master, Abū Sa'd b. al-Sam'ānī[306]—may Allah have mercy upon him. He is the author of *Al-Ansāb*.[307]
- The Imām and Ḥadīth master, Abū Bakr al-Bayhaqī—may Allah have mercy upon him. He is the author of many works that have spread around the world entire and that are considered well-pleasing to friend and foe alike.
- The Imām and Ḥadīth master, Ibn 'Asākir—may Allah have mercy upon him. He is the author of *Tārīkh Dimashq* —an encyclopaedic book in which he left nothing too small or great without mention.
- The Imām and Ḥadīth master, al-Khaṭīb al-Baghdādī—may Allah have mercy upon him. Al-Ḥāfiẓ Ibn 'Asākir mentioned him among the first of the fourth rank.[308]

---

303 Ibid.
304 See: *Al-Ṭabaqāt al-Kubrā*, 3:372.
305 See: *Tabyīn Kadhib al-Muftarī*, p. 227.
306 The Sam'ānī family are all either Ash'arīs or Māturīdīs.
307 See: *Al-Ṭabaqāt*: 3:372.
308 See: *Tabyīn Kadhib al-Muftarī*, p. 268.

- The Imām and Ḥadīth master, Muḥyī al-Dīn Yaḥyā b. Sharaf al-Dīn al-Nawawī—may Allah have mercy upon him. He is the author of many books for which Allah has placed acceptance in the world among people.
- The Imām and verifier, the remnant of the early Ḥadīth masters, Ṣalāḥ al-Dīn Khalīl b. Kīlkuldī al-ʿAlāʾī. He did not leave anyone after him as strong as him in Ḥadīth and he had no contemporary who could outmatch him in it.
- The Shaykh al-Islam and Ḥadīth master, Abū ʿAmr b. al-Ṣalāḥ—may Allah have mercy upon him. He was the first person placed in charge of Dar al-Ḥadīth al-Ashrafiyya, in which it was stipulated that only an Ashʿarī could take charge of it.
- The Imām and Ḥadīth master, Ibn Abī Jamra al-Andalūsī, the master narrator of the Maghreb—may Allah have mercy upon him and be pleased with him. He is the author of the book *Bahja al-Nufūs fī Sharḥ Miʾa Ḥadīth min Ṣaḥīḥ al-Bukhārī*.
- The Imām and Ḥadīth master, al-Kirmānī: Shams al-Dīn Muḥammad b. Yūsuf—may Allah have mercy upon him and be pleased with him. He is the author of the well-known commentary of *Ṣaḥīḥ al-Bukhārī*.
- The Imām and Ḥadīth master, al-Mundhirī—may Allah have mercy upon him. He is the author of *Al-Targhīb wal-Tarhīb*.
- The Imām and Ḥadīth master, al-Ubbī—may Allah have mercy upon him. He is the author of a commentary on *Ṣaḥīḥ Muslim*.
- The Imām and Ḥadīth master, Ibn Ḥajar al-ʿAsqalānī—may Allah have mercy upon him. He is the author of the greatest commentary on *Ṣaḥīḥ al-Bukhārī*: *Fatḥ al-Bārī*. Due to its high rank and general benefit, it has been said: "There is no migration after the *Fatḥ*."[309]

---

[309] This is taken from the Ḥadīth of the Prophet ﷺ: "There is no migration after the conquest [*fatḥ*] (of Mecca), but there remains struggle [*jihād*] and good intention." (Al-Bukhārī). This means there is no

- The Imām and Ḥadīth master, al-Sakhāwī—may Allah have mercy upon him.
- The Imām and Ḥadīth master, al-Suyūṭī—may Allah have mercy upon him.
- Imām al-Qasṭalānī—may Allah have mercy upon him—a commentator on *Ṣaḥīḥ al-Bukhārī.*
- The Imām and Ḥadīth master, al-Munāwī—may Allah have mercy upon him.

There are many other Imāms and Ḥadīth masters of the Umma that were from Ahl al-Sunna: the Ash'arīs and Māturīdīs.

Imām Tāj al-Dīn al-Subkī—may Allah have mercy upon him—said: "And it [the doctrine of al-Ash'arī] was the doctrine of the Ḥadīth scholars then and now."[310]

THE SENIOR JURISTS OF THE UMMA FROM THE ASH'ARĪS AND MĀTURĪDĪS

Al-Ḥāfiẓ Ibn 'Asākir—may Allah have mercy upon him—said:

> "Most of the scholars from all of the lands are upon it [the way of al-Ash'arī] and the Imāms of the of the capitals in all eras call to it, ...is there any of the jurists among the Ḥanafīs, Mālikīs, and Shāfi'īs except that he ascribes to it, or is pleased with its praiseworthy efforts in the religion of Allah, or lauds the great knowledge found within it?"[311]

Imām Tāj al-Dīn al-Subkī—may Allah have mercy upon him—said:

> Shaykh al-Islam, 'Izz al-Dīn b. 'Abd al-Salām mentioned that his [al-Ash'arī's] doctrine was unanimously agreed upon by the Shāfi'īs, Mālikīs, Ḥanafīs, and the virtuous Ḥanbalīs. [He mentioned] that his contemporaries who

---

migration in pursuit of Sacred Knowledge after the writing of *Fatḥ al-Bārī*, due to the vast amount of knowledge it contains. [t]

[310] *Al-Ṭabaqāt*, 4:32.

[311] *Tabyīn Kadhib al-Muftarī*, p. 410.

agreed with him included the Shaykh of the Mālikīs in his time, Abu ʿAmr b. al-Ḥājib, and the Shaykh of the Ḥanafīs, Jamāl al-Dīn al- Ḥaṣīrī.[312]

Imām Abū al-Muẓaffar al-Isfarāyīnī—may Allah have mercy upon him—said: "...and the science of jurisprudence; and those who delve deep into it are the traditionists and the people of analogy."[313]

The statements of these notables suffice us from mentioning the names of all of the scholars who surpassed the stars of the heavens in number and rank. Whoever would like to enumerate their names may go back to the biographical works on the jurists and see the reality of what we say.

THE NOTABLE SCHOLARS OF LANGUAGE AND LITERATURE FROM THE ASHʿARĪS AND MĀTURĪDĪS

Imām Abū Muẓaffar al-Isfarāyīnī—may Allah have mercy upon him—said:

> The general body of the Imāms in grammar and philology from the people of Basra and Kufa in the Islamic *dawla* [the ʿAbbāsid state] were from Ahl al-Sunna wal-Jamāʿa and the traditionists and the people of analogy... Furthermore, there was not a single Imām from the Imāms of literature except that he would censure severely the people of blameworthy innovation and be far removed from their innovations: such as Khalīl b. Aḥmad, Yūnus b. Ḥabīb, Sībawayh, al-Akhfash, al-Zajāj, al-Mubarrid, Abū Ḥātim al-Sijistānī, Ibn Darīd, al-Azharī, Ibn Fāris, and al-Fārābī.
>
> It is the same regarding the Imāms of grammar and philology, such as: al-Kasāʾī, al-Farrāʾ, al-Aṣmaʿī, Abū Zayd al-Anṣārī, Abū ʿUbayda, Abū ʿAmr al-Shaybānī, and Abū ʿUbayd al-Qāsim b. Sallām. There is not a single one among them except that there is found in his books allegiance to Ahl al-Sunna wal-Jamāʿa and refutation against the people of heresy and innovation. Not a single one among them in the ages from the early literary masters concurred

[312] *Al-Ṭabaqāt*, 3:365.
[313] *Al-Tabṣīr fī al-Dīn*, p. 189.

> with the innovations of the people of vain desires..., and whoever is marred by anything of that, it is impermissible to rely upon him in narrating the fundamentals of the language and citing the meanings of grammar; neither can he be relied upon in the interpretation of any reports or the exegesis of any verse from the Book of Allah, the Exalted.[314]

These were the early scholars of philology, grammar, and literature. After them came Imāms who followed the same straight path in creed without fail or alteration, such as Imām al-Anbārī, Ibn Sīda the author of *Al-Mukhaṣṣiṣ* in philology, Ibn Manẓūr the author of *Lisān al-ʿArab*, al-Jawharī author of *Al-Ṣiḥāḥ*, al-Majd al-Fayrūzābādī author of *Al-Qāmūs al-Muḥīṭ*, and al-Murtaḍā al-Zabīdī author of *Tāj al-ʿArūs*.

Among the grammarians there were Muḥammad b. Mālik the author of the famous *Alfiyya* in grammar, and its commentators such as Ibn ʿAqīl and Ibn Hishām and others whose works and writings no student or man of letters can do without. All of them were upon the doctrine of Ahl al-Sunna wal-Jamāʿa: the Ashʿarīs, Māturīdīs, and those who agreed with them.

AUTHORS ON THE PROPHETIC BIOGRAPHY [*SĪRA*] ﷺ FROM THE ASHʿARĪS AND MĀTURĪDĪS

Imām Abū al-Muẓaffar al-Isfarāyīnī—may Allah have mercy upon him—said: "Regarding the sciences related to the battles, biographies, and histories, and distinguishing the sound and unsound from that, there is no one from the people of blameworthy innovation who is a leader in any that. It is the specialty of Ahl al-Sunna wal-Jamāʿa."[315]

Some of those scholars among the Ashʿarīs and Māturīdīs whose books on battles and biographies are world renowned include:

- Imām al-Bayhaqī—may Allah have mercy upon him. He wrote *Dalāʾil al-Nubuwwa*.

---

[314] *Al-Farq bayn al-Firaq*, p. 183; *Itḥāf al-Sāda al-Muttaqīn*, 2:102.
[315] Ibid.

- Imām Abū Nuʿaym al-Aṣfahānī—may Allah have mercy upon him. He also wrote a book called *Dalāʾil al-Nubuwwa.*
- Qāḍī ʿIyāḍ—may Allah have mercy upon him. He wrote *Al-Shifā*, a book on the Prophetic characteristics and states, to which no other work of its like compares.
- Imām Ibn al-Jawzī[316]—may Allah have mercy upon him. He wrote *Al-Wafā bi-Aḥwāl al-Muṣṭafā* ﷺ.
- Imām al-Ḥalabī—may Allah have mercy upon him. He is the author of *Al-Sīra al-Ḥalabiyya* titled: *Insān al-ʿUyūn.*
- Imām al-Suhaylī—may Allah have mercy upon him. He wrote *Al-Rawḍ al-Unuf.*
- Imām al-Qasṭalānī—may Allah have mercy upon him. He wrote *Al-Mawāhib al-Laduniyya.*
- Imām al-Ṣāliḥī al-Dimashqī—may Allah have mercy upon him. He wrote *Subul al-Hudā wal-Rashād.*

The works of these Imāms are the relied upon references in the biography of al-Muṣṭafā ﷺ. All of them were upon the Ashʿarī or Māturīdī creed, following the early authors who compiled works on the Prophetic biography, such as Ibn Isḥāq, al-Wāqidī, Ibn Saʿd, Ibn Hishām, and others from the senior scholars of the Prophetic biography and battles.

The same may be said regarding the Imāms who compiled books on history. Most of them were from the Ashʿarīs or Māturīdīs, such as the Imām and Ḥadīth master Ibn ʿAsākir who wrote *Tārīkh Dimashq*, Imām Ibn al-Jawzī who wrote *Al-Muntaẓam*, Imām al-Khaṭīb al-Baghdādī who wrote *Tārīkh Baghdād*, Ibn Khaldūn, and Ibn Athīr.

---

[316] Our intent here is to mention those Imāms who either followed Imām al-Ashʿarī, or who were in agreement with him, such as Ibn al-Jawzī. He was not an Ashʿarī; however, he was in agreement with their doctrine. His criticisms against al-Ashʿarī, we believe, were the result of the interpolations that were inserted into the Imām's books in Baghdad. It is highly probable that Ibn al-Jawzī formed his view on Imām al-Ashʿarī based on these interpolated works. Anyone who reads about the issues that Ibn al-Jawzī attributed to the Imām will most likely agree with our assertion here.

The same may be said regarding the Imāms who wrote biographies, such as Imām al-Ṣafadī in his book *Al-Wāfī fī al-Wafiyāt* (that he abridged in his book *A'yān al-'Aṣr*) and before him Imām al-Bākharzī who wrote *Dimya al-Qaṣr*, Ibn Shākir al-Kutubī who wrote *Fawāt al-Wafiyāt*, Qāḍī al-Quḍāt Ibn Khallikān al-Shāfi'ī who wrote *Wafiyāt al-A'yān*, and the authors who wrote the biographies of those in the ranks of the scholars of the juridical schools and the authors who wrote biographies according to the generation, such as *Al-Durar al-Kāmina* and *Inbā' al-Ghamr*—both by al-Ḥāfiẓ Ibn Ḥajar—*Al-Ḍaw' al-Lāmi'* by al-Ḥāfiẓ al-Sakhāwī, *Mir'āt al-Zamān* by Sibṭ Ibn al-Jawzī, *Mir'āt al-Jinān* by al-Yāfi'ī, *Khulāṣa al-Athar* by al-Muḥibbī, *Silk al-Durar* by al-Murādī, *Al-Kawākib al-Sā'ira* by al-Ghazzī, and many others.

Other genres of literature related to the above include genealogy [*ansāb*] and geography, such as *Al-Ansāb* by Imām al-Sam'ānī, *Mu'jam al-Buldān* by Yāqūt al-Ḥamawī, *Mu'jam mā Istu'jima* by al-Bakrī, and many others. All of these authors were either Ash'arī or Māturīdī.

In all of the above we have sufficed with mentioning only those who are well known. Otherwise it is not possible [to enumerate all of them]. All of these scholars whose names we have mentioned and whose books we have listed, whether they pertain to the Qur'ān and its ancillary sciences, Ḥadīth, jurisprudence, legal theory, Arabic, history, battles, biography—all of them represent the main reference works in the Islamic library which no student or researcher can do without, no matter what science it is.

In general, history is the greatest witness and it provides the best testimony to the fact that the Ash'arī and Māturīdī schools (and those who agree with them from Ahl al-Sunna)—with all their groups—represent the vast majority. Wherever you go in the Islamic world, be it north, south, east, or west, you will see that the flags of Ahl al-Sunna are the highest. No matter how far you go back into history you will always find that their way was dominant over all others, and this is due to the Ḥadīth of the Prophet ﷺ: "My Umma shall never unite upon misguidance."

In addition, the esteemed institutions of learning that spread light to all of humanity, such as al-Azhar University in Egypt, al-Qarawiyīn in Morocco, al-Zaytūna University in Tunis, al-Jāmi' al-Umawī in Damascus, Nadwa al-'Ulamā' in India, and other beacons of science around the Islamic world—all of them adopted either the Ash'arī or Māturīdī creed.

Before them there were other schools in the Islamic world that established the Islamic civilization, such as the Niẓāmiyya schools that were ascribed to the Vizier Niẓām al-Mulk. There were so many branches of the Niẓāmiyya school that it was said that every city in Iraq and Khorasan had one. This is one of the most important reasons for the spread of the Sunni doctrine. The most famous Niẓāmiyya school was located in Baghdad and was the largest university in the world at that time.[317] It was presided over by Imām Abū Isḥāq al-Shīrāzī—may Allah have mercy upon him—and the Niẓāmiyya of Nisapour was presided over by Imām al-Juwaynī—may Allah have mercy upon him.

Among these lofty edifices of knowledge that had the greatest effect in the history of Islam is the Dār al-Ḥadīth al-Ashrafiyya school, in which the condition for being in charge over it was for one to be an Ash'arī. The first person to take charge of the school was al-Ḥāfiẓ Ibn al-Ṣalāḥ—may Allah have mercy upon him. He was followed by Imāms after him, such as the lordly Imām al-Ḥāfiẓ Yaḥyā b. Sharaf al-Nawawī—may Allah have mercy upon him, al-Ḥāfiẓ Jamāl al-Dīn al-Mizzī, al-Ḥāfiẓ al-Taqī al-Subkī, al-Ḥāfiẓ Ibn Kathīr, and many others. An innumerable group of scholars graduated from this institution and it continued to produce scholars, Imāms, Ḥadīth masters, jurists, and reciters for generations after.

Shaykh Muḥammad Muṭī' al-Ḥāfiẓ said:

> This continued up until the eleventh century, when weakness began to appear in it—as was the general phenomena the Islamic world over—until Allah prepared for it two noble scholars who, by their efforts, were able to return the school to its previous state. Gatherings of learning and the recitation and narration of Ḥadīth resumed there from the year 1272 AH. That was due to the efforts of Shaykh Yūsuf al-Maghribī and the assistance of Emir 'Abd al-Qādir al-Jazā'irī—who reopened the school by reading *Ṣaḥīḥ al-Bukhārī*.

---

[317] See: *Fatāwā al-Ṭanṭāwī*, 2:253.

> It was as if their work was a precursor to the appearance of the reviver of the fourteenth century: the great Ḥadīth scholar Muḥammad Badr al-Dīn al-Ḥasanī who took over the role of head Shaykh in the school and returned to its previous honour, glory, and pride. From Dār al-Ḥadīth and from the hands of the great Ḥadīth scholar the scholars of the Levant were produced. There is not a single scholar or student of Sacred Knowledge in Damascus today, except that he is either a student of his or a student of one of his students.[318]

Another proof that may be used to prove the virtue of the esteemed Ashʿarīs and Māturīdīs is the Ḥadīth in which prayers and praise are mentioned for the army that will conquer Constantinople and the Emir of that army. This is one of the amazing allusions of the Messenger of Allah ﷺ. Al-Bukhārī narrated it in *Al-Tārīkh al-Kabīr* and in *Al-Tārīkh al-Ṣaghīr*, Aḥmad in his *Musnad*, al-Bazzār, Ibn Khuzayma, al-Ṭabarānī, al-Ḥākim who authenticated it and was supported by al-Dhahabī, and pointed out as authentic by al-Suyūṭī in *Al-Jāmiʿ al-Ṣaghīr*. The Prophet ﷺ said: "Constantinople shall most certainly be conquered; what a good Emir is its Emir and what a good army is that army!"

This Ḥadīth has challenged and encouraged many of the Muslims from the time of the Companions and those after them to attempt time and time again to conquer Constantinople. They endeavoured to obtain the lofty portion and great praise of the Chosen one ﷺ. Allah, the Exalted, chose to deposit this nobility and honour with the Ottoman Sultan, Muḥammad al-Fātiḥ—may Allah have mercy upon him—and his brave army. Constantinople was conquered and al-Fātiḥ and his army triumphed with the praise of Allah's Messenger ﷺ.

Now, it is obvious to anyone who knows history that Muḥammad al-Fātiḥ and the Ottomans were all Ḥanafīs in their jurisprudence and Māturīdīs in their doctrine. So the question that must be asked here is: would the Messenger of Allah ﷺ praise an innovator and misguided person? Can this splendid praise be given to someone who is deviant in their beliefs?

---

318 *Dār al-Ḥadīth al-Ashrafiyya bi-Dimashq.*

Other [Ashʿarī or Māturīdī] conquerors and leaders of the Umma include the *mujāhid* and martyr, Nūr al-Dīn Maḥmūd—may Allah have mercy upon him, the *mujāhid* leader Ṣalāḥ al-Dīn al-Ayyūbī—may Allah have mercy upon him—who was honoured with purifying Masjid al-Aqṣā from the crusaders, and al-Malik al-Muẓaffar al-Taqī Quṭuz—may Allah have mercy upon him—who was honoured with repelling the Mongols from the Levant.

Some of the latter-day heroes and *mujāhids* who are the pride of Ahl al-Sunna include the ferocious lion, ʿUmar al-Mukhtār—may Allah have mercy upon him—who was one of the notable followers of the blessed Sanūsī movement; the erudite scholar, *mujāhid* and devout Sufi, *Badīʿ al-Zamān* [Saʿīd] al-Nūrsī—may Allah have mercy upon him—who was the reviver of Islam in Turkey after the winds of atheism nearly swept it away; the brave *mujāhid* ʿIzz al-Dīn al-Qassām—may Allah have mercy upon him—who was one of the notable scholars and devout Sufis and fighters; and the brave *mujāhid*, ʿAbd al-Qādir al-Jazāʾirī—may Allah have mercy upon him.

There are many others besides the above mentioned whose numbers only Allah knows. We have sufficed with mentioning the famous ones among them from both the common folk and the elite. The prides of Ahl al-Sunna do not fall under enumeration; how could we possibly weigh the ocean or count the stars? Those whom we have mentioned here are only to warm the heart and it is not meant as statement of proof; the proofs and evidence mentioned in the previous chapters are enough.

May Allah have mercy upon Imām ʿAbd al-Qādir al-Baghdādī who said: "There is not a single praiseworthy trait that is counted among the achievements of the people of Islam—from the sciences, branches of knowledge, and the various types of independent scholarly judgments, except that Ahl al-Sunna wal-Jamāʿa has had the most crucial impact and influence in it."[319]

[319] *Al-Farq bayn al-Firaq*, p. 283.

May Allah have mercy upon the erudite scholar, ʿAbdullāh b. ʿAlawī al-Ḥaddād who said:

> You should know that the doctrine of the Ashʿarīs in creed is that which the majority of the Umma of Islam and its scholars and notables were upon. Hence, those who ascribe themselves to them and those who traverse their way were the Imāms of the people of [religious] sciences one and all through the passing of days and years. They are the Imāms of the science of Divine Oneness and theology, Qurʾānic exegesis, canonical recitation, jurisprudence, legal theory, Ḥadīth and its ancillary sciences, Sufism, philology, and history.[320]

After all that has been mentioned, we have the right to ask: what is the objective behind attacking the notables of the Muslims and seeking to remove the awe and respect for them from the hearts of the Muslims? Why do some people insist on bringing down the lofty edifices of this religion by attacking its symbols? Do they think that it is not possible for the latter generations to attain honour except by attacking the honour of the early generations? Does the statement of the Prophet ﷺ apply to us: "The Final Hour will not be established until the latter part of this Umma curses the early part."

[320] *Nayl al-Marām*, p. 8.

CHAPTER ELEVEN

THE NOBLE EFFORTS OF AHL AL-SUNNA IN DEFENDING THE RELIGION AND REFUTING THE INNOVATORS

A CURSORY LOOK AT THE BOOKS on biography, history, and the other sciences—Islamic or otherwise—will convince any fair minded person who removes the covering of blind following from his eyes that the Ashʿarīs and Māturīdīs possess virtue.

The first thing noticed by anyone who reads the books of our heritage is the immense effort expended by the notable Muslims and Imāms of the religion from the Ashʿarīs and Māturīdīs in defence of Islam and its doctrine and in protection of its sanctities and fortification of its battle-trenches and in disseminating Sacred Knowledge around the world. These efforts are the highlight and crowning achievement of our history.

Imām ʿAbd al-Qādir al-Baghdādī—may Allah have mercy upon him—said:

> There is not a single praiseworthy trait that is counted among the achievements of the people of Islam—from the sciences, branches of knowledge, and the various types of independent scholarly judgments, except that Ahl al-Sunna wal-Jamāʿa has had the most crucial impact and decisive influence in it. You have the Imāms of the fundamentals of the religion and the scholars of theological rhetoric from Ahl al-Sunna; the first of their theologians from the Companions was ʿAlī b. Abī Ṭālib—may Allah ennoble his countenance..., then ʿAbdullāh b. ʿUmar..., the first theologian of Ahl al-Sunna from the followers was ʿUmar b. ʿAbd al-ʿAzīz who wrote a powerful refutation against the Qadariyya.
>
> Then there was Zayd b. ʿAlī Zayn al-ʿĀbidīn..., then al-Ḥasan al-Baṣrī..., then al-Shaʿbī..., then al-Zuhrī..., after this rank there was Jaʿfar b. Muḥammad al-Ṣādiq... The first of the theologians among the jurists and heads of the legal schools was Abū Ḥanīfa and al-Shāfiʿī..., and Abū al-ʿAbbās b. Surayj was the most skilled of the group in these sciences...

> After them came Imām Abū al-Ḥasan al-Ash'arī who became a thorn in the throats of the Qadariyya. His famous students include Abū al-Ḥasan al-Bāhilī and Abū 'Abdullāh b. Mujāhid; both of whom produced students who till this day are the luminaries of the time and the Imāms of the era, such as: Abū Bakr Muḥammad b. al-Ṭayyib al-Bāqillānī, Abū Isḥāq Ibrāhīm b. Muḥammad al-Isfarāyīnī, and Ibn Fūrak... Moreover, through the passing generations the Imāms of spiritual guidance and Sufism have been upon the same upright doctrine. Moreover, the majority of the scholars of grammar, linguistics, and literature have been upon the doctrine of Ahl al-Sunna... Moreover, the Imāms of the reciters and Qur'ānic exegetes via *riwāya* [narration] from the era of the Companions until the time of Muḥammad b. Jarīr al-Ṭabarī and his contemporaries and those after them —all of them were from Ahl al-Sunna. In addition, the Qur'ānic exegetes via *dirāya* [direct understanding and commentary] (minus some individuals from the people of innovation), in addition to the famous scholars of the historic battles, biographies, textual criticism, and the narrators—all of them were from Ahl al-Sunna wal-Jamā'a. May Allah, the Glorified, resurrect us within their ranks.[321]

He also said:

> The first part of this section explains the categories of Ahl al-Sunna wal-Jamā'a. Know, may Allah grant you felicity, that Ahl al-Sunna wal-Jamā'a are comprised of eight types of people:
>
> 1- A group that has comprehensive knowledge of the issues pertaining to Divine Oneness, prophecy, the rulings related to the Divine promise and Divine threat, punishment, reward, and the conditions of *ijtihād*, the Imāmate, and leadership...
>
> 2- The second group among them are the Imāms of jurisprudence from both the people of opinion [analogy], and the people of prophetic traditions among those who, in the matters of doctrine, took the schools of the *Ṣifātiyya*

[321] *Al-Farq bayn al-Firaq*, p. 283.

(those who affirm the Divine attributes) regarding Allah and His beginningless attributes, and who also declared their disavowal of the belief in *qadr* (that man creates his own works) and extreme rationalism [*'itizāl*]. They believed in the eternality of the delight of Paradise for its inhabitants as well as the eternality of the punishment of the Hellfire for the disbelievers. They believed in the Imāmate of Abū Bakr, 'Umar, 'Uthmān, and 'Alī, and they praised the pious predecessors of this Umma. They believed in the obligation of praying the Friday prayer behind the Imāms, and declared their disavowal of the people of desires and misguidance. They believed in the obligation of extracting the rulings of the Sacred Law from the Qur'ān, Sunna, and consensus of the Companions. This group includes the Companions of Mālik, al-Shāfi'ī, Abū Ḥanīfa, and Aḥmad b. Ḥanbal—may Allah be pleased with all of them.

3- The third group among them are those who gained a comprehensive knowledge of the routes of the reports and Sunna recorded from the Prophet ﷺ. They distinguished between that which was rigorously authentic among them as well as that which was weak. They knew the factors behind the praise or disparagement [of Ḥadīth narrators] and they did not mix their knowledge of this with anything of the innovations of the misguided people of desires.

4- The fourth group among them are those who gained comprehensive knowledge of most of the fields of literature, grammar, and morphology; following the way of the Imāms of the language, such as Khalīl, Abū 'Amr b. al-'Alā', and Sībawayh.

5- The fifth group among them are those who gained comprehensive knowledge of the various modes of reciting the Qur'ān as well as the various modes of its exegesis and interpretation in accordance with the way of Ahl al-Sunna, free from the interpretations of the people of misguided desires.

6- The sixth group among them are the ascetic Sufis who gained true insight [into the nature of the world] and [consequently] sufficed themselves with little; those who gained direct experience and took notice. They are those

> who were pleased with that which is decreed and were contented with little. They knew that the hearing, sights, and hearts shall be questioned regarding both good and evil, and that they shall all be taken to account for even an atom's weight. As a result, they prepared the best preparation for the Day of Resurrection. Their words reflected the two ways: outward expression and symbolic spiritual allusion in the manner of the people of Ḥadīth, as opposed to those who purchase vain talk. They do not perform works with ostentation, nor do they abstain from works out of shyness. Their religion consists of Divine Oneness and negation of resemblance. Their way is that of total reliance and trust upon Allah while submitting to His commands, being content with what He provides them, and turning away from opposition to Him: ﴾*That is the bounty of Allah that He gives to whom He wills, and Allah is the Possessor of great bounty.*﴿ [Al-Jumuʿa: 4]
>
> 7- The seventh group among them are those who stand vigilantly in the battle trenches manned by the Muslims in the face of the disbelievers; struggling against the enemies of the Muslims and safeguarding their border areas.
>
> 8- The eighth group among them are those in the lands in which the rites of Ahl al-Sunna dominate, as opposed to those areas in which the rites of the people of desire and misguidance dominate...[322]

Imām Abū al-Muẓaffar al-Isfarāyīnī—may Allah have mercy upon him—said:

> As for the sciences: the first of them is to ascend the levels of virtue and literature; that is the key to all sciences and it presents excellent benefits in this life and the next; there is no way to interpret the Qur'ān or reports from the Messenger ﷺ except with knowledge of literature. The general body of the Imāms in grammar and philology from the people of Basra and Kufa in the Islamic *dawla* [the ʿAbbāsid state] were from Ahl al-Sunna wal-Jamāʿa and the traditionists and the people of analogy...

---

[322] Ibid.

Furthermore, there was not a single Imām from the Imāms of literature except that he would censure severely the people of blameworthy innovation and be far removed from their innovations

The second of them is the science of Qur'ānic exegesis. The third of them is the science related to the Ḥadīth reports of the Chosen one ﷺ. The fourth of them is the science of jurisprudence; and those who delve deep into it are the traditionists and the people of analogy... The fifth of them is the science related to the battles, biographies, and histories, and distinguishing the sound and unsound from that, there is no one from the people of blameworthy innovation who is a leader in any that. It is the specialty of Ahl al-Sunna wal-Jamā'a... The sixth of them is the science of Sufism and spiritual allusion; never has a person from the people of innovation had any portion thereof...

The seventh of them is the science of the fundamentals of the religion: Ahl al-Sunna are singled out with the most number of books written in the field of doctrine and fundamentals...

As for the types of practical efforts [*ijtihādāt*] that revolve around Ahl al-Sunna in the lands of Islam, they are famous and well-known... From their practical effects is their filling the battle-trenches of Islam and guarding the frontiers such as the border areas near Europe and Armenia in which the trenches are filled with the blessings of the traditionists, and in the border areas in the Turkish lands in which the trenches are shared between the traditionists and the people of analogy...

The efforts of Ahl al-Sunna wal-Jamā'a in the sciences and physical struggles that we have mentioned to you here demonstrate that they are the people of scholarly effort and struggle...[323]

May Allah bless al-Ḥāfiẓ Ibn 'Asākir who said:

I wonder in amazement: what is it that causes the hearts to have aversion towards them [the Ash'arīs] and what is it that causes the innovators to have resentment towards

[323] *Al-Tabṣīr fī al-Dīn*, p. 187.

> them? Is it due to the profundity of their knowledge or their preponderant understanding? Is it due to their belief in Divine Oneness and transcendence or their avoidance of anthropomorphism [*tajsīm*] and corporealism [*tashbīh*]? Or is it due to their affirmation of the Divine attributes or their belief that the Lord is transcendent above parts and tools?[324]

He said elsewhere:

> Most of the scholars from all of the lands are upon it [the way of al-Ashʿarī] and the Imāms of the capitals in all eras call to it. Those who adhere to it are the reference points in [knowledge of the] Sacred Law; unto them [people] go for knowledge of the lawful and unlawful; they are the ones who deliver legal verdicts to the people concerning the difficult matters; and the creation rely upon them to clear up confusing and novel matters. Is there any of the jurists among the Ḥanafīs, Mālikīs, and Shāfiʿīs except that he ascribes to it, or is pleased with its praiseworthy efforts in the religion of Allah, or lauds the great knowledge found within it?[325]

Imām al-Murtaḍā al-Zabīdī—may Allah have mercy upon him—said:

> You should know that the adherents to the religion of Islam have universally concurred upon the belief that the Maker of the world does not resemble anything from the world, and that He has no likeness, similitude, or opposite; and that He, the Glorified, exists [*mawjūd*] without resemblance or nullification. After the aforementioned, they disagreed between themselves. Some of them believed in [going into] detail regarding that which agrees with the general precepts of their doctrine, and they did not violate [or mix] the fundamentals of Divine Oneness with its branches.

---

[324] *Tabyīn Kadhib al-Muftarī*, p. 367.
[325] Ibid.

They are the verifying scholars of Ahl al-Sunna wal-Jamāʿa: the traditionists and the people of analogy who held firmly to the fundamentals of the religion as it pertains to Divine Oneness and Prophecy.

They did not mix their doctrine with any type of innovation or misguidance... This was the way followed by all of the Imāms of the religion in jurisprudence, Ḥadīth, and independent scholarly judgment [*ijtihād*] in legal verdicts and rulings, such as Mālik, al-Shāfiʿī, Aḥmad, Abū Ḥanīfa, al-Awzāʿī, al-Thawrī, the jurists of Medina, all of the Imāms of the two Sacred Sanctuaries, the *ahl al-ẓāhir* (literalists),[326] and all whose divergent opinions are given proper consideration in jurisprudence.

This is the belief of the Imām of the affirmationist Ṣifātiyya from the theologians, such as ʿAbdullāh b. Saʿīd al-Qaṭṭān, al-Ḥārith b. Asad al-Muḥāsibī, ʿAbd al-ʿAzīz al-Makkī, al-Ḥusayn b. al-Faḍl al-Bajalī, Abū al-ʿAbbās al-Qalānisī, and Abū al-Ḥasan al-Ashʿarī, and those who followed them from the monotheists who were free from anthropomorphism [*tajsīm*] and extreme denial [*taʿṭīl*].

This is also the belief of the Imāms of Sufism, such as Abū Sulaymān al-Dārānī, Aḥmad b. Abī al-Ḥawārī, Sarrī al-Saqaṭī, Ibrāhīm b. Adham, al-Fuḍayl b. ʿIyāḍ, al-Junayd, Ruwaym, al-Nūrī, al-Kharrāz, al-Khawwāṣ, and those who took their path—not those who ascribed themselves to them from whom they are innocent, such as the incarnationists and others.

This is the path followed by the Imāms of the Muslims in the field of Ḥadīth, such as al-Zuhrī, Shuʿba, Qatāda, Ibn ʿUyayna, ʿAbd al-Raḥmān b. Mahdī, Yaḥyā b. Saʿīd, Yaḥyā b. Maʿīn, ʿAlī al-Madīnī, Aḥmad b. Ḥanbal, Isḥāq b. Rāhawayh, Yaḥyā b. Yaḥyā al-Tamīmī, and all of the Ḥadīth masters who preserved the Ḥadīth of Allah's Messenger ﷺ; those whose words were recorded in the science of *jarḥ wa-taʿdīl*[327] and distinguishing between what is sound and unsound from the narrations and reports.

---

[326] Followers of the legal school of Imām Dāwūd al-Ẓāhirī. [t]

[327] The recorded views on the creditation and discreditation of narrators. [t]

> [This path is also followed by] the Imāms from whom philology, grammar, the canonical modes of Qurʾānic recitation, and the grammatical analysis of the Qurʾān are taken. All of them were upon the path of Divine Oneness without any resemblance or extreme denial...
>
> And all of the Imāms of the religion today whose opinions are valid to use as proofs in philology, grammar, and the modes of recitation, all of them ascribe themselves to exactly what Ahl al-Sunna wal-Jamāʿa ascribes to in matters of Divine Oneness, affirming the attributes of praise for the One whom they worship, Glorified is He, and negating resemblance from Him.[328]

Earlier in this book we quoted the words of Imām al-Zabīdī: "When the term *Ahl al-Sunna wal-Jamāʿa* is used, it means the Ashʿarīs and Māturīdīs."[329] This proves that his statement above: "...all of them ascribe themselves to exactly what Ahl al-Sunna wal-Jamāʿa ascribes to..." means the Ashʿarīs, Māturīdīs, and those who agreed with them from the other groups of Ahl al-Sunna wal-Jamāʿa.

All of this clearly illustrates the rank of Ahl al-Sunna wal-Jamāʿa—the Ashʿarīs and Māturīdīs and traditionists—and their distinction above the people of base desires, deviation, and innovations. This shows the immense bounty granted to them by Allah and their raising of the banner of truth, guidance, and direction for all of creation.

---

[328] *Itḥāf al-Sāda al-Muttaqīn*, 2:102.
[329] Ibid., 2:6.

Chapter Twelve

Formal Legal Verdicts and Statements from the Scholars Regarding the Virtue of the Ashʿarīs and Harsh Words Against Those who Condemn Them

Allah, the Exalted, said: ﴾*Those who injure the believing men and women for other than what their [hands] earned, certainly that have carried a slander and clear sin.*﴿ Allah, the Exalted, said in a Ḥadīth *qudsī*: "Whoever takes a friend of Mine in enmity, I declare war against him."

The scholars are the friends of Allah and the elect of His creation. By them, the religion is spread and the beliefs and sanctities of the people are defended. The death of thousands of people causes less harm to the religion and worldly life than the death of a single scholar.

The sanctity of a scholar is from the sanctity of the religion; whoever extends to them the respect they are due and knows their true rank, it is the religion he is respecting. Whoever acts in a haughty manner towards them or belittles them, it is in fact the religion that he is belittling. Allah, the Exalted, said: ﴾*And whoever sanctifies the symbols of Allah, then that is from the piety of the hearts.*﴿

What feature of Islam is greater than its signposts and symbols by which it is established and the servants and lands are made secure? What duty is more binding and greater in reward than honouring them and acknowledging their virtue? What sin and enormity is worse than maligning them and detracting from their rank.

Highhandedness against the scholars—especially the senior ones among them—is one of the sins that shall proliferate in the last days. It is mentioned in the Ḥadīth that one of the portents of the Last Hour is the latter part of this Umma shall curse its early ones. This is an indication from him ﷺ pointing out the severity and odiousness of this sin—so much that it was delayed to the Last Days!

There are numerous statements from the scholars of Islam and many mass-transmitted legal verdicts from them in which they censure those who detract from the station of the notables of the

Sacred Law and the scholars of the Umma. In their legal verdicts they declared it a duty upon the leader of the Muslims to reprimand and punish those who detract from them.

An example of this is found in the legal verdict delivered by the exemplar of the Mālikīs of his time, Imām Ibn Rushd (al-Jadd)—may Allah have mercy upon him.

> ***Question***
> What does the noble and upright Qāḍī, Abū al-Walīd—may Allah cause him to arrive at His Divine success and strengthening, and cause him to tread every righteous path—say regarding Shaykh Abū al-Ḥasan al-Ashʿarī, Abū Isḥāq al-Isfarāyīnī, Abū Bakr al-Bāqillānī, Abū Bakr b. Fūrak, Abū al-Maʿālī, ...and their peers who adopted the way of theological rhetoric, spoke about the fundamentals of doctrine, and compiled books in refutation against the people of vain desires?
>
> What does he [Ibn Rushd] say about a people given to insulting them and detracting from them, insulting all who ally themselves with the Ashʿarī knowledge, imputing them with disbelief, disavowing themselves from them, and having enmity towards them and believing that they are upon misguidance and that they are involved in gross ignorance? What should be said to them and what should be done with them and what should be believed about them? Should they be left to their desires or should they be made to desist from their extremism?
>
> ***Answer***
> I have examined your question—may Allah protect you and me. Those whom you named from the scholars are Imāms of goodness and guidance whom it is obligatory to follow, because they stood up in defence of the Sacred Law and they refuted the specious doubts of the deviants and misguided people. They clarified the confusing matters and explained the doctrinal beliefs that must be believed in.
>
> By their knowledge of the fundamentals of doctrine and their knowledge of Allah تعالى and what is necessary for Him, possible for Him, and what is impossible and negated from Him they are the real scholars. It is not possible

> for you to know the branches until you know the fundamentals. Of that which is obligatory is to attest to their virtues and admit to their good actions. They were the ones meant in the statement of the Messenger of Allah ﷺ: "This knowledge will be carried in each generation by trustworthy ones who will negate from it the distortions of the extremists, the deviance of the deniers, and the false interpretations of the ignorant."
>
> Only a fool or deviant innovator who inclines away from the truth can believe that they are misguided or ignorant. And no one but a criminal can insult them or ascribe to them things contrary to their actual positions. Allah ﷻ said: ﴾*Those who injure the believing men and women for other than what their [hands] earned, certainly that have carried a slander and clear sin.*﴿
>
> Hence, the ignorant one from them must be enlightened and the reprobate must be reprimanded. Repentance must be sought from the innovator who deviates away from the truth if he seeks to make innovation palatable. If he repents [then all well and good], otherwise, if he does not, he should be hit until he repents—just as 'Umar b. al-Khaṭṭāb ﷺ did with Ṣabīgh who was accused of deviance in his beliefs. He was hit until he said: "O leader of the believers! If you wanted to treat me with medicine, the medicine has reached the source of illness; if you wanted to kill me, please carry it out!" He ['Umar] then left him alone. I ask Allah alone for protection and success by His mercy.[330]

Imām Abū al-Muẓaffar al-Isfarāyīnī—may Allah have mercy upon him—said after explaining the doctrine of Ahl al-Sunna: "And you know that everyone who follows this religion that we have described from the creed of the saved group is upon the truth and the straight path; so whoever imputes him with blameworthy innovation is an innovator, whoever imputes him with misguidance is misguided, and whoever imputes him with disbelief is a disbeliever."[331]

---

[330] *Fatāwā Ibn Rushd*, 2:802.

[331] *Al-Tabṣīr fī al-Dīn*, p. 111.

Imām al-Nawawī—may Allah have mercy upon him—was severe against those who detracted from the scholars. He said:

> Allah, the Exalted, said: ﴾*And whoever sanctifies the symbols of Allah, then that is from the piety of the hearts*﴿ and He said: ﴾*And whoever honours the sanctities of Allah then it is better for him with his Lord*﴿ and He said: ﴾*And lower you wing towards the believers*﴿ and He said: ﴾*Those who injure the believing men and women for other than what their* [*hands*] *earned, certainly that have carried a slander and clear sin.*﴿
>
> It is reported in *Ṣaḥīḥ al-Bukhārī* from Abū Hurayra ﷺ, from the Messenger of Allah ﷺ: "Indeed, Allah ﷻ says: 'Whoever injures a friend of mine I shall declare war against him.'" Al-Khaṭīb al-Baghdādī reported that both al-Shāfiʿī and Abū Ḥanīfa said: "If the jurists are not the friends of Allah then Allah does not have any friend." In al-Shāfiʿī's narration it is worded: "...the practicing jurists..."
>
> And from Ibn ʿAbbās ﷺ: "Whoever injures a jurist has injured the Messenger of Allah ﷺ and whoever injures the Messenger of Allah ﷺ has injured Allah ﷻ." In the *Ṣaḥīḥ* collection, the Messenger of Allah ﷺ said: "Whoever prays the morning prayer is in the guarantee of Allah, so do not let Allah seek you out with anything of His guarantee."[332]

If the notables of the Umma from the Ashʿarī and Māturīdī Imāms of the religion are not the friends of Allah, then who is?

Al-Ḥāfiẓ Ibn ʿAsākir—may Allah have mercy upon him—said:

> Know, dear brother, may Allah grant you and me success with His good pleasure and make us of those who fear Him and observe proper piety towards Him, that the flesh of the scholars is poison and the way of Allah in rendering the veils of those who detract from them is well-known. Whoever speaks ill of the scholars will be afflicted by Allah before his [physical] death with the death of his heart: ﴾*Let those who oppose his command beware lest they are tried with an affliction or tried with a painful punishment.*﴿[333]

---

[332] *Al-Majmūʿ*, 1:24.

[333] *Tabyīn Kadhib al-Muftarī*, p. 425; *Al-Majmūʿ*, 1:24.

Imām Ibn Ḥajar al-Haytamī—may Allah have mercy upon him—was asked about Imām Abū al-Ḥasan al-Ashʿarī, al-Bāqillānī, Ibn Fūrak, Imām al-Ḥaramayn [al-Juwaynī], al-Bājī, and others who followed the way of al-Ashʿarī. He responded:

> They are the Imāms of the religion and the sires among the scholars of the Muslims. It is obligatory to follow them because of their aid to the Sacred Law, their clarification of confusing matters, their refutations of the misconceptions of the people of heresy, and their explanations of what is obligatory in the realm of doctrine and religion. This is due to their knowledge of Allah and what is necessary for Him, impossible for Him, and possible...
>
> It is obligatory to acknowledge the virtue of the aforementioned Imāms as well as those who came before them, and to acknowledge that they are included among those meant by the statement of the Prophet ﷺ: "This knowledge will be carried in each generation by trustworthy ones who will negate from it the distortions of the extremists, the deviance of the deniers, and the false interpretations of the ignorant." Only an ignorant fool or deviant innovator believes that they are misguided, and no one but a reprobate insults them. It is therefore a must that the ignorant person be made aware, that the reprobate be reprimanded, and that repentance be sought from the innovator.[334]

Al-Ḥāfiẓ Ibn ʿAsākir cited a legal verdict by Imām Muḥammad b. ʿAlī al-Dāmighānī that was supported by Imām Abū Isḥāq al-Shīrāzī, Ibrāhīm b. ʿAlī al-Fayrūzābādī, and Imām Abū Bakr al-Shāshī. In this legal verdict he spoke about the virtue of the Ashʿarīs and the obligation of punishing those who detract from them or malign them.

This is the text of the legal verdict:

---

[334] *Al-Fatāwā al-Ḥadīthiyya*, p. 205.

In the name of Allah, All-Merciful, the Compassionate
What do the noble and esteemed Imāms and jurists—may Allah grant them a goodly success and be pleased with them—say regarding a folk who curse the Ash'arī group and charge them with disbelief? What should be done to them on account of that statement? Inform us of the legal verdict concerning that—may you be rewarded and bestowed with bounties, Allah willing.

The answer, and with Allah is all success:
All who put themselves forward to curse a group of the Muslims and charge them with disbelief have innovated and committed a sin. It is upon the one who looks into the matters [the ruler]—may Allah honour his victors—to censure them and reprimand them with that which will deter them and their ilk from committing further acts similar to it. *—Written by Muḥammad b. 'Alī al-Dāmighānī*

The answer, and with Allah is all success:
The Ash'arīs are the people of the Sunna and the helpers of the Sacred Law. They have been appointed to refute the innovators... Whoever insults them has insulted Ahl al-Sunna. If the matter of the one who does this is raised to the one in charge of looking after the affairs of the Muslims, it is obligatory upon him to reprimand him with that which will deter others. *—Written by Ibrāhīm b. 'Alī al-Fayrūzābādī and Abū Isḥāq al-Shīrāzī*

My response is same as the above. *—Written by Muḥammad b. Aḥmad al-Shāshī*

Al-Ḥāfiẓ Ibn 'Asākir said:

So these are the responses of the Imāms who were the scholars of the Umma in their time. As for Qāḍī al-Quḍāt Abū 'Abdullāh al-Ḥanafī al-Dāmighānī, it used to be said in his time that he was Abū Ḥanīfa the Second. As for the Shaykh and Imām Abū Isḥāq, mention of his virtue has extended beyond the horizons. As for the Shaykh and Imām Abū Bakr al-Shāshī, his rank is not hidden to either a senior scholar or beginner. Whomever Allah

> grants correctness and protects from sectarianism and obstinance will stop at what they mentioned and suffice themselves with what they reported. May Allah protect us from bearing false witness and engaging in slander.[335]

The erudite scholar and Sayyid, Muḥammad b. 'Alawī al-Mālikī al-Ḥasanī—may Allah have mercy upon him—said about the Ash'arīs and Māturīdīs:

> The Ash'arīs are the Imāms of the notable figures of guidance among the scholars of the Muslims, whose knowledge has filled the world from both East to West, and whom people have unanimously agreed regarding their excellence, scholarship, and piety. They include the first rank of scholars from Ahl al-Sunna and the most brilliant of their luminaries, confronted the excesses committed by the Mu'tazila.
>
> Shaykh al-Islām, Ibn Taymiyya said regarding them: "The scholars are the helpers of the religious sciences, and the Ash'arīs are the helpers of the fundamentals of the religion."[336]
>
> They include whole sections of the foremost Imāms of Ḥadīth, Sacred Law, and Qur'ānic exegesis. Shaykh al-Islām Ahmad b. Ḥajar al-'Asqalānī, the mentor of Ḥadīth scholars and author of the book *Fatḥ al-Bārī fī Sharḥ Ṣaḥīḥ al-Bukhārī*, which not a single scholar can dispense with, was an Ash'arī. The Shaykh of the scholars Ahl al-Sunna, Imām al-Nawawī, author of *Sharḥ Ṣaḥīḥ Muslim* and many other famous works, was an Ash'arī. The master of Qur'ānic exegetes, Imām al-Qurṭubī, author of *Al-Jāmi' li-Aḥkām al-Qur'ān*, was an Ash'arī. Shaykh al-Islām Ibn Ḥajar al-Haytamī, who wrote *Al-Zawājir 'an Iqtirāf al-Kabā'ir*, was an Ash'arī. The Shaykh of Sacred Law and Ḥadīth, the reliable proof Zakariyyā al-Anṣārī, was an Ash'arī. Imām Abū Bakr al-Bāqillānī, Imām al-'Asqalānī, Imām al-Nasafī, Imām al-Shirbīnī, Abū Ḥayyān al-Tawḥīdī, author of the Qur'ānic commentary *Al-Bahr al-Muḥīṭ*, Imām Ibn Juzayy, author of *Al-Tas'hīl fī 'Ulūm al-Tanzīl* and others—all of

---

[335] *Tabyīn Kadhib al-Muftarī*, p. 332.

[336] *Al-Fatāwā*, vol. 4.

> these were Imāms of the Ashʿarīs. If we wanted to name all of the top scholars of Ḥadīth, Qurʾānic exegesis, and Sacred Law who were Imāms of the Ashʿarīs, we would be hard pressed to do so and it would require volumes to merely list these virtuous figures whose knowledge has filled the earth from East to West. And it is obligatory upon us to give credit where credit is due, recognizing the merit of those of knowledge and virtue who have served the Sacred Law of the Greatest Messenger ﷺ. What good is to be hoped for us if we level our foremost scholars and righteous predecessors with charges of deviance and misguidance? How should Allah give us the benefit of their scholarship if we believe it is deviance and departure from the way of Islam?[337]

Legal verdict of the Sacred Law Committee in Dubai

This is the response we received to a question we posted to the website of the Sacred Law Committee in the United Arab Emirates:

> *In the name of Allah, the All-Merciful, the Compassionate*
> May the peace, mercy, and blessings of Allah be upon you. Thank you for contacting us. This is in response to the letter you sent to us.
>
> ***The question***
> Dear brothers! Peace be upon you, and the mercy and blessings of Allah. Who are the Ashʿarīs? Are they from Ahl al-Sunna wal-Jamāʿa? What is the ruling on the one who disparages them and imputes them with blameworthy innovation and misguidance?

---

[337] *Mafāhīm Yajib an Tuṣaḥḥaḥ* (*Notions That Must Be Corrected*). This is a blessed and beneficial book. It has received the commendations of a large number of senior Islamic scholars in the Islamic world. [Shaykh Muḥammad b. ʿAlawī al-Mālikī al-Ḥasanī's *Notions That Must Be Corrected* has been published by Sunni Publications in 2008. A second edition containing the aforementioned commendations has been published in 2010].

The answer, and with Allah is all success

The Ash'arīs are from Ahl al-Sunna wal-Jamā'a: from the followers of Abū al-Ḥasan al-Ash'arī who treaded the path of the Companions, the followers, and their followers. Their views that are ascribed to the *Salaf* and their views that are ascribed to the latter-day scholars are all sourced from proofs and revealed texts: whether the position is to pass on the outward wordings as they are or interpret them in a manner that coincides with the reports and the language.

Hence it impermissible to disparage them or impute them with blameworthy innovation or misguidance. The one who disparages them is in fact disparaged; the one who imputes them with blameworthy innovation is the innovator; and the one who imputes them with misguidance is the one who is misguided—because the Umma through all of its successive generations have met their statements with acceptance and their scholarly efforts with good-pleasure and fairness.

And with Allah is all success.

The formal legal verdict of Shaykh Aḥmad al-Ḥajjī al-Kurdī

Question

Can you please explain to us the foundations of this group [the Ash'arīs] and also something regarding its creed with respect to the names and attributes?

Answer

In the name of Allah, the All-Merciful, the Compassionate. All praise is due to Allah, the Lord of the worlds. May the most superior prayers and most complete salutations be upon our master Muḥammad, the seal of the Prophets and Messengers, and upon his progeny and Companions and those who follow their guidance with goodness until the Last Day. To proceed:

Imām Abū al-Ḥasan al-Ash'arī is the Imām of this group. It is a Sunni group that is followed by the general body of Muslims around the world. Its fundamentals are explained in the various books of Islamic creed such as *Al-ʿAqīda al-Ṭaḥāwiyya*. It would be good to refer to it for more details. And Allah, the Exalted, knows best.

—Shaykh Aḥmad al-Ḥajjī al-Kurdī

The formal legal verdict of the Mufti of Lebanon

All praise is due to Allah, the Lord of the worlds. May prayers and salutations be upon our master and Prophet, Muḥammad, the seal of the Prophets and Messengers, and upon his progeny and Companions and those who follow them with goodness until the Last Day. To proceed:

The Ashʿarīs are from Ahl al-Sunna wal-Jamāʿa. They ascribe themselves to Imām Abū al-Ḥasan ʿAlī b. Ismāʿīl al-Ashʿarī—may Allah have mercy upon him. The well-known view is that he was born in the year 260 AH in the city of Basra, and died in the year 324 AH. Imām Abū al-Ḥasan al-Ashʿarī—may Allah have mercy upon him—was a major Imām from the Imāms of Ahl al-Sunna wal-Jamāʿa.

The doctrine of the Ashʿarīs is the doctrine of Ahl al-Sunna wal-Jamāʿa: in affirming Allah's existence and Oneness, that there is nothing like unto Him, that He resembles nothing and that nothing resembles him, and that He is described with all attributes of perfection and exalted beyond all attributes of imperfection.

The Ashʿarīs refuted the opinions of the Muʿtazila who denied the vision of Allah in the Hereafter, and Allah affirmed that in the Holy Qur'ān when He said: ﴾*Faces on that day shall be bright. Looking upon their Lord.*﴿ Some of the distinguished Imāms of the Ashʿarīs include: Imām al-Juwaynī al-Shāfiʿī, Imām al-Ghazālī al-Shāfiʿī, Imām al-Laqqānī al-Mālikī, and many of the Ḥadīth scholars and jurists—may Allah be pleased with all of them.

Most of the Levant and other lands of the Muslims are upon the doctrine of Ahl al-Sunna wal-Jamāʿa: Ashʿarīs or Māturīdīs.

And Allah, the Exalted, knows best. May Allah send complete prayers and perfect salutations upon our master Muḥammad, and upon his Family and Companions. All praise is due to Allah, the Lord of the worlds.

Mufti of the Republic of Lebanon
Shaykh Muḥammad Rashīd Rāghib Qabbānī
Beirut, 12th *Ṣafar* 1425

The books of the scholars are filled with praise for the Ashʿarīs and Ahl al-Sunna entire. Hardly a single book is bereft of it. Their books are also filled with censure against those who disparaged them or attacked them.

What we have cited here should suffice those who are objective and fair-minded. As for those who are reckless, the bright sun on the horizon will not convince them that it is day time. To Allah we turn to help in the face of what they describe.

Ahl al-Sunna: The Ashʿarīs

The Testimony and Proofs of the Scholars

Chapter Thirteen

The Doctrine of Ahl al-Sunna wal-Jamāʿa

When someone reads the Sunni books of theology, he or she will see that the scholars affirmed only twenty attributes for Allah, the Exalted. Lest it be imagined that Ahl al-Sunna negated all else besides those twenty, we say:

The attributes of Allah, the Exalted, insofar as faith in them is concerned, are divided into two categories. The first category consists of that in which faith is obligatory and which must be known in a general sense. These are the attributes that are affirmed textually and rationally, namely all of the perfections that are perceived in the intellect such as justice, love, mercy, vengeance, forgiveness, wisdom, and every other attribute of perfection that belongs to Allah, the Exalted.

The second category consists of that in which detailed faith and detailed knowledge is obligatory. These are the attributes that are affirmed textually and rationally in detail, and they are the twenty attributes that the scholars call "the most important attributes" All other attributes are included within these attributes.[338]

Shaykh Muḥammad Saʿīd Ramaḍān al-Būṭī—may Allah have mercy upon him—said:

> It is obligatory upon you to know in a comprehensive and general word that Allah ﷻ possesses every attribute of perfection and is transcendent above every attribute of imperfection; His godhood entails in the highest order that He is described with absolute perfection.
>
> After that, we must become acquainted with the details of the most important of these attributes, explain their meanings and what they entail of doctrinal positions. In His Holy Book, Allah, the Exalted, described Himself with many different attributes; however, the particulars

[338] See: *Arkān al-Imān*, Shaykh Wahbī al-Ghāwjī, 1:41.

> of these attributes come together within twenty main attributes that are affirmed by the indications of the Book, as well as incontrovertible rational proof.[339]

In the commentary upon *Jawhara al-Tawḥīd* by Shaykh ʿAbd al-Karīm Tatān and Muḥammad Adīb al-Kaylānī it reads:

> Before speaking about "the necessary existence," we would like to explain that, in general, every perfection is necessary for Allah, the Exalted, and that He is transcendent above every imperfection, and that it is possible for Him to either do or leave off every contingently possible thing. In detail, there are twenty attributes that are necessary for Allah. The scholars divided them into four categories for the sake of teaching [people] that they are the main [attributes] that are necessary for Allah, the Exalted...[340]

The Imām and erudite scholar, al-Hud'hudī, said in his commentary on *Al-Sanūsiyya al-Ṣughrā*, explaining the words of the author: "From that which is necessary for our Master ﷻ are twenty attributes...":

> The governing particle "*from*" here means *some*; in other words "from some of what is necessary," because the necessary attributes of our Master ﷻ are not restricted to these twenty. His perfections are endless. Allah has not burdened us except with knowing what is provided to us with evidence, which are these twenty attributes. By His Divine generosity He has not made it obligatory upon us to know that which has not been provided with evidence.[341]

The statements of the scholars to this effect are numerous. What we have cited here should prove sufficient in clarifying the point.

---

339 *Kubrā al-Yaqīniyāt*, p. 108.

340 *Sharḥ Jawhara al-Tawḥīd*, 1:284.

341 *Sharḥ al-Sanūsiyya al-Ṣughrā*, pp. 45–46.

Ahl al-Sunna—the Ashʿarīs and Māturīdīs—are not extreme deniers of the attributes, nor do they believe that Allah resembles His creation. They affirm for Allah every perfection that is affirmed for Him textually and rationally, and they declare Him transcendent above the traits of imperfections and faults.

Consider—may Allah grant all of us guidance—the basic doctrine of Ahl al-Sunna, the Ashʿarīs, in order to realize the purity of this creed and its firm adherence to what is reported from the Messenger of Allah ﷺ and his Companions—may Allah be pleased with all of them.

Imām al-Ghazālī—may Allah have mercy upon him—said:

> All praise is due to Allah, Who originates all and returns them, Who does as He wills, the Possessor of the Noble Throne and overwhelming force, the Guide of His choice servants to the straight path and upright way, Who has blessed them after having had them attest to His Oneness, by preserving their doctrines from the darkness of doubt and misgivings, bringing them to follow His chosen Messenger and the example of his noble and honoured Companions; He Who manifests Himself and His acts to His servants through His sublime attributes, of which none possess knowledge save those who give heed with an attentive mind.
>
> He is one in his Being without partner, unique without peer, ultimate without opposite, alone without equal, He is One, Pre-eternal without a first, beginningless with a beginning, everlastingly abiding, unceasingly existent, eternally limitless, the ever self-subsisting through whom all else subsists, ever enduring, without end. He is, was, and ever will be possessed of all attributes of Majesty, unannihilated by dissolution or separation through the passage of time or terminus of interims. He is the First and the Last, the Outward and the Inward, and He has knowledge of everything.
>
> He is not a body with a form, or a limited quantitative substance. He does not resemble corporeal bodies and does not accept divisibility. He, the Exalted, is not a substance or qualified by a substance, and He is not an accident or qualified by accidents. Nay, He does not

resemble anything that exists, nor does anything that exists resemble Him. ﴾*There is nothing like unto Him*﴿ nor is He like unto anything. He is not limited by size, contained by places, encompassed by direction, or bounded by heavens or earth.

He is "established on the Throne" in the way in which He said and the meaning He intended; established in a manner that is transcendent above contact, settling, fixity, indwelling, or movement. The Throne does not carry Him, but is carried by the subtlety of His infinite power, as are the Angels who carry it, and all are powerless in His grasp. He is above the Throne, the heavens, and all else to the farthest reaches of the stars, with an aboveness that does not increase His nearness to the Throne or heavens, or His distance from the earth and what lies beneath it. He is as exalted in degree above the Throne and the heavens as He is above the earth and its depths, while He is also near to everything in existence. He is nearer to a servant than his own jugular vein, and is witness to everything. His nearness does not resemble the nearness of bodies to one another just as His Entity does not resemble the entities of bodies.

He does not indwell in anything, nor does anything indwell in Him. He is exalted above containment in space and He is transcendent above confinement in time. He was before creating time and space, and is now as He was. He is distinguished from His creation by His attributes. There is nothing in His Entity other than Him, nor is His Entity in what is other than Him. He is exalted beyond change and motion: contingent events neither occur within Him nor do changes befall Him. He remains in His attributes of Majesty exalted above change, and in the attributes of His perfection beyond needing any increase in perfection. The existence of His entity is known by human reason, and in the afterlife He is beheld by the eyesight of the righteous as a beatitude and favour, in the abode of permanence, to complete their joy with the sight of His Noble Countenance.

He, the Exalted, is living, almighty, over-mastering, and triumphant. He is unaffected by inability or weakness; unsusceptible to drowsiness, sleep, annihilation, or death; He is the possessor of absolute sovereignty and might, and honour and force. His is the Majesty and authority, the creation and command. He alone creates, begins, gives existence, and originates. He creates all beings and their acts, ordains their sustenance and time of death. Nothing possible is outside of His grasp and the disposal of no matter is beyond His power. The number of things He can do is limitless, the amount He knows is infinite.

He knows all things knowable, encompasses all that takes place from the depths of the earth to the highest heaven. He knows without an atom's weight in the earth or heavens escaping His knowledge. He knows the concealed and that which is even more hidden, the buried consciousness of hearts, the movement of thoughts, and the secrets of the inmost soul; with pre-eternal, beginningless knowledge that He has always possessed from the limitless reaches of past eternity, not with a renewed awareness originating within Him through being imparted or conveyed.

He, the Exalted, wills all that exists and directs all events. Nothing occurs in the physical or spiritual world—be it little or large, small or great, good or evil, of benefit or harm, faith or disbelief, knowledge or ignorance, triumph or loss, increase or decrease, obedience or sin—save through His ordinance, apportionment, wisdom, and decision. What He wills is, and what He does not will is not.

His will, like His other attributes, exists in His entity and He is eternally described with it. He has willed from pre-eternity the existence of all things at the exact times He has chosen. They occur at the times which He has destined from beginningless eternity, occurring neither before nor after, but taking place in accordance with His knowledge and will, without substitution or alteration. He directs events without successive thoughts or waiting for time to elapse, which is why nothing diverts Him from anything else.

The Imām and knower of Allah, Ḥabīb 'Abdullāh b. 'Alawī al-Ḥaddād ﷺ said:

> Every believer must protect his faith by learning the creed of one of the Imāms whose nobility and well-grounding in knowledge is agreed upon. And I cannot see anyone in pursuit of that finding that which is clearer, more comprehensive, and free from suspect and misleading things than the creed of Imām al-Ghazālī ﷺ that he placed in the first chapter of the volume on the foundations of beliefs in the *Iḥyā'*...[342]

Imām 'Abd al-Qādir al-Baghdādī—may Allah have mercy upon him—said: "So whoever believes in that which we have mentioned, and does not mix his faith with anything from the blameworthy innovations of the people of vain desires, then he is counted amongst the saved group—provided he dies upon it."[343]

Imām Abū al-Muẓaffar al-Isfarāyīnī—may Allah have mercy upon him—said: "And that you know that everyone who follows this religion that we have described from the creed of the saved group is upon the truth and the straight path; so whoever imputes him with blameworthy innovation is an innovator, whoever imputes him with misguidance is misguided, and whoever imputes him with disbelief is a disbeliever."[344]

May Allah, the Exalted, make us of those who hold firmly to this creed and act in accordance to it, and may He cause us to die upon in. Amen!

---

[342] *Risāla al-Mu'āwana*, p. 68.
[343] *Al-Farq bayn al-Firaq*, p. 20.
[344] *Al-Tabṣīr fī al-Dīn*: p. 111.

CONCLUSION

This marks the conclusion of our discussion on this topic that is frequently asked about and which is surrounded—despite its seriousness and importance—with general ignorance. This is a topic whose reality is at times covered by ignorance, and at other times covered by obstinate bigotry. The result of that is the current darkness that envelops most of the Umma.

It had occurred to us early on that this research would only span a few pages, but much to our surprise, it has exceeded two hundred and fifty pages [in the original Arabic]. Each time we endeavoured to speak on one topic, we were drawn to speak about other topics that are no less important. We hope that we have covered the topic and explained all the issues that were in need of elucidation; with all of its issues and topics of discussion, it is extremely important and pertinent.

Were it not that some people—may Allah guide them—delved into this topic and spoke badly, and had they not tainted the thoughts of the up-and-coming generation of Muslims, and gave them the idea that the scholars of Islam from the Ashʿarīs and Māturīdīs are misguided and deviated away from the path of the *Salaf*, we would not have entered this door, and we would have left it closed shut. However, what are we to do when some have opened this door and started to impute misguidance and innovation upon others without verification or proof? There is no movement or power except by Allah!

In this work, we have been keen to suffice with the quotes from the scholars, notables, and elite of the Umma. Those Imāms—through their quotes that we gathered—were the ones addressing the reader of this research. Let it be said, however, that the quotes we mentioned here are only a small sample in comparison to the quotes we decided to leave out for fear of being long winded.

We have sufficed with mentioning the scholars who are well-known to the common person. Had we wished to mention everyone, the time and place would be constricted. By Allah, we are not saying this out of surmise and conjecture. Nay, it is a reality attested to by history and the world.

No matter the case, this research is now the responsibility of the reader. He or she is duty bound to do their utmost and weigh the reality that is supported by textual and rational proofs and evidence. We are left only with presenting the conclusions of this research, which are stated in the following points.

- The Ashʿarīs and Māturīdīs are the followers of the two great Imāms: Abū al-Ḥasan al-Ashʿarī and Abū al-Manṣūr al-Māturīdī ﷺ—the two Imāms of Ahl al-Sunna wal-Jamāʿa. They did not invent a path that is different from the path of the pious predecessors and they did not found a new doctrine. They codified the doctrine of the *Salaf* and defended it with rational proofs. The only reason others ascribe themselves to these two Imāms is because they made the way of the *Salaf* well-known. They are akin to the four Imāms in jurisprudence; just as the one who ascribes himself to one of the four Imāms is in reality following the *Salaf* and is not in opposition to them; similarly, the one who follows one of these two Imāms is also following the *Salaf* and not departing from their way.
- According to the scholars, the term *Ahl al-Sunna wal-Jamāʿa* refers to the Ashʿarīs, the Māturīdīs, and the traditionists [*ahl al-Ḥadīth*]. They are the great bulk and majority throughout history and most of the Islamic lands, from the time of the *Salaf* until today. Before that, they were called the *Muthbita* (people of affirmation) because they affirmed the attributes that the Muʿtazila negated. After that, they were called Ahl al-Sunna, after the appearance of the two Imāms of Ahl al-Sunna, al-Ashʿarī and al-Māturīdī, because they aided the Sunna and defeated blameworthy innovation.
- Regarding the ambiguous texts that pertain to the Divine attributes, there are only two valid approaches according to the scholars: the way of *tafwīḍ*—which was the position of the majority of the *Salaf*—and the way of *taʾwīl*—which was the position of some groups among the *Salaf* and the position of the majority of the latter-day scholars.

Nothing remains after these two approaches besides extreme denial [*taʿṭīl*] or resemblance [*tashbīh*].

- There is no real disagreement between the position of *tafwīḍ* and figurative interpretation; both are based on declaring Allah transcendent above the outward and literal meanings of the ambiguous texts; meanings that are impossible for Allah, the Exalted. The disagreement between the two approaches is within the fold of allowable disagreements that do not necessitate accusations of misguidance or innovation. Both positions are reported from the *Salaf.*
- Figurative interpretation that conforms to the prerequisites outlined by the scholars is a Sunni method. There is no way to gain a correct understanding of the Book of Allah, the Exalted, and the Sunna of His Prophet ﷺ without it. It is inescapable and even those who decry its use are bound to use it for some texts.
- The Sunni method of figurative interpretation is not extreme denial or a path that leads to extreme denial. Anyone who accuses the latter-day scholars of the Umma of extreme denial due to their use of figurative interpretation is in fact accusing the *Salaf* of this Umma, because groups of them are reported to have engaged in figurative interpretation. We have cited a sample of their statements and interpretations in this research.
- It is enough as a testament to the Ashʿarīs and Māturīdīs and their virtues, merits, and righteous acts in service to Allah's religion, what is filled in the Islamic library; sciences and branches of knowledge that are like an exquisite pearl or crown. Whoever is fair-minded and give a cursory glance to the Islamic library and its sections, be it the Qurʾān and its ancillary disciplines, Ḥadīth studies, jurisprudence and its theory, hagiography, battles, history, language, literature, and more, will with certainty, know the virtue of the scholars of this Umma from the Ashʿarīs and Māturīdīs. He will know with clarity, the stupendous efforts of those notables in defence of the religion and the Muslims.

- There are innumerable legal verdicts from the scholars of the Umma in every era, in which they spoke highly of the Ashʿarīs and Māturīdīs and mentioned their merits and virtue, just as there are innumerable statements from them in which they censured, rebuked, and ordered disciplinary action and punishment against those who disparaged them.

We know for certain that we will not be able to convince everyone who reads this book, even if we were covetous of that and tried our best. That is an unreachable aspiration: ﴾*They will not cease differing with each other. Except the one shown mercy by Your Lord*﴿

The least that can be done is to observe fair-mindedness and good relations; and Allah shall judge between His servants regarding that in which they differed. It is sufficient for us that we have aided the true reality that has been adopted by the Umma in its long history. Ignorance of that reality will not decrease it or make it any weaker, nor will it transform it into falsehood. Ignorance will only be a shame for its people after it is unveiled in the near future.

We beseech Allah and ask Him to unite the ranks of the Muslims and remove the causes of splitting between them. We ask that He guides us and all of our brothers to that which He loves and is pleased with, and that He unites us in one rank.

In closing, we say to every Muslim: let us cast our gaze at every cause of unity and agreement that Allah called us to. Let us cast to the side everything that sullies unity. Let us keep in front of us the words of the Real [Allah], Exalted is He: ﴾*Do not dispute and thus lose courage and then your strength would depart*﴿

Our final call is: All praise is due to Allah, the Lord of the worlds. May prayers and salutations be upon His servant and Messenger, Muḥammad, and upon his Family and Companions.

الحمد لله رب العالمين

BIBLIOGRAPHY

Andalūsī, Abū Ḥayyān al-,
Al-Baḥr al-Muḥīṭ wal-Nahr al-Mād min al-Baḥr
Aṣfahānī, Abū Nuʿaym Rāghib al-. *Al-Mufradāt fī Gharīb al-Qurʾān*
--------*Dalāʾil al-Nubuwwa*
Ashʿarī, Abū al-Ḥasan al-, *Al-Ibāna* (ed. Fawqiyya Ḥusayn)
Athīr, Mubārak b. Muḥammad b. al-, *Al-Nihāya fī Gharīb al-Ḥadīth*
--------*Al-Kāmil*
Ayūb, Ḥasan, *Tabṣīṭ al-ʿAqāʾid al-Islāmiyya*
Ālūsī al-, Maḥmūd b. ʿAbdullāh al-Ḥusaynī, *Tafsīr Rūḥ al-Maʿānī*
ʿAbd al-Barr, Yūsuf b. ʿAbdullāh b., *Al-Istīʿāb fī Maʿrifa al-Aṣḥāb*
--------*Al-Istidhkār*
ʿAjība, Aḥmad b., *Al-Baḥr al-Madīd fī Tafsīr al-Qurʾān al-Majīd*
ʿAlawī al-Mālikī al-Ḥasanī, Muḥammad b.,
Mafāhīm Yajib An Tuṣaḥḥaḥ
ʿArabī, Abū Bakr b. al-, *Sharḥ al-Muwaṭṭāʾ*
--------*Tuḥfa al-Aḥwadhī Sharḥ Jāmiʿ* al-Tirmidhī
ʿAsākir, ʿAlī b. al-Ḥasan b.,
Tabyīn Kadhib al-Muftarī (ed. Muḥammad Zāhid al-Kawtharī)
--------*Tārīkh Madīna Dimashq*
ʿĀbidīn b., Muḥammad Amīn b. ʿUmar,
Al-ʿUqūd al-Durriyya fī Tanqīḥ al-Fatāwā al-Ḥāmidiyya
Badawī, ʿAbd al-Raḥmān, *Madhāhib al-Islāmiyyīn*
Baghawī, Masʿūd b. Muḥammad al-Farrāʾ al-, *Sharḥ al-Sunna*
--------*Tafsīr al-Baghawī*
Baghdādī, ʿAbd al-Qādir al-, *Al-Farq bayn al-Firaq*
Bannā, Ḥasan al-, *Majmūʿa Rasāʾil al-Imām*
Bashkuwāl, Abū al-Qāsim Khalaf b., *Al-Ṣila fī Tārīkh Aʾimma al-Andalus*
Bāqillānī, Abū Bakr al-, *Al-Inṣāf*
--------*Al-Tamhīd*
Bayāḍī, Kamāl al-Dīn al-, *Ishārāt al-Marām min ʿIbārāt al-Imām* (ed. Muḥammad Zāhid al-Kawtharī)
Bayhaqī, Aḥmad b. Ḥusayn al-,
Al-Asmāʾ wal-Ṣifāt (ed. Muḥammad Zāhid al-Kawtharī)
--------*Al-ʿItiqād*
--------*Al-Muḥīṭ*
--------*Dalāʾil al-Nubuwwa*
Bayṭār, Bahja al-, *Ḥilya al-Bashar*
Bābartī, Akmal al-Dīn al-, *Sharḥ al-Ṭaḥāwiyya*

Bukhārī, Muḥammad b. Ismā'īl al-, *Khalq Af'āl al-'Ibād*
--------*Al-Tārīkh al-Kabīr*
--------*Al-Tārīkh al-Ṣaghīr*
--------*Al-Jāmi' al-Ṣaḥīḥ*
Būṭī, Muḥammad Sa'īd Ramaḍān al-, *Kubrā al-Yaqīniyāt al-Kawniyya*
Dardīr, Aḥmad al-, *Al-Kharīda al-Bahiyya*
Dawānī, Jalāl al-Dīn al-, *Sharḥ al-'Aqīda al-'Aḍudiyya*
Dānī, Abū 'Amr al-, *Risāla al-Wāfiya*
--------*Al-Risāla al-Wāfiya li-Madhhab Ahl al-Sunna fī al-'Itiqādāt*
Dhahabī, Muḥammad b. Aḥmad al-,
Siyar 'Alām al-Nubalā' [ed. Shu'ayb al-Arna'ūṭ]
--------*Mīzān al-'Itidāl*
--------*Al-'Uluw*
--------*Tadhkira al-Ḥuffāẓ*
Dānī, Abū 'Amr al-,
Al-Risāla al-Wāfiya fī Mu'taqad Ahl al-Sunna wal-Jamā'a
Duḥayān, 'Abdullāh b. Khalaf al-Duḥayān, *Tabṣīr al-Qāni' fī al-Jami' bayn Sharḥayn Ibn Shaṭṭī wa-Ibn Māni' 'alā al-'Aqīda al-Safārīniyya*
Farhūn, Ibrāhīm b., *Al-Dībāj al-Mudhahhab*
Ghazālī, Abū Ḥāmid al-. *Iḥyā' 'Ulūm al-Dīn*
--------*Iljām al-'Awām 'an 'Ilm al-Kalām*
Ghāwjī, Wahbī al-,
Naẓra 'Ilmiyya fī Nisba Kitāb Al-Ibāna Jamī'hi ilā al-Imām Abī al-Ḥasan
-------- *Arkān al-Imān*
Haytamī, Shihāb al-Dīn b. Ḥajar al-, *Al-Fatāwā al-Ḥadīthiyya*
--------*Al-Zawājir 'an Iqtirāf al-Kabā'ir*
Hud'hudī, Muhammad b. Manṣūr al-, *Sharḥ al-Sanūsiyya al-Ṣughrā*
Ḥaddād, 'Abdullāh b. 'Alawī al-, *Nayl al-Marām*
--------*Kitāb Risāla al-Mu'āwana*
Ḥajar al-'Asqalānī, Shihāb al-Dīn b., *Fatḥ al-Bārī Sharḥ Ṣaḥīḥ al-Bukhārī*
--------*Lisān al-Mīzān*
--------*Hadī al-Sārī*
Ḥanbal, Aḥmad b., *Musnad*
Ḥawwā, Sa'īd, *Jawalāt fī al-Fiqhayn; Al-Kabīr wal-Akbar*
Ḥāmid, Muḥammad al-, *Rudūd 'alā Abāṭīl*
Ḥūt al-Bayrūtī, Muḥammad b. Darwīsh al-,
Rasā'il fī Bayān 'Aqā'id Ahl al-Sunna wal-Jamā'a
Isnawī, Jamāl al-Dīn al-, *Ṭabaqāt al-Shāfi'iyya*
Isfarāyīnī, Abū al-Muẓaffar al-, *Al-Tabṣīr fī al-Dīn*
Ījī, 'Aḍud al-Dīn al-, *Al-Mawāqif*
'Iyāḍ, Abū Faḍl Qāḍī, *Al-Shifā' bi-Ta'rīf Ḥuqūq al-Muṣṭafā* ﷺ

Jamā'a, Badr al-Dīn b., *Īḍāḥ al-Dalīl fī Qaṭi' Ḥujaj Ahl al-Ta'ṭīl*
Jawzī, Abū al-Faraj b. al-, *Ṣayd al-Khāṭir*
--------*Dafa' Shubh al-Tashbīh*
Juwaynī, al-, *Al-Niẓāmiyya*
--------*Al-Irshād*
--------*Kifāya al-Mu'taqad*
Kathīr, Ismā'īl b. 'Umar b., *Tafsīr al-Qur'ān al-'Aẓīm*
--------*Al-Bidāya wal-Nihāya*
--------*Ṭabaqāt al-Fuqahā' al-Shāfi'īn*
Kattānī, 'Abd al-Ḥayy b. 'Abd al-Kabīr, *Fahras al-Fahāris wal-Ashbāt wa-Mu'jam al-Mu'ājim wal-Mashyakha wal-Musalsalāt*
Kāndahlawī, Muḥammad Zakariyyā al-, *Awjaz al-Masālik*
Khaldūn, 'Abd al-Raḥmān b., *Muqaddima*
Khallikān, Aḥmad b. Muḥammad b., *Wafiyāt al-A'yān wa-Abnā' Abnā' al-Zamān*
Khaṭīb, Ḍiyā' al-Dīn al-, *Ghāya al-Marām fī 'Ilm al-Kalām*
Khaṭṭābī, Abū Sulaymān Aḥmad al-, *Ma'ālim al-Sunan Sharḥ Abī Dāwūd*
Khāzin, 'Alī b. Muḥammad al-, *Al-Musammā li-Bāb al-Ta'wīl fī Ma'ānī al-Tanzīl*
Makhlūf, Muḥammad b. Muḥammad, *Shajara al-Nūr al-Zakiyya fī Ṭabaqāt al-Mālikiyya*
Maydānī, Al-Ghunaymī al-, *Sharḥ al-Ṭaḥāwiyya*
Mawāhibī al-Ḥanbalī, 'Abd al-Bāqī al, *Al-'Ayn wal-Athar*
Munīr al-Sakandarī al-Mālikī, Nāṣir al-Dīn b. al-, *Al-Muntaqā fī Sharaf al-Muṣṭafā* ﷺ
Musāfir, 'Adī b., *'Itiqād Ahl al-Sunna wal-Jamā'a*
Muslim b. al-Ḥajjāj al-Naysabūrī, *Ṣaḥīḥ Muslim*
Muṭī' al-Ḥāfiẓ, Muḥammad, *Dār al-Ḥadīth al-Ashrafiyya bi-Dimashq*
Nadwī, Abū al-Ḥasan al-, *Rijāl al-Fikr wal-Da'wa fī al-Islām*
Nasafī, Abū Ḥafṣ al-, *Al-Taysīr fī 'Ilm al-Tafsīr*
Nawawī, Yaḥyā b. Sharaf al-Dīn al-, *Sharḥ Ṣaḥīḥ Muslim*
--------*Al-Majmū'*
--------*Rawḍa al-Ṭālibīn*
Qasṭalānī, Aḥmad b. Muhammad al-, *Mawāhib al-Laduniyya*
Qayrawānī, b. Abī Zayd, *Al-Nawādir wal-Ziyādāt*
Qārī, 'Alī al-, *Mirqāt al-Mafātīḥ*
Qaṭṭān, Abū al-Ḥasan 'Alī b. al-, *Al-Iqnā' fī Masā'il al-Ijmā'*
Quḍā'ī, Salāma al-'Azzāmī al-, *Furqān al-Qur'ān*
Qurṭubī, Abī 'Abdullāh Muḥammad al-, *Al-Tadhkira*
--------*Tafsīr al-Qurṭubī*
--------*Al-Mufhim*

Qutayba, Abū Muḥammad b.,
Al-Ikhtilāf fī al-Lafẓ (ed. Muḥammad Zāhid al-Kawtharī)
Quṭb, Sayyid, *Fī Ẓilāl al-Qur'ān*
Rajab al-Ḥanbalī, Zayn al-Dīn b., *Ṭabaqāt al-Ḥanābila*
Rāzī, Fakhr al-Dīn al-, *Tafsīr Mafātīḥ al-Ghayb*
--------*Ṭabaqāt al-Aṭṭibā'*
Rushd al-Jadd, Abū al-Walīd Muḥammad b., *Al-Bayān wal-Taḥṣīl*
--------*Fatāwā Ibn Rushd*
Safārīnī, Sulaymān al-, *Lawāmi' al-Anwār al-Bahiyya*
Salām, al-'Izz b. 'Abd al-, *Fatāwā al-'Izz b. 'Abd al-Salām*
--------*Al-Ishāra ilā al-Ījāz*
--------*Tafsīr al-'Izz b. 'Abd al-Salām*
Salūm, Muḥammad b. 'Alī b., *Sharḥ al-Durra al-Maḍiyya*
Subkī, Maḥmūd Khaṭṭāb al-, *Itḥāf al-Kā'ināt bi-Bayān Madhhab al-Salaf wal-Khalaf fī al-Mutashābihāt*
--------*Al-Dīn al-Khāliṣ*
Subkī, Taqī al-Dīn al-, *Al-Sayf al-Ṣaqīl fī al-Radd 'alā b. Zafīl* (ed. Muḥammad Zāhid al-Kawtharī)
Subkī, Tāj al-Dīn al-, *Ṭabaqāt al-Shāfi'iyya al-Kubrā*
Suhaylī, Abū al-Qāsim 'Abd al-Raḥmān al-, *Al-Rawḍ al-Unuf*
Suyūṭī, Jalāl al-Dīn al-, *Al-Itqān fī 'Ulūm al-Qur'ān*
--------*Al-Jāmi' al-Ṣaghīr*
Shahrastānī, Tāj al-Dīn al-, *Al-Milal wal-Niḥal*
Shawkānī, Muḥammad al- *Irshād al-Fuḥūl*
Shāmī, 'Adī b. Musāfir al-, *'Itiqād Ahl al-Sunna wal-Jamā'a*
Shāṭibī, Abī Isḥāq al-, *Al-Muwāfaqāt*
--------*Al-I'tiṣām*
Shīrāzī, Abū Isḥāq al-, *Ṭabaqāt al-Shāfi'iyya*
Ṣafadī, Ṣalāḥ al-Dīn, *Al-Wāfī fī al-Wafiyāt*
Ṣāliḥī al-Dimashqī, Muḥammad b. Yūsuf al-,
Subul al-Hudā wal-Rashād
Tatān, 'Abd al-Karīm & Kaylānī, Muḥammad Adīb al-,
Sharḥ Jawhara al-Tawḥīd
Taymiyya, Aḥmad b., *Al-Fatāwā*
Tilmisānī, 'Umar al-, *Ba'ḍ mā 'Allamanī al-Ikhwān*
Tirmidhī, Aḥmad b. 'Īsā al-, *Al-Jāmi' al-Ṣaḥīḥ*
Ṭabarī, Abū Ja'far b. Jarīr al-, *Tafsīr al-Ṭabarī*
Ṭaḥāwī, Abū Ja'far al-, *Al-'Aqīda al-Ṭaḥāwiyya*
Ṭanṭāwī, 'Alī al-, *Ta'rīf 'Ām bi-Dīn al-Islām*
--------*Fatāwā al-Ṭanṭāwī*

Ṭāshkopruzāde, Muṣṭafā, *Miftāḥ al-Sa'āda*
Ubbī, Abū 'Abdullāh al-, *Sharḥ Ṣaḥīḥ Muslim*
Zabīdī, Murtaḍā al-, *Ithāf al-Sāda al-Muttaqīn*
--------*Al-Luma'* (ed. Ḥamūda Ghurāba)
Zahra, Muḥammad Abū, *Tārīkh al-Madhāhib al-Islāmiyya*
Zarkashī, Abū 'Abdullāh *Al-Burhān fī 'Ulūm al-Qur'ān*
Zurqānī, Muḥammad al-, *Manāhil al-'Irfān*

The Foundational Proofs of Imam al-Sanusi is one of the foundational works in Islamic theology and is considered historically as an elemental text in traditional Islamic education. Studied for centuries and memorized by children throughout the Islamic world, *The Foundational Proofs* offers readers a methodical outline of Islamic doctrine that satisfies the mind and the heart alike. In this age of mass confusion and intellectual malaise, where fundamental Islamic beliefs are misunderstood and credulity is championed as faith, *The Foundational Proofs* explains the tenets of faith and supports them both rationally and textually.

Further enhancing the value of this work is the engaging and relevant additions of Shaykh Saʿid Foudah, one of the world's leading Islamic theologians today, who presents Imam al-Sanusi's work with the interlineal commentary of Imam Ahmad b. ʿIsa al-Ansari and engaging and detailed footnotes collated from a variety of famous commentaries, such as those by Imam al-Bajuri, Imam al-Battawi, Imam al-Sawi, Imam al-Marghani, and others, as well as his own insightful comments.

> "One of the most important tasks for a person to engage in is earnest research into the doctrines of the Islamic faith. That is because the religion of Islam is based upon proofs and sound evidence; it does not contradict science or violate the fundamentals of rationality. Fundamentally, the religion of Islam is based upon rationality, and while it is true that it does not ignore the emotional aspect of religion, faith that is not grounded in the intellect is not considered perfect faith, nor is it capable of withstanding or confronting false beliefs, specious arguments, or the doubts that are spread in each age. Here Shaykh Saʿid Foudah has taken it upon himself to explicate the foundational beliefs of Islam and tenets of faith as based on the intellect, and to demonstrate their congruity with and non-contradiction to logic and science."
>
> —*Shaykh Galal al-Jihani*

The translation and publication of the present book, *ʿUlama' al-Sufiyya Hum al-Salafiyya al-Haqiqiyyun*, is a welcome event for seekers of spiritual guidance and self-purification in our time.

This praiseworthy effort offers to the English-speaking public a contemporary explanation of the immutable principles of Sufism, which are one and the same with the three principles of Religion: submission [*islam*], faith [*iman*], and excellence [*ihsan*].

The book contains Shaykh ʿAbd al-Hadi's carefully presented anthology of the wisdom of the Sufi masters of old and their summations of doctrine [*ʿaqida*] and of the various spiritual diseases and spiritual stations and states of the wayfarer. They were gleaned from the bio-sapiental classics of the genre such as *Tabaqat al-Sufiyya*, the *Lumaʿ*, the *Risala*, the *Ihya'*, and can be found in later works such as *Tabaqat al-Awliya'* and *al-Kawakib al-Durriyya fi Tarajim al-Sufiyya*.

The vehemence of the title—shown in the emphatic-exclusive personal pronoun and translatable as *The Scholars of the Sufis*: [*Only*] *They are the Genuine Followers of the Salaf*!—is a reminder of the tireless efforts of the last two hundred years of Ahl al-Sunna wal-Jamaʿa scholarship demonstrating the Islamic orthodoxy of *tasawwuf* and denouncing the heresy of Wahhabism and pseudo-Salafism.

It is its unique gems that make *ʿUlama' al-Sufiyya* stand out such as, for example, the title's emphasis on knowledge: it is never about the Sufis at large but about their Gnostics; as for would-be-Sufi [*mutasawwif*] claimants who are nescient of the Sacred Law or not even concerned by it: they are also heretics and completely undesirable no matter how big they grow their beard, turban, *jubba*, or voice! This is a theme stressed by many of our *salaf al-salih* (pious predecessors).

—*Shaykh Gibril Fouad Haddad*

أهل السنة الأشاعرة

شهادة علماء الأمة وأدلتهم

AHL AL-SUNNA: THE ASHʿARĪS

The Testimony and Proofs of the Scholars

Shaykh Ḥamad al-Sinān
Shaykh Fawzī al-ʿAnjarī

Forewords by
Shaykh Wahba al-Zuḥaylī
Shaykh Muḥammad Saʿīd Ramaḍān al-Būṭī

Translated by
Abdul Aziz Suraqah

SUNNI PUBLICATIONS